Cybersecurity in the Transportation Industry

Scrivener Publishing
100 Cummings Center, Suite 541J
Beverly, MA 01915-6106

Publishers at Scrivener
Martin Scrivener (martin@scrivenerpublishing.com)
Phillip Carmical (pcarmical@scrivenerpublishing.com)

Cybersecurity in the Transportation Industry

Edited by
Imdad Ali Shah
and
Noor Zaman Jhanjhi

Scrivener
Publishing

WILEY

This edition first published 2024 by John Wiley & Sons, Inc., 111 River Street, Hoboken, NJ 07030, USA and Scrivener Publishing LLC, 100 Cummings Center, Suite 541J, Beverly, MA 01915, USA
© 2024 Scrivener Publishing LLC
For more information about Scrivener publications please visit www.scrivenerpublishing.com.

Wiley Global Headquarters
111 River Street, Hoboken, NJ 07030, USA

For details of our global editorial offices, customer services, and more information about Wiley products visit us at www.wiley.com.

Limit of Liability/Disclaimer of Warranty

Library of Congress Cataloging-in-Publication Data

ISBN 9781394204267

Front cover images supplied by Pixabay.com and Adobe FireFly
Cover design by Russell Richardson

Set in size of 11pt and Minion Pro by Manila Typesetting Company, Makati, Philippines

Printed in the USA

10 9 8 7 6 5 4 3 2 1

Contents

Acknowledgments

We would like to express our thanks to Almighty Allah SWT for his all blessings and then great appreciation to all of those we have had the pleasure to work with during this project. The completion of this project could not have been accomplished without their support. First, the editors would like to express deep and sincere gratitude to all the authors who shared their ideas, expertise, and experience by submitting chapters to this book and adhering to its timeline. Second, the editors wish to acknowledge the extraordinary contributions of the reviewers for their valuable and constructive suggestions and recommendations to improve the quality, coherence, and content presentation of chapters. Most of the authors also served as referees. Their willingness to give time so generously is highly appreciated. Finally, our heartfelt gratitude goes to our family members and friends for their love, prayers, caring, and sacrifices in completing this project well in time.

Imdad Ali Shah,
Scholar
School of Computing Science, Taylor's University, Malaysia
Prof. Dr. Noor Zaman Jhanjhi,
Taylor's University, Subang Jaya, Selangor Malaysia
Program Director for Postgraduate Research Programs

Cybersecurity Issues and Challenges in Civil Aviation Security

Imdad Ali Shah[1]*, N.Z. Jhanjhi[1] and Sarfraz Brohi[2]

*[1]School of Computing Science, Taylor's University, Kuala Lumpur,
Selangor, Malaysia*
[2]University of the West of England (UWE), Bristol, United Kingdom

Abstract

It is crucial to remember that security protocols for civil aviation are constantly updated and assessed to reflect new threats and technological advancements. Even though these precautions greatly increase security, there is always a chance of hijacking. However, the objective is to reduce the risk of such situations occurring and to assure immediate response and resolution in the event that they do. Aviation security is an essential aspect of modern-day air travel. It involves a range of measures designed to protect passengers, crew, and aircraft from unlawful interference such as hijacking, terrorism, and sabotage. The software components of these systems are increasingly at risk due to their interconnectedness. These concerns are expected to increase as the aviation industry rolls out increasingly electronic-enabled planes and smart airports. Trends and lessons from a 20-year analysis of aviation cybersecurity risks and attack surfaces might guide future frameworks to defend a vital industry. Cybercriminals, especially nation-state actors and terrorists, are increasingly drawn to the aviation industry as it grows more digitised and dependent on wireless technology. Malicious actors can take advantage of vulnerabilities in designing and implementing the vast number of linked devices and subsystems. The aim of this chapter is to provide an overview of the aviation infrastructure's weak spots in terms of the threat actors and attack methods that are most likely to be used during persistent attack operations. The sector will benefit from the analyses by better understanding its current and future cybersecurity measures. According to information currently available, state actors and persistent advanced threat groups working together to enhance local aviation capacities and track, permeate, and compromise the abilities of other sovereign

---

**Corresponding author*: shahsyedimdadali@gmail.com

Imdad Ali Shah and Noor Zaman Jhanjhi (eds.) Cybersecurity in the Transportation Industry,
(1–24) © 2024 Scrivener Publishing LLC

countries pose the greatest risks to the aerospace industry. Malicious hacking is the most common attack on the aviation industry's computer infrastructure. Air Traffic Management (ATM) uses Safety Management Systems (SMS) to implement safety policies, practices, and procedures in compliance with international standards. SMS effectiveness is crucial to ATM safety in a changing operating environment. The primary objective of this chapter is to peer-review civil aviation security issues and challenges. Our recommendations and ideas will help the civil aviation industry and new researchers.

Keywords: Cybersecurity risk, aviation, security issues and challenges and management systems

1.1   Introduction

Protecting airports, airspace, aircraft, passengers, crew, and the public, checked and carry-on luggage, freight, mail, and food service supplies from criminal activities like hijacking, sabotage, and terrorism is what aviation security is all about.

Concerns about the durability of existing cybersecurity protection frameworks have arisen considering the continued trend toward greater Information and Communications Technology (ICT) tools and mechanical instruments that are often employed in the field of aviation. With the introduction of "smart airports" and "e-enabled aircraft infrastructures," the aviation industry faces new challenges, one of which is meeting the sector's requirements for cybersecurity compliance [1–3]. When it comes to connecting different countries, the aviation industry is in a prime position. Since even seemingly minor mistakes can have catastrophic results, such as the loss of life or the exposure of sensitive information belonging to stakeholders, employees, and customers, or the theft of credentials, intellectual property, or intelligence, it is crucial that the infrastructures supporting its operational integrity be robust [4–6]. Significant threat actors are working with state actors to steal aerospace secrets and improve their own domestic aerospace capabilities while also monitoring, infiltrating, and subverting the capabilities of other countries. The operational security of a vital sector of the economy must be safeguarded from cybercriminals, making it an urgent priority to develop and deploy effective cyber defences. Figure 1.1 presents the cyberattack types.

The fact that there are so many airports in the United States (5,080 public and 14,556 private as of 2019) may have something to do with the high

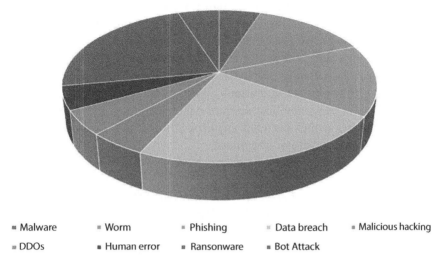

- Malware   - Worm   - Phishing   - Data breach   - Malicious hacking
- DDOs   - Human error   - Ransonware   - Bot Attack

Figure 1.1 Cyberattacks by type.

number of occurrences. Britain tops the list of countries attacked by a wide margin, with the rest of Europe coming in second at a rate of 44%. Airports in Africa have never been the target of a cyberattack, and Asia ranks third with 8%. The frequency with which airports were closed and the length of time aeroplanes were grounded because of cyber incidents varies [7–9]. We compile information from the literature on the various types of cyberattacks, the actors behind them, and their motivations. Figure 1.2 presents the cyberattacks in aviation.

The third section analyses the recorded cyberattacks over the past two decades, while the fourth identifies potential entry points for cybercriminals in airports and aviation systems. Cybersecurity threats in the civil

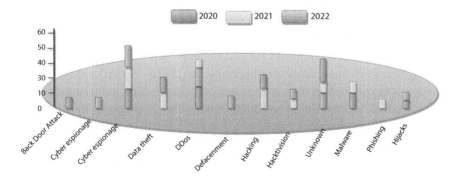

Figure 1.2 Cyberattacks on aviation.

aviation sector are discussed. Although traditional risks may appear differently during and after the Covid-19 pandemic, incident management, teamwork, and security assurance remain critically important throughout [10–12]. Furthermore, the sector must consistently adapt to the evolving regulations and challenges imposed by the global security environment to expand and evolve its operations. While bolstered security is always an advantage, it can also boost operational efficiencies inside a company, strengthen relationships between airports, airlines, and aviation authorities, and increase consumer happiness.

The chapter focuses on the following points:

- Peer-reviews cybersecurity measures in civil aviation
- Technologies in the civil aviation sector
- Security issues and challenges in the civil aviation sector
- Cyberattacks and hijacking incidents in the aviation industry
- Cyber issues and challenges.

1.2   Literature Review

There are several threats to civil aviation that must be addressed with consistent resources. To overcome these obstacles and guarantee the safety of air travel for passengers and crew, a cooperative strategy including governments, airlines, airports, and security agencies is essential. Cybersecurity is a major concern in the aviation industry because of the widespread adoption of digital technologies. Aircraft and their data are vulnerable to cyber risks such as hacking, malware, and phishing [13–15]. The aviation industry, including airports and airlines, is susceptible to insider threats from anyone having access to restricted areas, such as employees. Airline security relies heavily on the screening of passengers. Procedures for screening passengers and their belongings must be thorough enough to identify forbidden objects, including firearms, explosives, and other harmful materials. Passenger screening has certain benefits, but it also has drawbacks, such as lengthy lines, delays, and privacy issues [16–19]. Aviation security must continually adapt to new and emerging threats [20], including drones, which could be used for terrorist attacks or other malicious purposes, and new types of explosives or weapons that are difficult to detect. Civil aviation security is a global issue that requires international coordination and cooperation. The lack of consistency in security measures across different countries and regions can create vulnerabilities and increase the risk of incidents. Figure 1.3 presents the cyberattack types.

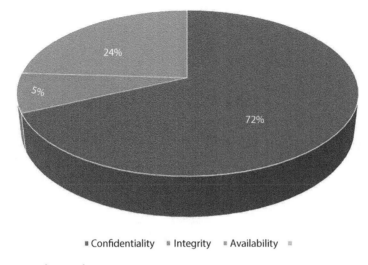

Confidentiality   Integrity   Availability

Figure 1.3 Cyberattack types.

North America is home to the most cyberattacks in the aviation industry, with 11 of the 26 occurrences occurring in the United States of America (USA) and only one in Canada. There were 5,080 public and 14,556 private airports in the United States in 2019, according to [21–23]. Therefore, the high number of occurrences may be related to this high concentration of airports. Britain tops the list of countries attacked by a wide margin, with the rest of Europe coming in second at a rate of 44%. Airports in Africa have never been the target of a cyberattack, and Asia ranks third with 8%. The frequency with which airports closed and the length of time airplanes were grounded because of cyber incidents varies. Figure 1.4 shows the Taxonomy of Civil Aviation Security.

The likelihood of cyber mishaps has increased due to the growing dependence on data integrity and privacy for the efficient operation of daily commercial operations. A significant pillar of the development of [24–26] next-generation systems, increased automation opens more entry points for malicious actors. According to Cyber Risk International [27–30], the proliferation of cybersecurity threats is due to a confluence of factors, including digital transformation, increased interconnectedness, segmentation, and complexity, and new industry solutions to accommodate the rising demand for international travel. The most important takeaways are as follows: Increased risk of cyberattacks is a direct result of the industry's increasing reliance on IT infrastructure to keep up service quality, as well as other factors such as the proliferation of new players and the persistence

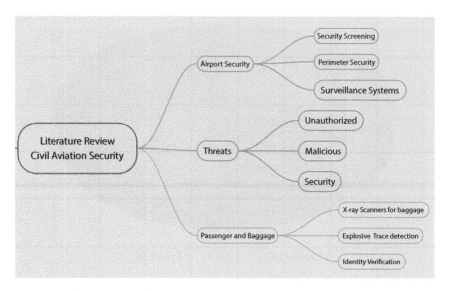

Figure 1.4 The taxonomy of civil aviation security.

of long-standing problems in the IT infrastructure that were never intended to deal with the threats posed by cybercriminals [31–33]. In addition to a lack of money, manpower, and current operational technologies like Supervisory Control and Data Acquisition (SCADA) and Industrial Control Systems (ICS), insider threats and the inability to upgrade legacy systems are also cited as problems. Solutions include creating a culture of security and executing effective measures of prevention and proactivity. There are growing threats and difficulties in ensuring adequate cybersecurity due to the rising reliance on data-driven operations to boost company efficiency and citizen well-being. Integration of technologies has unquestionably improved the security and efficacy of air travel. Nevertheless, increased human mobility and hyperconnectivity open the floodgates to a cascading impact, where a cyber incident at one airport becomes a worldwide problem with social and economic ramifications [34–36]. Industry must consequently take the initiative to supply effective defences against any new type of attack.

1.3 Research Methods

There are four platforms used for the collected data for this chapter; the procedure flowchart for gathering data is shown in Figure 1.5. We used

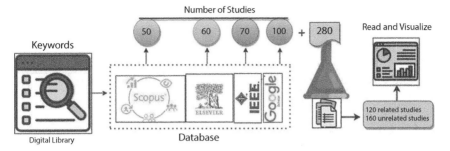

Figure 1.5 Overview of data-collection process flowchart.

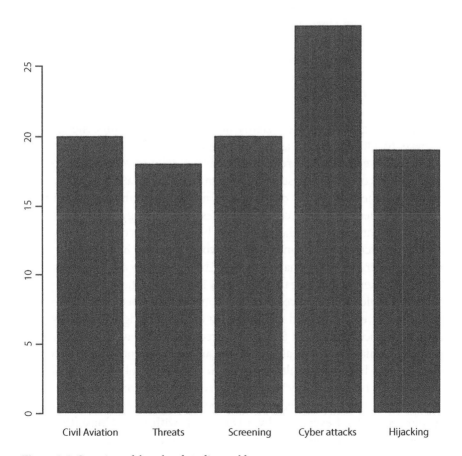

Figure 1.6 Overview of the related studies problems.

the keyword "Civil Aviation, Security Issues and Challenges." We selected these databases because they contain many research papers, book chapters and online information on numerous subjects.

There are 220 studies that have been filtered for problems from 160 unrelated studies. An overview of the studies is shown in Figure 1.6.

1.4   Cyber Risk in Aviation

Cyber risk in aviation is the potential threat that cyberattacks, like those on air traffic control systems, airport security systems, and airline computer networks, could pose to aircraft systems and related infrastructure. More and more computerised systems, like avionics and communication systems, are used in aviation. This has made the industry vulnerable to cyber threats. Cyberattacks on aviation systems can have serious consequences, including losing aircraft control, disrupting air traffic control systems, and compromising sensitive data [37–39]. Cyber threats to aviation can come from various sources, including state-sponsored hackers, criminal organizations, and individual actors. To mitigate the risks associated with cyber threats, stakeholders in the aviation industry have implemented various measures, such as increasing cybersecurity training for employees, implementing more secure systems, and collaborating with cybersecurity experts to [40–42] detect and prevent attacks. Additionally, government agencies have established regulations and guidelines to ensure the safety and security of aviation systems. Companies in the aviation industry need to stay on the lookout for cyber threats and keep producing and putting into place effective cybersecurity measures as technology changes and new threats appear. Figure 1.7 shows major cyberattacks by country, 2006-2020.

The repercussions of committing a cybercrime can be devastating. If a hacker undermines national security by breaking into a U.S. government agency, hackers might face up to 20 years in prison. Attacks on an airport's telecommunications service have been commonplace because of its importance to the economy and the difficulty of penetrating its defences. The first attack occurred when a teenager used a known flaw in the system to launch a denial-of-service assault on the airport's network. There have also been remote hacking assaults, with the air traffic control system, airplanes, and airports being primary targets. The assaults raise concerns about passport control, passenger safety, and luggage control [43–45]. One Australian airport is attacked every day by a consultant with CQR Consulting. The European Aviation Agency estimates that around 1,000 hacks happen in

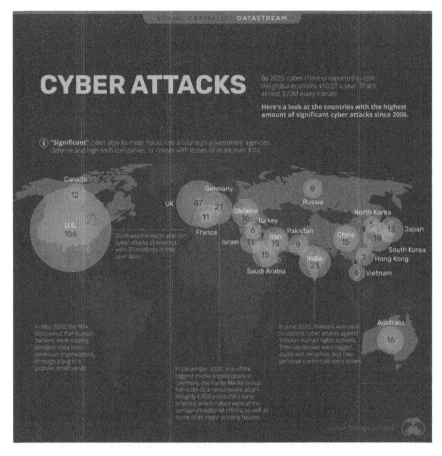

Figure 1.7 Major cyberattacks by country, 2006-2020 [77].

airports every month. A hacker from Tunisia breached a U.S. airport's computer and communication systems in 2014. LOT, a Polish airline, had an attack on its airport's flight operating system due to a distributed denial-of-service attack in 2015. This incident caused the cancellation of roughly 22 flights and forced about 1,400 people to abandon their flights [46–49]. Distributed denial-of-service (DDoS) assaults are frequent in the aviation sector and allow threat actors to disable the system and get access to it. Airports, air buses, air transportation, etc., are all part of the aviation industry's infrastructure. This study suggests that air travel is an essential part of the aviation industry's key infrastructure.

1.4.1   Voice (Very High Frequency – VHF)

The primary method of communication between air traffic control and the plane is via the human voice, known as voice communication. It is used to transmit reports and requests from the aircraft to air traffic control and vice versa. The weather, flight details, and airport-specific updates are just some of the things that are aired. Very high-frequency (VHF) and high-frequency (HF) radios are responsible for this interaction (high frequency). This service is vulnerable to DoS attacks because it relies on a shared frequency for communication between planes and air traffic controllers [50–53]. Several authorities have speculated that the attackers are using unlicensed aviation transceivers or pirate radio stations to target aeroplanes. Spoofing in voice communication has been documented, highlighting the importance of protecting these systems. Attacks like jamming can essentially disable a VHF, leading the plane to use an unauthenticated data channel that is simpler to hack into. VHF intruder detection rates are between 30% and 40%.

1.4.2   Automatic Dependent Surveillance-Broadcast (ADS-B)

Aircraft use this system to transmit data such as their unique identifier, speed, location, and any important messages. The aircraft's identifier is sent out once every five seconds. The position and speed are sent out twice every second. Because of the improved precision of location, this is a crucial application in both European and American airspaces [54–56]. There is no encryption or authentication for sent communications, making this system vulnerable to attack. A researcher called Andrei Costin presented an attack against ADS-B at the Black Hat USA conference. For this assault, he employed an ADS-B receiver to spoof the messages that were being acknowledged by the other receiver, which cost him a total of $1,000 for the software-defined radio. This example proved that these signals are easily intercepted and spoofed by attackers [57]. Attackers can install a replay attack, for instance, to intercept flight data packets and then retransmit them to the targeted system.

1.4.3   Importance of Satellite Navigation (GPS)

The NextGen system, in which the Global Positioning System (GPS) will feature prominently, was recently introduced. GPS has suffered from numerous security flaws since its inception. The feeble transmissions on the single civilian frequency have been shown in research to make GPS susceptible to hacking. In addition, GPS jammers can be purchased or constructed with little effort. Jamming and other forms of attack against GPS systems can prevent them from getting any signal, leading to poor performance. Deception of pilots and control systems due to spoofing can potentially have severe consequences [58–60]. Radio frequency assaults are a type of serious attack that may inflict harm on both people and their gadgets. Satellite communication is extremely vulnerable to interference since it relies on radio waves to transmit power.

1.5   Distributed Denial of Service (DDoS)

Distributed Denial of Service is referred to as DDoS. It is a kind of cyber-attack in which a target system or network is bombarded with an excessive volume of traffic or requests using a number of hacked machines or devices. A DDoS assault aims to stop the target from operating normally and make it inaccessible to authorized users.

1.5.1   Impact of DDoS on Air Transportation

DDoS attacks can have a big effect on air transportation systems, especially on the computer systems and networks of communication that keep the industry running. Several of the above attacks have happened, and it was also found that the aviation industry has many weak spots, making it easy for attackers to get into the fastest-growing industry. A distributed denial-of-service attack was found to be the most common type of attack against aircraft and the systems that support it earlier in the investigation. Websites and other online services are the primary targets of this kind of assault. The goal of this type of assault is to disrupt or slow down the target by sending an excessive amount of traffic to it [61–63]. There are a variety of ways that information might be used inappropriately, from outright destruction of technology to encrypted data held for ransom.

1.6   Discussion

Cybersecurity is becoming increasingly important in the aviation industry due to the growing number of cyberattacks and the increased reliance on technology in aviation systems to ensure civil aviation security. Understanding the aviation system's inner workings is necessary before implementing aviation security. Communication, navigation, and surveillance are the three primary functions of the aviation system's subsystems and wireless technologies. Airline safety is also a major focus for CNS [64–67]. The airfield serves as a landing spot for planes. It does this with the use of ground stations, satellites, and similar aircraft. Using established communication methods, the pilot exchanges information with the ground station and satellite by voice call or text message. It flies and lands safely thanks to the employment of navigation protocols, the Instrument Landing System (ILS), and Distance Measuring Equipment (DME). To monitor air traffic and look for trespassers, ground control uses surveillance protocols such as primary surveillance radar, secondary surveillance radar, and automatic dependent surveillance broadcast (ADS-B). During take-off, flight, and landing, these systems are always operating. Connectivity in the aviation sector is managed by the Air Traffic Management (ATM) system. So, when connecting with aeroplanes and satellites, the ATM system relies on air traffic control (ATC) as its central hub. With the help of ATC, networks on the ground may communicate with data centres and vice versa. Satellites and other features, such as aeroplane networks, are within the purview of ground networks. Connectivity between ground stations and aeroplanes is vital to the aviation system's operation. Contact with an incoming aircraft is often initiated by the ground station. Connectivity with supplementary ground units is handled by an ATC, which is part of the ground station.

1.6.1   Importance of IoT in Civil Aviation

The Internet of Things (IoT) is a network that enables previously disconnected devices and infrastructure to exchange data and perform tasks together. The IoT offers several potential uses in the aviation industry, including boosting plane efficiency, cutting down on repair bills, and providing a more enjoyable ride for passengers. Aircraft maintenance is one of the most important uses of the IoT in the aviation industry. The engines, landing gear, and avionics are just some of the systems and components that might benefit from being monitored by IoT sensors [68–70]. This information may be analysed in real time, letting maintenance teams see problems before they escalate and plan their work more effectively. By analysing weather and air traffic patterns in real time, IoT may also enhance aircraft performance. Airlines can save money in the long term by using this data to plot more efficient flight patterns that need less fuel. Smart airports are another manner in which the Internet of Things may enhance the travel experience for travellers. With the use of IoT sensors, airports can monitor passenger flow, queue lengths, and wait times. Figure 1.8 shows IoT applications.

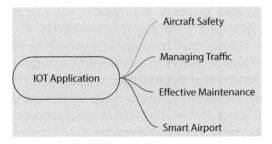

Figure 1.8 IoT applications.

This aids airports in controlling the flow of passengers and decreasing wait times [71–73]. The Internet of Things may also be utilised to provide passengers with individualised services, such as tailored itineraries and recommendations for in-flight entertainment and dining. The Internet of Things has the potential to revolutionise the aviation business by increasing productivity, cutting costs, and enhancing the travel experience for passengers.

1.6.2   Cybersecurity Challenges in Civil Aviation

Today's hot topic is cybersecurity and concern in aviation due to the critical nature of the systems involved [74–76]. Some of the challenges faced by the aviation industry in the context of cybersecurity are mentioned below.

1. Human Factors: One of the biggest challenges in aviation cybersecurity is the human factor. Pilots, maintenance workers, and other employees may unintentionally introduce security vulnerabilities or fail to follow proper security protocols.
2. Legacy Systems: Many of the systems used in aviation were developed before the age of the internet and were not designed with cybersecurity in mind. These legacy systems may have vulnerabilities that can be exploited by hackers.
3. Lack of Awareness: There is often a lack of awareness among aviation professionals about the importance of cybersecurity and how to properly secure systems.
4. International standards and coordination: Cybersecurity threats to aviation are global and addressing them requires international coordination and standardization. Without

a coordinated approach, vulnerabilities in one part of the world can impact aviation systems worldwide.

5. Human Factors and Training: acknowledging the significance of human factors in cybersecurity and funding training and awareness initiatives for aviation staff. This entails instilling a culture of cybersecurity awareness within the aviation sector and training staff members about cybersecurity risks and recommended practices.

6. Emerging Technologies: Addressing the cybersecurity issues presented by the introduction of new aviation technology, including unmanned aerial vehicles (UAVs) and autonomous systems. This includes performing risk analyses, creating security policies, and putting precautions in place to prevent any vulnerabilities.

7. Incident Response and Recovery: establishing reliable incident response protocols and plans to handle and recover from cyber incidents. To lessen the effects of cyberattacks, this includes creating incident response teams, holding frequent drills and exercises, and encouraging coordination among pertinent parties.

8. Threat Intelligence and Information Sharing: improving communication and information exchange between aviation stakeholders, such as airports, airlines, regulatory bodies, and cybersecurity organizations. This can aid in more accurately recognizing and countering new cyber threats.

Chapter's Contribution

To keep up with the yearly rise in passenger traffic, new aviation technologies are being made all the time. For this reason, all airlines strive to use cutting-edge technology inside their operations, making air travel a more satisfying experience for passengers and boosting their standing in the market. The increased usage of smart devices in this business has led to a corresponding increase in the associated risks and dangers. Here, we elaborate on the current systems in use in civil aviation. These systems' common flaws were also discussed. The industry would collapse without critical infrastructure, so any disruption to it would be catastrophic. Considering that the primary function of the airline business is the movement of people, goods, and so on, this sector was singled out as a crucial infrastructure. The most prevalent type of attack, distributed denial of service (DDoS), was examined to demonstrate the severity of the effects. Threats were also properly countered, and the threat modelling tool STRIDE was used.

Increased international tourism has brought with it several digital transformation, connectivity, segmentation, and complexity issues for the business, all of which will continue to present cybersecurity concerns. The industry is becoming more vulnerable to cyber assaults as more and more integration and automation are used to meet the demands of the market. Without a doubt, advancements in technology will boost service quality and delight customers, but at the cost of opening up new attack vectors for cybercriminals. Additionally, the sector has a responsibility to safeguard legacy IT infrastructures and established procedures, which is made more difficult by the industry's fragmentation and the fact that many of the systems in use were not built to be resistant to cybercrime. In this light, it remains an open problem that limits innovation in securing comprehensive and reliable data on the type and scale of cyber events inside the sector. The sensitive nature of the business and the dominance of government-owned organisations mean that news outlets, blogs, and corporate websites give little information about cyber breaches. While this is acceptable from a business standpoint, it creates obstacles for academics working to find answers that will help the industry advance. In order to make sense of data that may be biased, developers often resort to quantitative analysis. Hence, it is becoming increasingly obvious that there is a need for the development of AI-based cybersecurity solutions to deal with the key risks to the aviation industry's operational integrity. There is a wealth of potential in developing new, offensively focused defences to safeguard the more automated avionic infrastructures that are becoming increasingly vulnerable.

1.7   Conclusion

This review made a map of what has happened in the civil aviation business over the past 20 years by looking at published literature and recorded cyberattacks. Because their goals are the same as the industry's, the results show that advanced persistent threat (APT) groups working with state actors pose the greatest cyber threat to the aerospace industry. These groups want to get their hands on intellectual property and intelligence so they can improve their own country's aerospace capabilities and spy on, infiltrate, and destroy the capabilities of other countries. Like every other industry, the aviation industry is always looking for ways to give passengers more value. To meet the business need, the approach is to increase the level of system integration, add automation where it makes sense, and use data more. Internet of Things (IoT) technologies are largely responsible for the current state of affairs, as they serve to increase connectivity on the ground, in the air, and between the two, the latter of which is used to enhance the on-ground (smart airport) customer experience. Since rising degrees of integration and connection present a spectrum of new cyberattack surfaces, the cyber integrity of the rapidly expanding Smart Airport and e-enabled aircraft systems requires quick action to build complete cyber-defence mechanisms. Nevertheless, without safeguards in place, APT groups might expand their attacks to include in-flight aircraft, where they could potentially inflict catastrophic damage and even loss of life using very sophisticated remote attack tools.

1.8 Future Work

Aviation for civil purposes: It is anticipated that cybersecurity will change and advance in response to new threats and technological developments, improving communication and information exchange between aviation stakeholders, such as airports, airlines, regulatory bodies, and cybersecurity organizations. This can aid in more accurately recognizing and countering new cyber threats. Intelligent Threat Detection and Mitigation is developing and implementing cutting-edge cybersecurity tools and methods to quickly identify and counteract online threats. This can involve using big data analytics, machine learning, and artificial intelligence to spot anomalies and possible security breaches. To enhance the security and resilience of aviation systems and operations, civil aviation cybersecurity will prioritize staying ahead of emerging threats, improving collaboration and information sharing, embracing cutting-edge technology, and putting proactive measures into place.

References

[1] Duchamp, H.; Bayram, I.; Korhani, R. Cyber-Security, a new challenge for the aviation and automotive industries. In *Seminar in Information Systems: Applied Cybersecurity Strategy for Managers*; 2016; pp. 1–4. Available online: https://archive.blogs.harvard.edu/cybersecurity/files/2017/01/Cybersecurity-aviation-strategic-report.pdf (accessed on 20 September 2020).
[2] Monteagudo, J. Aviation Cybersecurity—High Level Analysis, Major Challenges and Where the Industry Is Heading. *Cyber Startup Observatory*, 2020. Available online: https://cyberstartupobservatory.com/aviation-cyber-security-major-challenges/ (accessed on 26 September 2020).

[3] Bellekens, X.; Jayasekara, G.; Hindy, H.; Bures, M.; Brosset, D.; Tachtatzis, C.; Atkinson, R. From cyber-security deception to manipulation and gratification through gamification. In *International Conference on Human-Computer Interaction*; Springer: Berlin/Heidelberg, Germany, 2019; pp. 99–114.

[4] ICAO. Security and Facilitation Strategic Objective: Aviation Cybersecurity Strategy. 2019. Available online: https://www.icao.i nt/cybersecurity/ Documents/AVIATIONCYBERSECURITYSTRATEGY.EN.pdf (accessed on 6 December 2021).

[5] Okoli, C.; Schabram, K. A Guide to Conducting a Systematic Literature Review of Information Systems Research. 2010. Available online: https:// asset-pdf.scinapse.io/prod/1539987097/1539987097.pdf (accessed on 6 December 2021).

[6] Okoli, C. A Guide to Conducting a Standalone Systematic Literature Review. 2015. Available online: https://aisel.aisnet.org/cais/vol37/iss1/43/ (accessed on 6 December 2021).

[7] IATA. Compilation of Cyber Security Regulations, Standards, and Guidance Applicable to Civil Aviation. 2021. Available online: https://www.iata.org/ contentassets/4c51b00fb25e4b60b38376a4935e278b/compilation-of-cyber-regulations-standards-and-guidance_3.0.pdf (accessed on 6 December 2021).

[8] Haass, J.; Sampigethaya, R.; Capezzuto, V. Aviation and cybersecurity: Opportunities for applied research. *TR News* 2016, 304, 39.

[9] Lykou, G.; Anagnostopoulou, A.; Gritzalis, D. Implementing cyber-security measures in airports to improve cyber-resilience. In *Proceedings of the 2018 Global Internet of Things Summit (GIoTS), Bilbao, Spain, 4–7 June 2018*; pp. 1–6.

[10] Lykou, G.; Anagnostopoulou, A.; Gritzalis, D. Smart airport cybersecurity: Threat mitigation and cyber resilience controls. *Sensors* 2019, 19, 19. [CrossRef] [PubMed]

[11] Gopalakrishnan, K.; Govindarasu, M.; Jacobson, D.W.; Phares, B.M. Cyber security for airports. *Int. J. Traffic Transp. Eng.* 2013, 3, 365–376. [CrossRef]

[12] Mathew, A.R. Airport Cyber Security and Cyber Resilience Controls. arXiv 2019, arXiv:1908.09894.

[13] Suciu, G.; Scheianu, A.; Vulpe, A.; Petre, I.; Suciu, V. Cyber-attacks–The impact over airports security and prevention modalities. In *World Conference on Information Systems and Technologies*; Springer: Berlin/Heidelberg, Germany, 2018; pp. 154–162.

[14] Corretjer, P.J. A Cybersecurity Analysis of Today's Commercial Aircrafts and Aviation Industry Systems. Master's Thesis, Utica College, Utica, NY, USA, 2018; p. 22.

[15] Kagalwalla, N.; Churi, P.P. Cybersecurity in Aviation: An Intrinsic Review. In *Proceedings of the 2019 5th International Conference on Computing, Communication, Control and Automation (ICCUBEA), Pune, India, 19–21 September 2019*; pp. 1–6.

[16] Lehto, M. Cyber Security in Aviation, Maritime and Automotive. In *Computation and Big Data for Transport*; Springer: Berlin/Heidelberg, Germany, 2020; pp. 19–32.

[17] CyberRisk, I. Cyber Threats to the Aviation Industry. 2020. Available online: https://cyberriskinternational.com/2020/04/06/cyber-threats-to-the-aviation-industry/ (accessed on 19 September 2020).

[18] Fireeye. Cyber Threats to the Aerospace and Defense Industries. 2016. Available online: https://www.fireeye.com/content/dam/fireeye-www/current-threats/pdfs/ib-aerospace.pdf (accessed on 24 September 2020).

[19] Varonis. 9 Infamous APT Groups: Fast Fact Trading Cards. 2020. Available online: https://www.varonis.com/blog/apt-groups (accessed on 6 December 2021).

[20] Kessler, G.C.; Craiger, J.P. Aviation Cybersecurity: An Overview. 2018. Available online: https://commons.erau.edu/ntas/2018/presentations/37/ (accessed on 6 December 2021).

[21] Abeyratne, R. Aviation and Cybersecurity in the Digital World. In *Aviation in the Digital Age*; Springer: Berlin/Heidelberg, Germany, 2020; pp. 173–211.

[22] Arampatzis, A. The State of Civil Aviation Cybersecurity. 2020. Available online: https://www.tripwire.com/state-of-security/security-data-protection/civil-aviation-cybersecurity/ (accessed on 30 September 2020).

[23] Viveros, C.A.P. Analysis of the Cyber Attacks against ADS-B Perspective of Aviation Experts. Master's Thesis, University of Tartu, Tartu, Estonia, 2016.

[24] Goodin, D. US Air Traffic Faces "Serious Harm" from Cyber Attackers. *The Register*, May 7, 2009. Available online: https://www.theregister.com/2009/05/07/air_traffic_cyber_attack/ (accessed on 19 September 2020).

[25] Ellinor, M. Report: Hackers Broke into FAA Air Traffic Control Systems. 2009. Available online: https://www.cnet.com/tech/services-and-software/report-hackers-broke-into-faa-air-traffic-control-systems/ (accessed on 19 September 2020).

[26] Shah, I. A. (2022). Cybersecurity Issues and Challenges for E-Government during COVID-19: A Review. *Cybersecurity Measures for E-Government Frameworks*, 187–222.

[27] Welsh, W. Phishing Scam Targeted 75 US Airports. *Information Week*, June 23, 2014. Available online: https://www.informationweek.com/cyber-resilience/phishing-scam-targeted-75-us-airports (accessed on 19 September 2020).

[28] Brewster, T. Attack on LOT Polish Airline Grounds 10 Flights. *Forbes*, June 22, 2015. Available online: https://www.forbes.com/sites/thomasbrewster/2015/06/22/lot-airline-hacked/?sh=6e4015fe124e (accessed on 19 September 2020).

[29] Kirkliauskaite, K. Main Cyber-Security Challenges in Aviation. 2020. Available online: https://www.aerotime.aero/25150-main-cyber-security-challenges-in-aviation (accessed on 19 September 2020).

[30] Polityuk, P.; Prentice, A. Ukraine Says to Review Cyber Defenses after Airport Targeted from Russia. 2016. Reuters, January 18, 2016. Available online: https://www.reuters.com/article/us-ukraine-cybersecurity-malware-idUSKCN0UW0R0 (accessed on 6 October 2020).

[31] Park, K. Cathay Pacific Cyber Attack Is World's Biggest Airline Data Breach. *Insurance Journal*, October 26, 2018. Available online: https://www.insurancejou rnal.com/news/international/2018/10/26/505699.html (accessed on 19 September 2020).

[32] Sandle, P. British Airways Says "Sophisticated" Hacker Stole Data on 380,000 Customers. *Insurance Journal*, September 10, 2018. Available online: https://www.insurancejournal.com/news/international/2018/09/10/500566.htm (accessed on 19 September 2020).

[33] Shah, I. A., Wassan, S., & Usmani, M. H. (2022). E-Government Security and Privacy Issues: Challenges and Preventive Approaches. In *Cybersecurity Measures for E-Government Frameworks* (pp. 61-76). IGI Global.

[34] Srinivasan, K., Garg, L., Datta, D., Alaboudi, A. A., Jhanjhi, N. Z., Agarwal, R., & Thomas, A. G. (2021). Performance comparison of deep CNN models for detecting driver's distraction. *CMC-Computers, Materials & Continua*, 68(3), 4109–4124.

[35] Paganini, P. Istanbul Ataturk International Airport Targeted by a Cyber-Attack. *Security Affairs*, July 28, 2013. Available online: https://securityaffairs.co/wordpress/16721/hacking/istanbul-ataturk-international-airport-targeted-by-cyber-attack.html (accessed on 19 September 2020).

[36] Khalil, M. I., Jhanjhi, N. Z., Humayun, M., Sivanesan, S., Masud, M., & Hossain, M. S. (2021). Hybrid smart grid with sustainable energy efficient resources for smart cities. *Sustainable Energy Technologies and Assessments*, 46, 101211.

[37] K. Hussain, S. J. Hussain, N. Jhanjhi and M. Humayun, SYN Flood Attack Detection based on Bayes Estimator (SFADBE) for MANET, *2019 International Conference on Computer and Information Sciences (ICCIS)*, Sakaka, Saudi Arabia, 2019, pp. 1–4, doi: 10.1109/ICCISci.2019.8716416.

[38] A. Almusaylim, Z., Jhanjhi, N. Z., & Alhumam, A. (2020). Detection and mitigation of RPL rank and version number attacks in the internet of things: SRPL-RP. *Sensors*, 20(21), 5997.

[39] Jhanjhi, N. Z., Brohi, S. N., Malik, N. A., & Humayun, M. (2020, October). Proposing a hybrid rpl protocol for rank and wormhole attack mitigation using machine learning. In *2020 2nd International Conference on Computer and Information Sciences (ICCIS)* (pp. 1–6). IEEE.

[40] Shah, I. A., Jhanjhi, N. Z., Humayun, M., & Ghosh, U. (2022). Impact of COVID-19 on Higher and Post-secondary Education Systems. In *How COVID-19 Is Accelerating the Digital Revolution* (pp. 71–83). Springer, Cham.

[41] Jhanjhi, N. Z., Brohi, S. N., Malik, N. A., & Humayun, M. (2020, October). Proposing a hybrid rpl protocol for rank and wormhole attack mitigation

using machine learning. In *2020 2nd International Conference on Computer and Information Sciences (ICCIS)* (pp. 1–6). IEEE.

[42] A. Almusaylim, Z., Jhanjhi, N. Z., & Alhumam, A. (2020). Detection and mitigation of RPL rank and version number attacks in the internet of things: SRPL-RP. *Sensors, 20*(21), 5997.

[43] K. Hussain, S. J. Hussain, N. Jhanjhi and M. Humayun, SYN Flood Attack Detection based on Bayes Estimator (SFADBE) for MANET, *2019 International Conference on Computer and Information Sciences (ICCIS)*, Sakaka, Saudi Arabia, 2019, pp. 1–4, doi: 10.1109/ICCISci.2019.8716416.

[44] Shah, I. A., Sial, Q., Jhanjhi, N. Z., & Gaur, L. (2023). The Role of the IoT and Digital Twin in the Healthcare Digitalization Process: IoT and Digital Twin in the Healthcare Digitalization Process. In *Digital Twins and Healthcare: Trends, Techniques, and Challenges* (pp. 20–34). IGI Global.

[45] Srinivasan, K., Garg, L., Datta, D., Alaboudi, A. A., Jhanjhi, N. Z., Agarwal, R., & Thomas, A. G. (2021). Performance comparison of deep CNN models for detecting driver's distraction. *CMC-Computers, Materials & Continua, 68*(3), 4109–4124.

[46] Shah, I. A., Jhanjhi, N. Z., & Laraib, A. (2023). Cybersecurity and Blockchain Usage in Contemporary Business. In *Handbook of Research on Cybersecurity Issues and Challenges for Business and FinTech Applications* (pp. 49–64). IGI Global.

[47] Khalil, M. I., Jhanjhi, N. Z., Humayun, M., Sivanesan, S., Masud, M., & Hossain, M. S. (2021). Hybrid smart grid with sustainable energy efficient resources for smart cities. *Sustainable Energy Technologies and Assessments, 46*, 101211.

[48] Singh, K. Delta, Sears Report Data Breach by Service Provider. *Insurance Journal*, April 5, 2018. Available online: https://www.insurancejournal.com/news/national/2018/04/05/485440.htm (accessed on 19 September 2020).

[49] Ukwandu, E., Ben-Farah, M.A., Hindy, H., Bures, M., Atkinson, R., Tachtatzis, C., Andonovic, I. and Bellekens, X., 2022. Cyber-security challenges in aviation industry: A review of current and future trends. *Information, 13*(3), p.146.

[50] Sandle, T. Air Canada Suffers Major App Data Breach of 20,000 Customers. *Digital Journal*, August 30, 2018. Available online: https://www.digitaljournal.com/business/air-canada-in-major-app-data-breach/article/530763 (accessed on 19 September 2020).

[51] Gibbs, B. Potential Personally Identifiable Information (PII) Compromise of NASA Servers. 2018. Available online: http://spaceref.com/news/viewsr.html?pid=52074/ (accessed on 22 September 2020).

[52] Gates, D. Boeing Hit by WannaCry Virus, but Says Attack Caused Little Damage. *Seattle Times*, March 18, 2018. Available online: https://www.seattletimes.com/business/boeing-aerospace/boeing-hit-by-wannacry-virus-fears-it-could-cripple-some-jet-production/ (accessed on 22 September 2020).

[53] Solomon, S. Israeli Airports Fend Off 3 Million Attempted Attacks a Day, Cyber Head Says. *Times of Israel*, February 12, 2019. Available online: https://www.timesofisrael.com/israeli-airports-fend-off-3-million-attempted-attacks-a-day-cyber-head-says/ (accessed on 19 September 2020).

[54] Duvelleroy, M. Airbus Statement on Cyber Incident. 2019. Available online: https://www.airbus.com/en/newsroom/press-releases/2019-01-airbus-statement-on-cyber-incident (accessed on 22 September 2020).

[55] Goud, N. Ransomware Attack on Albany Airport on Christmas 2019. *Cybersecurity Insiders*, 2019. Available online: https://www.cybersecurity-insiders.com/ransomware-attack-on-albany-airport-on-christmas-2019/ (accessed on 25 September 2020).

[56] Team, N. Cryptocurrency Miners Infected More than 50% of the European Airport Workstations. *Cyber Defense Magazine*, October 18, 2019. Available online: https: //www.cyberdefensemagazine.com/cryptocurrency-miners-infected-more-than-50-of-the-european-airport-workstations/ (accessed on 25 September 2020).

[57] Narendra, M. Privacy: Air New Zealand Experiences Data Breach. 2019. Available online: https://www.grcworldforums.com/news/2019/08/16/privacy-air-new-zealand-experiences-data-breach/ (accessed on 25 September 2020).

[58] Montalbano, E. DoppelPaymer Ransomware Used to Steal Data from Supplier to SpaceX, Tesla. 2020. Available online: https://threatpost.com/doppelpaymer-ransomware-used-to-steal-data-from-supplier-to-spacex-tesla/153393/ (accessed on 22 September 2020).

[59] Chua, A. Ransomware Attack hits ST Engineering's USA Aerospace Unit. *FlightGlobal*, June 7, 2020. Available online: https://www.flightglobal.com/aerospace/ransomware-attack-hits-st-engineerings-usa-aerospace-unit/138722.article (accessed on 23 September 2020).

[60] Claburn, T. Airline Software Super-Bug: Flight Loads Miscalculated Because Women Using "Miss" Were Treated as Children. *The Register*, April 8, 2021. Available online: https://www.theregister.com/2021/04/08/tui_software_mistake/ (accessed on 9 April 2021).

[61] Mazareanu, E. Number of Public and Private Airports in the United States from 1990 to 2019. 2020. Available online: https://www.statista.com/statistics/183496/number-of-airports-in-the-united-states-since-1990/ (accessed on 28 November 2020).

[62] Paganini, P. Cyber Threats against the Aviation Industry. 2014. Available online: https://resources.infosecinstitute.com/topic/cyber-threats/ (accessed on 19 September 2020).

[63] Thales. Overcoming the Cyber Threat in Aviation. 2016. Available online: https://onboard.thalesgroup.com/overcoming-cyber-threat-aviation/ (accessed on 24 September 2020).

[64] Zetter, K. Feds Say that Banned Researcher Commandeered a Plane. *Wired*, May 15, 2015. Available online: https://www.wired.com/2015/05/feds-say-banned-researcher-commandeered-plane/ (accessed on 18 January 2022).

[65] Freiherr, G. Will Your Airliner Get Hacked? *Smithsonian Magazine*, February 2021. Available online: https://www.smithsonianmag.com/air-space-magazine/will-your-airliner-get-hacked-180976752/ (accessed on 18 January 2022).

[66] Efe, A.; Tuzlupınar, B.; Cavlan, A.C. Air Traffic Security against Cyber Threats. *Bilge Int. J. Sci. Technol. Res.* 2021, 3, 135–143. Available online: https://dergipark.org.tr/en/pub/bilgesci/issue/49118/405074 (accessed on 18 January 2021).

[67] Santamarta, R. A Wake-Up Call for SATCOM Security. Technical White Paper. 2014. Available online: https://www.secnews.gr/wp-content/uploads/Files/Satcom_Security.pdf (accessed on 19 September 2020).

[68] Biesecker, C. Boeing 757 Testing Shows Airplanes Vulnerable to Hacking, DHS Says; *Avionics International*: New York, NY, USA, 2017.

[69] Papp, D.; Ma, Z.; Buttyan, L. Embedded systems security: Threats, vulnerabilities, and attack taxonomy. In *Proceedings of the 2015 13th Annual Conference on Privacy, Security and Trust (PST), Izmir, Turkey, 21–23 July 2015*; pp. 145–152. 57. GAO. Aviation Cybersecurity. 2020. Available online: https://www.gao.gov/assets/gao-21-86.pdf (accessed on 12 May 2020).

[70] Kumar, T.M., Reddy, K.S., Rinaldi, S., Parameshachari, B.D. and Arunachalam, K., 2021. A Low Area High Speed FPGA Implementation of AES Architecture for Cryptography Application. *Electronics*, 10(16), p. 2023.

[71] Parameshachari, B.D., 2021, March. Logistic Sine Map (LSM) Based Partial Image Encryption. In 2021 *National Computing Colleges Conference (NCCC)* (pp. 1–6). IEEE.

[72] Kowsalya, T., Babu, R.G., Parameshachari, B.D., Nayyar, A. and Mehmood, R.M., 2021. Low Area PRESENT Cryptography in FPGA Using TRNGPRNG Key Generation. *CMC-Computers Materials & Continua*, 68(2), pp.1447–1465.

[73] Trend Micro, Cyberattacks from the Frontlines: Incident Response Playbook for Beginners - Security News, 2020. https://www.trendmicro.com/vinfo/us/security/news/managed-detection-and-response/cyberattacksfrom-the-frontlines-incident-response-playbookfor-beginners (accessed May 4, 2021).

[74] Touhid, Different Types of Computer Security, *Cyber Threat and Security Portal*, 2019. https://cyberthreatportal.com/types-of-computer-security/ (accessed May 04, 2021). [27] E-Council, "What is STRIDE methodology in Threat Modeling?" https://blog.eccouncil.org/whatis-stride-methodology-in-threat-modeling/ (accessed May 4, 2021).

[75] D. Fayez Alqushayri, Cybersecurity Vulnerability Analysis and Countermeasures of Cybersecurity Vulnerability Analysis and Countermeasures of Commercial Aircraft Avionic Systems Commercial Aircraft Avionic Systems, Scholarly Commons Citation, 2020. Accessed: May 02, 2021. [Online]. Available: https://commons.erau.edu/edt/519.

[76] L. Zhen, Y. Zhang, K. Yu, N. Kumar, A. Barnawi and Y. Xie, Early Collision Detection for Massive Random Access in Satellite-Based Internet of Things,

IEEE Transactions on Vehicular Technology, vol. 70, no. 5, pp. 5184–5189, May 2021, doi: 10.1109/TVT.2021.3076015.

[77] Visual capitalist, https://www.visualcapitalist.com/cyber-attacks-worldwide-2006-2020/

Addressing Security Issues and Challenges in Smart Logistics Using Smart Technologies

Aneela Kiran Ansari[1*] and Raja Majid Ali Ujjan[2]

[1]Department of Computer Science, Shah Abdul Latif University, Khairpur, Sindh, Pakistan
[2]School of Computer Engineering & Physical Science, University of the West, Paisley, Scotland

Abstract

Smart logistics systems (SLSs) gather, store, and transmit sensitive data, such as customer information, shipping information, and financial records. Unauthorized persons having access to sensitive data can cause data breaches, which can result in theft and misuse. Sensors, RFID tags, and other tracking and monitoring devices found in the Internet of Things (IoT) are crucial to the success of smart logistics. Intruders might potentially obtain unauthorized access and risk data integrity by exploiting security flaws in these devices. Cybersecurity concerns can arise from insiders who have permission to access an SLS, such as workers or contractors. These people may endanger the system's security inadvertently, resulting in data breaches, illegal access, or sabotage. Insider risks may be reduced by implementing appropriate access restrictions, monitoring systems for anomalous activity, and regularly performing security training. Cybersecurity procedures are designed to protect electronic data and systems from unauthorized access and theft. To safeguard oneself and one's business, a variety of cybersecurity measures can be used. We focus on some of the most significant cybersecurity measures by looking at requests for information like "Explain the cybersecurity measures." Efficiency and speed are increasingly valued as a result of technological advancements. Modern means of transportation are included in this category. There has been a lot of focus on these vehicles from IT companies. Statistically speaking, they are far safer than regular cars. Innovations in autonomous and crewless vehicles have, like any new

---

*Corresponding author: Aneelakiranansari73@gmail.com

Imdad Ali Shah and Noor Zaman Jhanjhi (eds.) Cybersecurity in the Transportation Industry, (25–48) © 2024 Scrivener Publishing LLC

technology, given rise to cyberattack dangers. Hackers believe they can break into any targeted vehicle's system, and access the owner's private data without permission Therefore, the companies that produce hackers perceive numerous entry points and think they can break the security of any targeted vehicle system, steal the owner's personal identification information, and cause mechanical damage. Therefore, businesses developing autonomous vehicles must implement a robust cybersecurity architecture to protect against cyberattacks. They must better understand the nature of cybersecurity threats to autonomous vehicle systems. The dangers associated with cybersecurity are numerous for both individuals and corporations. Malicious actors, software flaws, and hardware flaws are only a few examples of the causes of these dangers. Human error, such as negligent internet browsing or clicking on dangerous links, can also result in cybersecurity issues. Many people agree that autonomous vehicles (AVs) have positive outcomes, but they worry about this technology's potential hazards and side effects. This chapter aims to peer-review the cybersecurity issues and challenges in the context of emerging technologies in transportation from the public's perspective. The results of our study will help the new research group and transportation companies.

Keywords: Cybersecurity, security issues, transportation, electric data, and emerging technologies

2.1   Introduction

Transportation technology supports movement on land, in water, the air, and even in space by using vehicles and infrastructure like highways and railroads. Innovations in transportation technology are mostly driven by the need to make transportation more efficient, convenient, and safe. Together, experts in the transportation industry and the scientific community collaborate to improve these new technologies' efficiency, safety, and sustainability so that more people and goods can be transported. This is why, for example, slow, coal-powered trains have given way to fast, super-efficient bullet trains; expensive, fuel-hungry planes have given way to quiet, cost-saving, eco-friendly models; and big, gas-hungry cars have given way to all-electric ones [1–3]. Vehicles will also increase in sophistication as AI, data science, manufacturing, and deep learning mature. Everything from self-driving cars and space exploration to ride-hailing apps like Uber and Lyft relies on advancements in these domains. Transportation technology is one of the fastest-growing and most competitive industries in the world because of the vast opportunities it presents. Thousands of new companies are competing to develop the "next big thing" in the transportation industry [4–6]. Scientists and transportation industry professionals work together to optimize the use of these new technologies to convey more people and goods more efficiently and sustainably. Figure 2.1 presents the smart logistics connection.

Germany hopes to reduce Europe's CO2 emissions significantly. France and the United Kingdom (UK) have set a target date of 2040 to end domestic sales of conventional automobiles. The UK offers plug-in vehicle subsidies, the United States (US) provides the clean car rebate programme, and both Japan and China have implemented initiatives to encourage the purchase of green vehicles [7–9]. The most common neighborhood electric vehicles (NEVs) that use unconventional energy sources are electric vehicles (EVs), hydrogen vehicles, natural gas vehicles, and vehicles powered by methanol and ethanol. Among these NEVs, EVs have the most significant potential for promoting positive social and environmental outcomes [10]. The government and private sector efforts to improve EV technology and infrastructure are much appreciated. Figure 2.2 presents major cyberattacks on transportation, and logistics, in the 2nd half of 2021.

Today's two well-known developing technologies are artificial intelligence and blockchain technology, which have several admirable qualities like automation, decentralization, security, and justice. Since 2008, there has been an increase in interest in blockchain-related technology; blockchain technology is capturing attention and may be used as a dominant topic.

The chapter focuses on the following points:

- Cybersecurity issues and challenges in smart logistics
- Smart technologies and their components

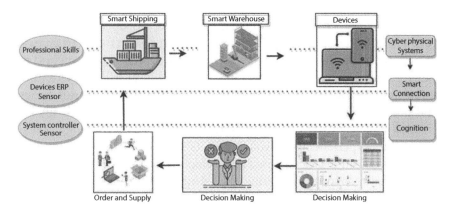

Figure 2.1 Smart logistics connection.

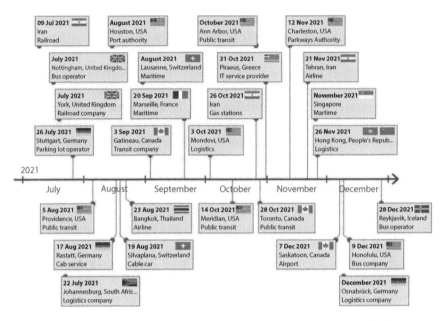

Figure 2.2 Major cyberattacks on transportation, and logistics in the 2nd half of 2021, adapted from [11].

- Types of transportation
- Transportation development.

2.2   Literature Review

Investors must find a comprehensive solution to the intelligent city's privacy and security challenges to avoid these issues and stay outside this intelligent network. The creation of the necessary smart system for smart cities is something that smart city planners and security experts should support to achieve this enormous aim. Recent initiatives and ideas will help us ensure future systems for sustainable smart towns by addressing these difficulties and obstacles [12]. Blockchain is one of the most reliable platforms for creating intelligent transportation systems. Blockchain technology, which is currently experiencing a revolution in its usage and can construct such kinds of applications, can be used to develop transport system applications for developing smart towns. Using blockchain technology in smart cities, a sizable connected network of automobiles will serve as the transportation system for independent vehicle control.

The human aspect, which plays a significant part in all types of technology, will change significantly because of smart transportation systems (STS), which consider managing traveller information and vehicle design. Additionally, it is a legitimate industry for moving things from one location to another. As time passes, the transportation industry examines a variety of difficulties and problems, including traffic congestion, a high accident rate, carbon emissions, and air pollution [13–15]. Additionally, because the transportation industry is inherently public, using wireless technology raises several privacy and security concerns for transportation solutions. Figure 2.3 presents the taxonomy of the literature review.

The Internet of Things (IoT) has used blockchain technology in recent years to boost connectivity. An intelligent vehicle system, an example of a distributed system, keeps track of every linked component and can determine what actions are being taken by which device [16, 17]. IoT devices with smart contracts can connect to the internet and communicate with one another because there is no requirement for a centralized authority to conduct this type of device-to-device interaction. In contrast to purely automated systems, autonomous systems can make judgements in the face of ambiguity. The military, personal hygiene, and transportation are just a few areas that have benefited from the development of autonomous systems as humans will no longer be required to perform routine vehicle

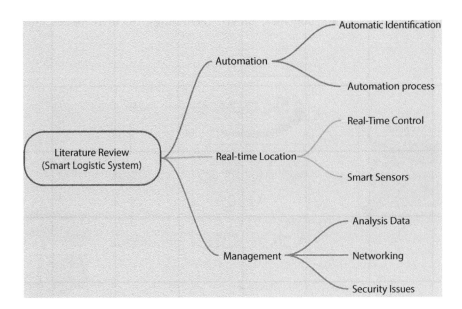

Figure 2.3 Taxonomy of literature review.

operations like lane changing, parking, and accident avoidance [18, 19]. Companies are investing in software development, forming partnerships with top university research centres, and implementing road testing to gain a slice of the expanding autonomous vehicle (AV) industry. The strategic attractiveness of AVs must be weighed against the risks that come with this technology, and most governments recognize the necessity of adapting to these rapid technological changes. There are significant economic and societal gains associated with AVs.

The United Kingdom, the United States, China, and Japan are just a few countries dedicated to creating AVs. They want to increase mobility for the elderly and the disabled, improve safety, and become more competitive in the automobile sector [20, 21]. China plans to dominate the global market for EVs and AVs by the year 2030. Countries like Singapore and Japan, experiencing severe labour shortages in the transportation industry, can significantly benefit from adopting AV technology. Autonomous vehicles can also aid in achieving other national goals, such as better fuel economy and less congestion and pollution [22, 23].

2.3   Methodology

There are three platforms used for the collected data for this chapter; the procedure flowchart for gathering data is shown in Figure 2.4. We used the keyword "Smart Logistics, Smart Technology, Security Issues and

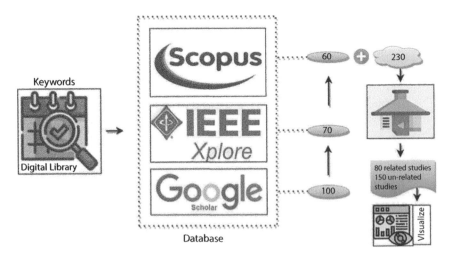

Figure 2.4 Flow chart of the data collection.

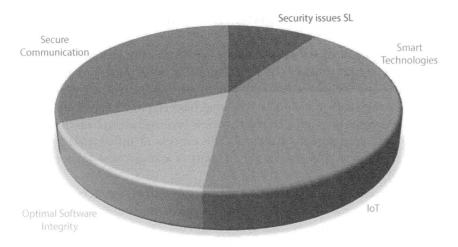

Figure 2.5 Related studies.

Challenges." We selected these databases because they contain many research papers, book chapters and online information on numerous subjects.

There are 280 studies that have been filtered for problems from 130 unrelated studies. An overview of the studies appears in Figure 2.5.

The use of AVs, however, is not without its dangers. The management of such threats is the subject of this piece. To be more precise, we look at how technology's unintended consequences are managed in terms of governance. Based on their characteristics, AVs are sorted into various groups. Vehicles with autonomous capabilities can be broken down into five distinct groups, as defined by the Society of Automotive Engineers (SAE) [24]. Blockchain is a decentralized method that can be used as a public record of all communications in a distributed network. All transactions are mathematically related to one another using private and [25, 26] public keys, allowing participants to track and identify these transactions without needing record retention.

Critical Review

There are 232 studies that have been collected from different databases which are mentioned in Figure 2.4 [Secure Communication, Security issues, Smart Technologies, IoT, and Optimal Software Integrity], and 120 only related ones have been filtered for this chapter, such as 13% in 2019, 20% in 2020, 18% in 2021, 28% in 2022 and 21% in 2023.

2.4 Evaluation of Logistics and Smart Technologies

The development of smart technology has drastically changed logistics. Therefore, for practitioners and academics to better empower logistical tasks, it is essential to understand how smart technologies are utilized. It will be conceptually crucial to assess what has been investigated and draw valuable insights through a literature review because research on this topic is fresh and considerably dispersed. The process of informatization has accelerated, but the informatization of logistics management did not begin until much later.

Smart technology, sometimes referred to as smart gadgets or smart systems, is the incorporation of cutting-edge technologies and connection characteristics into regular systems and objects to give them the ability to function more effectively, autonomously, and interactively. To link systems and objects to the internet and enable communication and data exchange, these technologies often make use of the Internet of Things (IoT). Appliances, wearable technology, home automation systems, automobiles, and industrial systems are just a few of the many products that fall under the umbrella of "smart technology." These devices can gather data, evaluate it, and take appropriate action since they are equipped with sensors, actuators, CPUs, and connection capabilities. Figure 2.6 shows an overview of the smart technology component.

2.4.1 Connectivity

Smart devices may be accessed, controlled, and communicated with remotely thanks to their internet connectivity. They frequently use cellular, Wi-Fi, or Bluetooth networks to establish connections and send data.

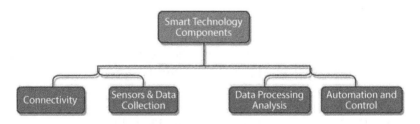

Figure 2.6 Overview of smart technology component.

2.4.2   Sensors Collection

Several types of sensors used by smart devices to gather information about their environment or their own operation are temperature sensors, motion detectors, light detectors, and global positioning system (GPS) receivers. Tracking, analysis, and decision-making are just a few of the immediate uses for the data that these sensors can collect.

2.4.3   Data Processing Analysis

The processing and analysis of the gathered data are made possible by the processors and software capabilities found in smart devices. They can use data analytics, machine learning, or artificial intelligence (AI) algorithms to make sense of the data, draw conclusions, or initiate particular actions.

2.4.4   Automation and Control

Devices and systems may be automated and controlled thanks to smart technology. A smart home system, for instance, can automate lighting, climate control, security systems, and entertainment gadgets in accordance with user preferences or established criteria.

2.4.5   Remote Monitoring and Management

Through specialized programs or web interfaces, smart devices may be remotely managed, controlled, and monitored. With an internet connection, users can access and manage their devices from anywhere, which improves ease and effectiveness.

How we travel will continue to develop and improve as transportation technology does. As evidenced by the rise of electric vehicles and biofuel-powered aeroplanes, the transportation industry has the potential to assist humanity in developing more environmentally friendly modes of transportation. Being a significant industry player, it has acknowledged the importance of greener air travel by announcing that by 2030, it will have delivered fully biofuel-powered planes. Also, transportation advancements mean that people and cargo may reach their destinations more quickly. Time and money are two resources that businesses and customers can benefit from when transportation systems, such as railroads or delivery networks, are made more efficient [27, 28]. To a lesser extent, but significantly, the logistics sector stands to gain from these developments in transportation, as it frequently collaborates with the transport sector to ensure the most cost-effective and efficient movement of goods. More advanced transportation technologies like connected vehicles and freight trucks may help streamline logistics. With an increasing number of Internet of Things (IoT) sensors in CCTV cameras installed along main thoroughfares and delivery routes, more accurate information will be collected to reduce traffic and congestion [29, 30]. With IoT vehicles' knowledge about the phase and timing of signals, connected cars can also predict traffic patterns. Even though self-driving cars are not currently widely available, manufacturers and innovators in the sector have high hopes that they will eventually make millions of people safer. In 2020, about 40,000 Americans lost their lives in traffic-related incidents. The annual toll from car accidents will be substantially altered as the technology behind autonomous vehicles improves, and they can detect and avoid potential collisions.

2.5   Transportation Technology's Types

The transportation industry is experiencing a golden age of innovation, with new technologies allowing us to go farther and faster than ever. An overview of transportation technology types is shown in Figure 2.7. Here are some of the most innovative transportation options available today:

2.5.1   Underground Tunneling

The term "underground transit" refers to transporting passengers or cargo via tunnel networks buried deep below the planet's surface. Elon Musk's Boring Company, the idea which came to him while he was stuck in Los Angeles traffic, is a tunnelling and infrastructure firm that aims to reduce traffic congestion and increase travel time for motorists by constructing tunnels beneath the city [31, 32]. The company has built the LVCC Loop

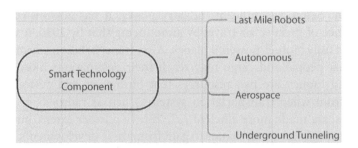

Figure 2.7 Overview of transportation technology's types.

system in Las Vegas, which consists of a tunnel. The 45-minute walk to the LVCC New Exhibit Hall is estimated to be reduced to about two minutes in the car, thanks to the three-station tunnel system that connects the two. Though still in its infancy, underground tunneling is an intriguing concept with the potential to alleviate traffic congestion and lessen the environmental impact of current car travel.

2.5.2   Aerospace

For the time being, though, aerospace is a fascinating mode of transportation. The race is on to be the first firm to offer commercial space flights, and companies like SpaceX, Blue Origin, and Virgin Galactic are all in the mix. The days of needing to be a NASA astronaut to fulfil your goal of space travel are over. Reusable rocket boosters are just one example of the tremendous technological development made possible by the advent of commercial space flight. Historically, rockets would drop their boosters two minutes after take-off [34, 35]. These single-use boosters would crash in a blazing heap after their mission. Boosters created by SpaceX can safely and accurately guide themselves down to Earth using their propulsion systems. The capacity to reuse these rockets is a breakthrough in environmentally friendly transportation technology that makes space travel accessible to the public. Modern transportation is being pushed to its limits by the "Space Race." The innovations are genuinely remarkable. Bringing down the price of space travel from a projected $500 billion to an estimated $60 million per journey encourages us to imagine a future in which humans reside on the moon, Mars, and beyond.

2.5.3   Autonomous Vehicles

The fight over self-driving cars is heating up as well. Every major automaker and start-up is racing to develop the first commercially viable generation of autonomous vehicles. Imagine getting in your car, inputting your destination's location, and relaxing as the automobile takes you there without you having to take control of the wheel or worry about getting lost in the city [36–38]. For many years, this seemed like an impossible goal, but it's finally starting to materialize. The sensors in these cars are continually taking in data from the environment, such as the number of pedestrians crossing the street, the speed of nearby vehicles, and the presence or absence of any animals that might dart into traffic. GPS can find the quickest way to get to a place, but it can also inform you about accidents and traffic jams you can avoid [39–42]. The primary issue with driverless vehicles is how to ensure passenger safety. On the road, anything may happen. How may a car mimic a human's thoughtful reactions to these situations? Each manufacturer and start-up teaches these vehicles to drive responsibly and with the same reasoning as a human. Even though they're still at the prototype stage, autonomous cars are making significant advances in transportation technology that will have far-reaching implications for how we get around.

2.5.4 Last-Mile Robots

Technology in the transportation sector is more comprehensive than vehicles. This category may also include technology that facilitates the transportation of goods from point A to point B. Last-mile robotics is one of the most significant developments in transportation technology for the shipping sector. Companies already use robots that can navigate cities and glide down sidewalks to carry packages to customers' front doors, eliminating the need for a human delivery person [43–45]. Domino's Pizza and Amazon Prime now use robots to ensure on-time delivery of food orders within a set distance from their respective fulfilment centres.

2.5.5 Electric Vehicles

The widespread availability of electric vehicles has profoundly impacted our mobility, both locally and nationally. Electric cars, made famous by manufacturers like Tesla and Nissan, rely entirely on batteries to get us from one place to another. To get back on the road, drivers of electric vehicles must recharge their batteries rather than fill them up with gasoline [46–48]. The range of the most cutting-edge electric vehicles available today is between 150 and 350 miles. Fantastic examples of transportation technology, these cars are altering how automobiles function and are propelled.

2.6 Transportation Technology in Development

Several emerging technologies are influencing the transportation sector. Significant progress has been made in the area of autonomous cars. The potential for this technology to transform urban transportation is enormous, despite its newness. We might see less traffic, less pollution, and more safety on our roads thanks to self-driving cars. New technologies, such as driverless buses and electric vehicles, are reshaping the public transportation sector and private auto markets alike [48–451]. These developments make moving around town without a car more accessible and convenient.

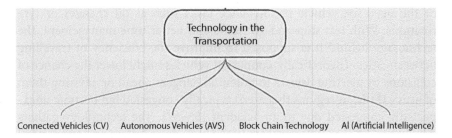

Figure 2.8 Overview of emerging technology in transportation.

This is terrific news for the planet and our overcrowded, polluted urban centres. An overview of emerging technology in transportation is shown in Figure 2.8.

Artificial intelligence (AI) is the first category of emerging technology. By automating processes like data analysis, decision-making, and even customer service interactions through chatbots or virtual assistants, this technology enables organizations to enhance their supply chains. AI has been used to automate many transportation-related tasks, such as navigation systems, car maintenance schedules, and even monitoring fuel efficiency.

2.6.1   Blockchain Technology

Blockchain technology is an additional emerging technology type that is utilized in transportation. With this technology, companies may enhance their supply chains by recording all transactions in a digital ledger that can be viewed later [51–53]. Businesses may also track shipments and inventory levels at any time, which lowers costs by allowing them to know precisely what products are available at any given time.

2.6.2   Autonomous Vehicles

Like Google's self-driving cars, which were originally unveiled in 2009, autonomous vehicles are self-driving cars that can manage their driving. We'll have to wait and watch how long it takes for them to become [54] widespread on our roads, as they have been in development for years and aren't anticipated to be completely operational until around 2020.

2.6.3   Connected Vehicles

Connected vehicles communicate with one another to share information about traffic conditions, other important issues concerning road safety, or the need for vehicle maintenance tasks such as oil changes or tyre rotations. With less stop-and-go traffic and better time management, the technology behind it is supposed to improve the efficiency of travelling between cities. Theoretically, connected vehicles might lower the chance of collisions by alerting drivers to potential dangers ahead or advising them of heavy traffic in regions that aren't typically congested but become unexpectedly congested due to an accident [55–57]. The technology gathers data from GPS and video sensors in the car, which is then sent to a central server where it is examined for pertinent information.

2.7   Discussion

This chapter is on cybersecurity issues and challenges and logistic smart technology. The widespread adoption of digital tools by transportation and logistics firms has boosted the supply chain and the logistics network. With these newfound efficiencies, we can focus on growing our revenue sources like never before [58–60]. One drawback is that transportation and logistics (T&L) have become increasingly susceptible to cyberattacks as a result of several weaknesses that have been highlighted by digitization. Logistics, shipping, trucking, courier services, and everything in between are feeling the pinch. When sensitive consumer data is compromised, the impact is financially devastating, operationally disruptive, and even liability-creating [61–63]. The heightened danger stems from several different sources. One reason is that hackers easily break into transportation and logistics firms because of the widespread adoption of operational technology (OT), which provides new wired and wireless communication channels directly linked to these firms' digital ecosystems. Cybersecurity rules and standards, cybersecurity education, and the availability of qualified cyber defenders are all areas in which the T&L sector lags.

Formerly, the T&L industry would suffer cyberattacks once every few years. Two a month are the norm now. In particular, a few stand out. For instance, in May 2021, a cyberattack essentially disabled the Colonial Pipeline, which supplied gasoline to almost half of the East Coast of the United States, for nearly a week. As a result of the ransom and business interruption, the total cost could exceed $50 million, the company said [64–66]. Even though email and supply chain disruptions are common targets of other cyber assaults, they tend to garner less coverage in the media. In addition, hackers are making more and more attempts to steal information from networks essential to the development and expansion of the T&L sector since they facilitate a more effective and engaging client experience. Automated ordering, shipping monitoring, and account access are just a few of the digital conveniences made possible by these networks [66–68]. While immensely beneficial, customer-focused initiatives like these necessitate storing sensitive data gathered via internet platforms, phone apps, and other mobile devices—some of the most vulnerable access points because of the lack of robust cyber-protection mechanisms. There has been a dramatic reduction in the price of a successful cyberattack on the transportation and logistics industry as the target area for such attacks has grown and the nature of the risk has diversified.

This increased urgency has prompted BCG to investigate the root causes of the industry's susceptibility to cyberattacks in the present day. Our team has developed interconnected tools businesses may use to lessen their vulnerability and build effective, long-lasting defences against these threats. Technology, legislation, and people and procedures are the three main areas where T&L businesses are most vulnerable to cyberattacks. Because of new risks to the sector as a whole, each of these areas needs careful thought. The increased cyberattack surface is visible across the whole T&L industry. When it comes to the maritime industry, hackers are drawn to these systems because they are constantly collecting, integrating, and analyzing data on board to keep tabs on where ships are, what they are carrying, what problems they are having with their upkeep, and how the ocean's environment is affecting all these factors.

Similarly, the railroad sector is transitioning from wired train control and management systems (TCMS) to wireless standards like GSM-Railway, a widespread network connecting trains to railway regulation control centres. T&L companies, like all mobility providers today, use vehicle infotainment systems and other equipment to broaden the scope of possible internet-based interactions.

Chapter's Contribution

As transportation technology advances, so will the methods we travel. As evidenced by the rise of electric vehicles and biofuel-powered planes, the transportation industry has the potential to assist humanity in developing more environmentally friendly modes of transportation. The developments in transportation imply that passengers and freight may travel shorter distances and arrive at their destinations sooner than ever. When transportation systems, like railroads or distribution networks, are optimized, businesses and customers save time and money. The logistics industry stands to benefit less from these transportation innovations, but substantially because it routinely partners with the transport industry to ensure the most cost-effective and efficient transfer of goods. Logistics could be simplified using cutting-edge transportation technologies like connected autos and freight trucks. CCTV cameras equipped with IoT sensors are being increasingly deployed along significant thoroughfares and delivery routes to gather more precise data to reduce traffic and congestion. Connected cars can predict traffic patterns using data collected by IoT vehicles regarding the phase and timing of signals. Manufacturers and industry leaders believe that self-driving cars will make millions of lives safer, even though they are not yet commercially available.

Multiple emerging technologies are influencing the transportation sector. One of the most revolutionary developments in the improvement of self-driving vehicles. Although this technology is just starting, it could completely alter how we think about urban areas. As more people begin to use autonomous vehicles, we may see a reduction in traffic, cleaner air, and a decrease in fatalities. Technology advancements in other areas are also impacting the transportation sector, such as electric vehicles, ride-sharing services, and innovative forms of public transit like driverless buses. Because of these developments, getting around town without a car is becoming less of a hassle. This is good news for the planet and the cleanliness and sanity of our overpopulated and polluted urban centres.

Given the critical nature of the issue, BCG has launched an investigation into the underlying factors that make the industry vulnerable to cyberattacks in the first place. Our team has built a set of interconnected technologies to help organizations protect themselves from cybercriminals and other long-term risks. Telecommunications and media companies are particularly susceptible to cyberattacks because of technological weaknesses, laws, personnel, and processes. Each of these facets requires careful consideration as new threats emerge in the industry. All sectors of the T&L industry are increasingly vulnerable to cyberattacks due to their expanded digital footprint, for example, in the maritime sector.

Players in the transit business are under pressure to modernize because of factors like rapid technological innovation, increased urbanization, and rising expectations from customers and governments. Transit data is sought after by commuters, city planners, emergency personnel, and others. Collaboration between transit agencies' security and operations staff is essential for agencies to maintain their competitive edge. However, most transportation authorities have used separate, proprietary systems for a long time. As the number of Internet of Things (IoT) devices used by transportation agencies grows, so does the number of potential network vulnerabilities that must be addressed. To maintain people's faith, these threats must be reduced. Together, improved collaboration decreased security threats, facilitated data gathering and sharing amongst stakeholders, and optimized daily chores are all possible thanks to a modern, unified security system. It lays out an obvious development strategy, free from the arbitrary limitations of closed platforms.

Protecting passengers and staff, decreasing crime and vandalism along transportation routes, responding quickly to crises, settling liability claims, and ensuring compliance with privacy and municipal regulations are all significant obstacles. To address these issues, operators should implement a scalable enterprise video management system that unifies mobile and fixed video surveillance under a single management platform and interface. Adaptive and transformative AI, cloud computing, and remote on-demand services are now prerequisites for all solutions since the future is just as crucial as the present when making investments and forming partnerships.

A significant change in the transportation business is imminent, as with many other industries, thanks to the rise of digital technologies. Regarding transit times, better loading and unloading procedures, prompt product delivery, increased safety, and higher operational efficiency, users see how the cloud and connected devices promote a more rapid and dependable transportation network. The advantages of cloud computing in this business, such as streamlined workflows and increased safety, are undeniable. Some companies have optimized order management and production planning across warehouse locations using cloud-based warehouse management systems, while others have revolutionized shipment tracking with innovative mobile applications. Today's security managers are adapting to the new realities of video and AI-powered analytics made possible by cloud-based security platform solutions (AI). Insights from untapped sources, such as video surveillance and unstructured IoT data, can be mined using AI technology.

2.8   Conclusion

New technologies are significantly impacting the transportation system's rapid evolution. How we get about cities is evolving due to new technologies, such as driverless vehicles and on-demand services. There may be numerous upsides to these developments, but they also have the potential to alter the transportation landscape significantly. Cybersecurity measures stop unauthorized users from getting into computers and other electronic devices and stealing information. Numerous cybersecurity tools are available to ensure the safety of your data and your business. By investigating requests for information like "Explain the cybersecurity measures," we hope to shed light on some essential methods for keeping sensitive data safe online. Efficiency and speed are increasingly valued because of technological advancements. Innovative modes of transportation are included in this category. There has been a lot of appreciation and interest in these cars from tech companies. Cyberattacks against autonomous vehicles, for example, pose a significant threat to passenger safety even though studies show they are statistically safer than traditional vehicles. Cybersecurity threats have emerged with other new technologies, and autonomous and uncrewed vehicles are no exception. We can see multiple attack vectors, so hackers think we can hack into any vehicle's system, steal the owner's personal information, and compromise the vehicle's security. There is a widespread belief among hackers that they can gain access to and compromise any targeted automotive system, allowing them to obtain the owner's identifiers and inflict physical harm to the vehicle. As a result, companies working on autonomous vehicles need to protect themselves from intrusions by establishing a solid cybersecurity architecture and learning more about the cybersecurity threats to independent vehicle infrastructure. As a result, numerous cybersecurity threats can harm both individuals and businesses. Various factors, including malicious actors, software bugs, and hardware failures, can bring on these risks. Human error, such as careless web browsing or clicking on malicious links, is another source of cybersecurity issues. While most people recognize the benefits of AVs, some are concerned about the technology's downsides. Therefore, we begin by defining AVs and highlighting the many technological risks associated with their use. After outlining the issues, we get into governments' new directions regarding AV security and the possible remedies to these issues. According to our findings, governments have so far avoided enacting binding measures to foster AV developments, with most responses being voluntary and centred on establishing councils or working groups to explore the repercussions of AVs better. Laws have been drafted in the United States to address privacy and cybersecurity issues, and the country has taken an active role in this process. Liability concerns have been legislated for in the UK and Germany, while most other nations are aware of the issue but have yet to implement any fixes.

2.9   Future Work

Various measures have been taken to address privacy and cybersecurity issues, including forming working groups and introducing or revising non-AV-specific legislation. While environmental and employment issues have been mostly ignored, numerous governments have begun retraining programmes for people who may be severely impacted. Accidents can happen anytime during transit, making it challenging when the video is only downloaded from these cameras at set intervals. If the video stream is still being transmitted, security staff cannot see it in real time or conduct any investigations. Even though advancements like dynamic resolution scaling and higher remote bandwidth capacities have made this process much more accessible, it still needs to be improved in more remote areas.

References

[1] Leman AM, Rahman F, Jajuli A, Zakaria S, Feriyanto D. Emission treatment towards cold start and back pressure in internal combustion engine against performance of catalytic converter: a review. *MATEC Web Conf* 2017;87: 02021.

[2] Alptekin Ertan. Emission, injection and combustion characteristics of biodiesel and oxygenated fuel blends in a common rail diesel engine. *Energy* 2017;119 (Jan. 15):44e52.

[3] Zhi C, Fang G. Preparation and heat transfer characteristics of microencapsulated phase change material slurry: a review. *Renew Sustain Energy Rev* 2011;15(9):4624e32.

[4] Dawson, M., & Walker, D. (2022). Argument for Improved Security in Local Governments Within the Economic Community of West African States. *Cybersecurity Measures for E-Government Frameworks*, 96-106.

[5] Huang Z, Hao C. J W. Analysis of vehicle contaminants emission in China. *Environ Protect* 2017;13:42e7.

[6] Fu-qiang A, Hong-liang Z, Zhi C, Yi-cheng QJ, Wei-nan Z, Ping L. Development status and research progress of power battery for pure electric vehicles. *Chin J Eng* 2019;41(1):25e45.

[7] Ujjan, R. M. A., Pervez, Z., Dahal, K., Bashir, A. K., Mumtaz, R., & González, J. (2020). Towards sFlow and adaptive polling sampling for deep learning based DDoS detection in SDN. *Future Generation Computer Systems*, *111*, 763-779.

[8] Chesti, I. A., Humayun, M., Sama, N. U., & Jhanjhi, N. Z. (2020, October). Evolution, mitigation, and prevention of ransomware. In *2020 2nd International Conference on Computer and Information Sciences (ICCIS)* (pp. 1-6). IEEE.

[9] Gaur, L., Solanki, A., Wamba, S. F., & Jhanjhi, N. Z. (Eds.). (2021). *Advanced AI techniques and applications in bioinformatics*. CRC Press.

[10] Nitta, N, Wu F, Lee J.T., Yushin, G. Li ion battery materials: present and future. *Mater Today* 2014;18(5):252e64.

[11] Statistics: Cyber Attacks on Transportation, Transit, Logistics, in the 2nd Half of 2021. *Kon Briefing*, March 7, 2022. https://konbriefing.com/en-topics/cyber-attacks-2021-ind-transportation-h2.html

[12] Aneke M, Wang M. Energy storage technologies and real life applications e a state of the art review. *Appl Energy* 2016;179:350e77.

[13] Basu S, Hariharan KS, Kolake SM, Song T, Sohn DK, Yeo T. Coupled electro-chemical thermal modelling of a novel Li-ion battery pack thermal management system. *Appl Energy* 2016;181:1e13.

[14] Zhang X, Kong X, Li G, Li J. Thermodynamic assessment of active cooling/heating methods for lithium-ion batteries of electric vehicles in extreme conditions. *Energy* 2014;64:1092e101.

[15] Huang C-K, Sakamoto JS, Wolfenstine J, Surampudi S. The limits of low temperature performance of Li-ion cells. *J Electrochem Soc* 2000;17(8): 2893e6.

[16] Shah, I. A., Jhanjhi, N. Z., & Laraib, A. (2023). Cybersecurity and Blockchain Usage in Contemporary Business. In *Handbook of Research on Cybersecurity Issues and Challenges for Business and FinTech Applications* (pp. 49-64). IGI Global.

[17] Raijmakers LHJ, Danilov DL, Eichel RA, Notten PHL. A review on various temperature-indication methods for Li-ion batteries. *Appl Energy* 2019;240 (Apr. 15):918e45.

[18] Xie Y. Li. W, Hu. X, Zou. C, f F. Novel mesoscale electrothermal modeling for lithium-ion batteries. *IEEE Trans Power Electron* 2020;35(3):2595e614.

[19] Xie Y, Li W, Hu X, Lin X, Yue H. An enhanced online temperature estimation for lithium-ion batteries. *IEEE Trans Transport Electrific* 2020;6(2):375e90.

[20] Wu S, Xiong R, Li H, Nian V, Ma S. The state of the art on preheating lithiumion batteries in cold weather. *J Energy Storage* 2020;27(Feb.). 101059.101051-101059.101013.

[21] Vidal C, Gross O, Gu R, Kollmeyer P, Emadi A. Xev LI-ion battery low temperature effects - review. *IEEE Trans Veh Technol* 2019;68(5):4560e72.

[22] Jaguemont J, Mierlo JV. A comprehensive review of future thermal management systems for battery-electrified vehicles. *J Energy Storage* 2020;31: 101551.

[23] Shah, I. A., Jhanjhi, N. Z., Humayun, M., & Ghosh, U. (2022). Impact of COVID-19 on Higher and Post-secondary Education Systems. In *How COVID-19 Is Accelerating the Digital Revolution* (pp. 71-83). Springer, Cham.

[24] Chen J, Kang S, Jiaqiang E, Huang Z, Liao G. Effects of different phase change material thermal management strategies on the cooling performance of the power lithium ion batteries: a review. *J Power Sources* 2019;442:227228.

[25] Solyali D, Akinlabi AHA. Configuration, design, and optimization of air-cooled battery thermal management system for electric vehicles: a review. *Renew Sustain Energy Rev* 2020;125:109815.

[26] Choudhari VG, Dhoble DAS, Sathe TM. A review on effect of heat generation and various thermal management systems for lithium ion battery used for electric vehicle. *J Energy Storage* 2020;32:101729.

[27] Shah, I. A., Jhanjhi, N. Z., Humayun, M., & Ghosh, U. (2022). Health Care Digital Revolution during COVID-19. In *How COVID-19 Is Accelerating the Digital Revolution* (pp. 17-30). Springer, Cham.

[28] Saito Y, Kanari K, Takano K. Thermal studies of a lithium-ion battery. *J Power Sources* 1997;68(2):451e4.

[29] Wang Q, Jiang B, Li B, Yan Y. A critical review of thermal management models and solutions of lithium-ion batteries for the development of pure electric vehicles. *Renew Sustain Energy Rev* 2016;64:106e28.

[30] Alkhulaifi YM, Qasem NAA, Zubair SM. Improving the performance of thermal management system for electric and hybrid electric vehicles by adding an ejector. *Energy Convers Manag* 2019:201.

[31] Zhang C, Jiang J, Gao Y, Zhang W, Liu Q, Hu X. Charging optimization in lithium-ion batteries based on temperature rise and charge time. *Appl Energy* 2017:194.

[32] Jaguemont J, Boulon L, Dube Y, Martel F. Thermal management of a hybrid electric vehicle in cold weather. *IEEE Trans Energy Convers* 2016;31(3): 1110e20.

[33] Shah, I. A., Sial, Q., Jhanjhi, N. Z., & Gaur, L. (2023). Use Cases for Digital Twin. In *Digital Twins and Healthcare: Trends, Techniques, and Challenges* (pp. 102-118). IGI Global.

[34] Lei Z, Zhang C, Li J, Fan G, Lin Z. A study on the low-temperature performance of lithium-ion battery for electric vehicles. *Automot Eng* 2013;35(10): 927e33.

[35] Rao Z, Wang S. A review of power battery thermal energy management. *Renew Sustain Energy Rev* 2011;15(9):4554e71.

[36] Chen Z, Xiong R, Lu J, Li X. Temperature rise prediction of lithium-ion battery suffering external short circuit for all-climate electric vehicles application. *Appl Energy* 2018;213:375e83.

[37] Joris DH, Joris J, Mohamed AM, Peter VDB, Joeri VM, Noshin O. Combining an electrothermal and impedance aging model to investigate thermal degradation caused by fast charging. Energies 2018;11(4). 804.

[38] Ouyang D, Chen M, Huang Q, Weng J, Wang J. A review on the thermal hazards of the lithium-ion battery and the corresponding countermeasures. *Appl Sci* 2019;9(12):2483e528.

[39] Xiaoqing Z, Zhenpo W, Hsin W, Cong W. Review of thermal runaway and safety management for lithium-ion traction batteries in electric vehicles. *J Mech Eng* 2020;56(14):91e118.

[40] De Santoli L, Paiolo R. Lo Basso G. An overview on safety issues related to hydrogen and methane blend applications in domestic and industrial use. *Energy Procedia* 2017;126:297e304.

[41] Wu W, Wang S, Chen K, Hong S, Lai Y. A critical review of battery thermal performance and liquid based battery thermal management. *Energy Convers Manag* 2019;182:262e81.

[42] Lei Z, Maotao Z, Xiaoming X, Junkui G. Thermal runaway characteristics on NCM lithium-ion batteries triggered by local heating under different heat dissipation conditions. *Appl Therm Eng* 2019;159:113847.

[43] Al-Zareer M, Dincer I, Rosen MA. A novel approach for performance improvement of liquid to vapor based battery cooling systems. *Energy Convers Manag* 2019;187:191e204.

[44] Al-Zareer M, Dincer I, Rosen MA. A novel phase change based cooling system for prismatic lithium ion batteries. *Int J Refrig* 2017;86:203e17.

[45] Srinivasan, K., Garg, L., Datta, D., Alaboudi, A. A., Jhanjhi, N. Z., Agarwal, R., & Thomas, A. G. (2021). Performance comparison of deep CNN models for detecting driver's distraction. *CMC-Computers, Materials & Continua*, 68(3), 4109-4124.

[46] Khalil, M. I., Jhanjhi, N. Z., Humayun, M., Sivanesan, S., Masud, M., & Hossain, M. S. (2021). Hybrid smart grid with sustainable energy efficient resources for smart cities. *Sustainable Energy Technologies and Assessments*, 46, 101211.

[47] A. Almusaylim, Z., Jhanjhi, N. Z., & Alhumam, A. (2020). Detection and mitigation of RPL rank and version number attacks in the internet of things: SRPL-RP. *Sensors*, 20(21), 5997.

[48] Shah, I. A., Sial, Q., Jhanjhi, N. Z., & Gaur, L. (2023). The Role of the IoT and Digital Twin in the Healthcare Digitalization Process: IoT and Digital Twin in the Healthcare Digitalization Process. In *Digital Twins and Healthcare: Trends, Techniques, and Challenges* (pp. 20-34). IGI Global.

[49] Jhanjhi, N. Z., Brohi, S. N., Malik, N. A., & Humayun, M. (2020, October). Proposing a hybrid rpl protocol for rank and wormhole attack mitigation using machine learning. In *2020 2nd International Conference on Computer and Information Sciences (ICCIS)* (pp. 1-6). IEEE.

[50] K. Hussain, S. J. Hussain, N. Jhanjhi and M. Humayun, SYN Flood Attack Detection based on Bayes Estimator (SFADBE) For MANET, *2019 International Conference on Computer and Information Sciences (ICCIS)*, Sakaka, Saudi Arabia, 2019, pp. 1-4, doi: 10.1109/ICCISci.2019.8716416.

[51] Balakrishnan, S., Ruskhan, B., Zhen, L. W., Huang, T. S., Soong, W. T. Y., & Shah, I. A. (2023). Down2Park: Finding New Ways to Park. *Journal of Survey in Fisheries Sciences*, 322-338.

[52] Zaman, N. (Ed.). (2012). *Wireless Sensor Networks and Energy Efficiency: Protocols, Routing and Management: Protocols, Routing and Management*. IGI Global.

[53] Nanglia, S., Muneer Ahmad, Fawad Ali Khan, and N. Z. Jhanjhi. An enhanced Predictive heterogeneous ensemble model for breast cancer prediction. *Biomedical Signal Processing and Control* 72 (2022): 103279.

[54] Shahid, H., Ashraf, H., Javed, H., Humayun, M., Jhanjhi, N. Z., & AlZain, M. A. (2021). Energy optimised security against wormhole attack in iot-based wireless sensor networks. *Comput. Mater. Contin*, 68(2), 1967-81.

[55] Ujjan, R. M. A., Pervez, Z., & Dahal, K. (2018, June). Suspicious traffic detection in SDN with collaborative techniques of snort and deep neural networks. In *2018 IEEE 20th International Conference on High Performance Computing and Communications; IEEE 16th International Conference on Smart City; IEEE 4th International Conference on Data Science and Systems (HPCC/SmartCity/DSS)* (pp. 915-920). IEEE.

[56] Brohi, S. N., Jhanjhi, N. Z., Brohi, N. N., & Brohi, M. N. (2020). Key applications of state-of-the-art technologies to mitigate and eliminate COVID-19.

[57] Almusaylim, Z. A., Zaman, N., & Jung, L. T. (2018, August). Proposing a data privacy aware protocol for roadside accident video reporting service using 5G in Vehicular Cloud Networks Environment. In *2018 4th International conference on computer and information sciences (ICCOINS)* (pp. 1-5). IEEE.

[58] Ujjan, R. M. A., Khan, N. A., & Gaur, L. (2022). E-Government Privacy and Security Challenges in the Context of Internet of Things. In *Cybersecurity Measures for E-Government Frameworks* (pp. 22-42). IGI Global.

[59] Lim, M., Abdullah, A., Jhanjhi, N. Z., Khan, M. K., & Supramaniam, M. (2019). Link prediction in time-evolving criminal network with deep reinforcement learning technique. *IEEE Access, 7*, 184797-184807.

[60] Diwaker, C., Tomar, P., Solanki, A., Nayyar, A., Jhanjhi, N. Z., Abdullah, A., & Supramaniam, M. (2019). A new model for predicting component-based software reliability using soft computing. *IEEE Access, 7*, 147191-147203.

[61] Sennan, S., Somula, R., Luhach, A. K., Deverajan, G. G., Alnumay, W., Jhanjhi, N. Z., ... & Sharma, P. (2021). Energy efficient optimal parent selection based routing protocol for Internet of Things using firefly optimization algorithm. *Transactions on Emerging Telecommunications Technologies, 32*(8), e4171.

[62] Gaur, L., Afaq, A., Solanki, A., Singh, G., Sharma, S., Jhanjhi, N. Z., ... & Le, D. N. (2021). Capitalizing on big data and revolutionary 5G technology: Extracting and visualizing ratings and reviews of global chain hotels. *Computers and Electrical Engineering, 95*, 107374.

[63] Ujjan, R.M.A., Taj, I. and Brohi, S.N., 2022. E-Government Cybersecurity Modeling in the Context of Software-Defined Networks. In *Cybersecurity Measures for E-Government Frameworks* (pp. 1-21). IGI Global.

[64] Muzafar, S., Humayun, M., & Hussain, S. J. (2022). Emerging Cybersecurity Threats in the Eye of E-Governance in the Current Era. In *Cybersecurity Measures for E-Government Frameworks* (pp. 43-60). IGI Global.

[65] Hussain, M., Talpur, M.S.H. and Humayun, M., 2022. The Consequences of Integrity Attacks on E-Governance: Privacy and Security Violation. In *Cybersecurity Measures for E-Government Frameworks* (pp. 141-156). IGI Global.

[66] Ujjan, R. M. A., Hussain, K., & Brohi, S. N. (2022). The Impact of Blockchain Technology on Advanced Security Measures for E-Government. In *Cybersecurity Measures for E-Government Frameworks* (pp. 157-174). IGI Global.

[67] Chhajed, G. J., & Garg, B. R. (2022). Applying Decision Tree for Hiding Data in Binary Images for Secure and Secret Information Flow. In *Cybersecurity Measures for E-Government Frameworks* (pp. 175-186). IGI Global.

[68] Alkinani, M. H., Almazroi, A. A., Jhanjhi, N. Z., & Khan, N. A. (2021). 5G and IoT based reporting and accident detection (RAD) system to deliver first aid box using unmanned aerial vehicle. *Sensors, 21*(20), 6905.

Global Navigation Satellite Systems for Logistics: Cybersecurity Issues and Challenges

Noor Zaman Jhanjhi[1]*, Loveleen Gaur[2] and Navid Ali Khan[3]

[1]School of Computing Science, Taylor's University, Kuala Lumpur, Selangor, Malaysia
[2]Amity University Noida, Noida, Uttar Pradesh, India
[3]School of Computer Science and Engineering, SCE, Taylor's University, Subang Jaya, Selangor, Malaysia

Abstract

The availability of accurate location, navigation, and timing data made possible by Global Navigation Satellite Systems (GNSS) technology has had a profound impact on the logistics industry. They are now crucial to the logistics industry's supply chain management, route optimization, asset protection, and overall operational efficiency. Positioning, navigation, and timing services are made available to customers all around the world thanks to the GNSS networks of satellites. Most people are familiar with the United States Global Positioning System (GPS), the most widely used GNSS. GNSS receivers on the ground may be able to pick up signals that a network of satellites in Earth's orbit sends out. The receivers use the signals to determine their position, velocity, and time, allowing for more precise navigation and timing measures. Transportation, mapping, surveying, and time synchronization are just a few of the many fields where GNSS has become indispensable. The military, police, and emergency services rely on it for navigation and communication as well. Like any other technology dependent on communication and computer systems, GNSS is susceptible to cyberattacks. Navigation, timing, and synchronization are just a few of the many uses for Global Navigation Satellite Systems, including GPS, GLONASS, Galileo, and BeiDou. However, their reliance on wireless signals and computer systems makes them vulnerable to cyberattacks. GNSS system operators have implemented various security measures to address

---

*Corresponding author: noorzaman.jhanjhi@taylors.edu.my

Imdad Ali Shah and Noor Zaman Jhanjhi (eds.) Cybersecurity in the Transportation Industry, (49–68) © 2024 Scrivener Publishing LLC

these cybersecurity threats, including encryption of signals, redundancy in the system design, and monitoring for signal anomalies. It is essential to continue improving cybersecurity measures to ensure the reliability and accuracy of GNSS systems. The primary object of this chapter is to measure cybersecurity for Global Navigation Satellite Systems in emerging technologies and provide recommendations to the practitioners, and this study opens doors for new researchers.

Keywords: GNSS, cyberattacks, cybersecurity, emerging technologies, and applications

3.1   Introduction

Global Navigation Satellite Systems (GNSS) are satellite-based systems that provide location, timing, and navigation services to users on a global scale. These systems use a network of orbiting satellites, ground control stations, and user receivers to determine the precise position and time information. Unidentified entities were making bogus claims to be warships belonging

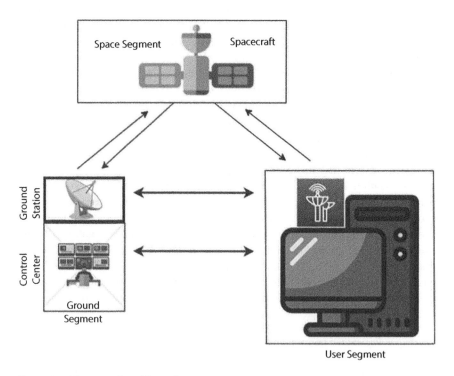

Figure 3.1 The typical satellite architecture.

to the United States or a coalition close to the Strait of Hormuz [1–3]. These sources say artificial intelligence systems have already been used nationally or militarily. Flaws of this sensitive and potentially hazardous kind in computer security still need to be adequately studied in academic circles. Less than a handful of studies have investigated these kinds of issues. Figure 3.1 presents the typical satellite architecture.

Yet, to navigate the wide canals, every vessel must adhere to the present Automatic Identification System (AIS) technology, which is insecure by design. AIS receivers are also becoming increasingly diverse daily. There is also widespread use of smartphone-based navigation applications in addition to the conventional onboard AIS configuration [4–7]. The seven smartphone-based navigation programs that were utilized in this research were downloaded roughly 43,000 times from the Google Play Store. This statistic does not consider the download counts of other applications that were not evaluated or the iOS platform. Using a Wi-Fi connection, the navigation data are sent from the receiver to the mobile application, where they are displayed. These receiving configurations that are based on smartphones are gaining popularity among private users since they have an appealing graphical user interface, are inexpensive, and are simple to

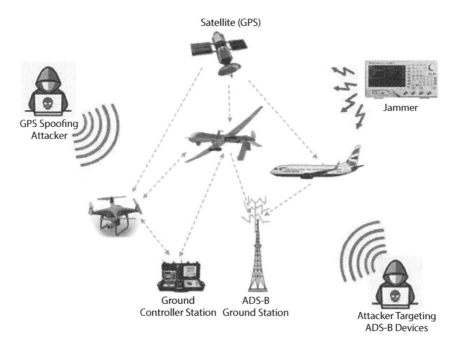

Figure 3.2 Cyberattacks on the GPS network [10].

install [8, 9]. The term "New Space" describes the adaptability pattern that emerged from using standard modules and components to lower the cost of space travel and increase its prevalence across sectors. Figure 3.2 presents the cyberattacks on the GPS network.

Further developments in this "ecology," include the manufacture of tiny satellites (weighing 600 kg or less) and massive satellite constellations numbering in the hundreds of thousands. Six times as many tiny satellites were launched, with half of them being used for commercial reasons [11, 12]. Components available commercially off-the-shelf (COTS) are increasingly used in satellites and ground control systems, reducing development times and prices.

The chapter focuses on the following points:

- Peer-reviews Global Navigation Satellite Systems
- GNSS and Logistic
- Technologies in Logistics
- Security issues and challenges in the GNSS.

3.2   Literature Review

After that, the matching filter implementation demodulates each channel individually. The recovered bit synchronization is then used in conjunction with a correlator to determine the training sequence, which allows the transmitted bits to be calculated. The authors put their receiver through its paces on a stratospheric balloon journey at 24 kilometres. The findings of the tests demonstrated that AIS signals might be received from around 500 kilometres and presented the first SDR-based AIS assaults that they had successfully performed. The authors built a software called AISTX [13–15] based on the Python programming language to generate an AIS payload per the protocol. The IQs of the signal were generated with the assistance of the GNU Radio Companion (GRC). Then they were sent into the air with the aid of the Universal Software Radio Peripheral (USRP). Three separate receivers independently validated the receipt of the forged signal. The AIS protocol specifications were susceptible to hacks such as spoofing, a fake collision threat, and disruption of service availability since several threats influenced them. The authors constructed the final AIS frame with the assistance of AISTX and encoded the message with the algorithm [16–18]. They tried sending type 1 messages across an RF connection and tested how well it worked. To test the reception, an additional SDR-based receiver equipped with a chart-plotting program known as Open CPN was utilized.

Their investigation's primary goal was to develop an AIS transponder that could be produced at a reasonable cost and carry out a study that was quite comparable to this one. The authors broadcast the location of a ship by using an SDR that was enabled for transmission, as well as GRC and AISTX [19–21]. They determined the difference between the data that had been transmitted and the data that had been received at the receiver end. Upon comparing the original data to the data received, they discovered that the ship's location was off by an average of seven meters. Fake AIS broadcasts are not the only tactic that may be used in attacks on ships. Figure 3.3 presents the taxonomy of GLONASS.

A group of researchers from the University of Texas at Austin could take control of an $80 million boat by using a relatively inexpensive GPS spoofing technique [22–24]. In yet another experiment, faking the GPS resulted in an incredible increase in ship speed. The authors investigated AIS vulnerabilities and obstacles. They conducted an in-depth investigation on a spoofing event that took place close to Elba in December 2019. Because of the phony signals, a genuine ship was put in a potentially hazardous scenario. More than a dozen bogus ships were discovered to be heading in the same direction as that ship. The researchers concluded that the marine sector is not immune to cyberattacks and needs to adequately prepare for the hazards connected with using contemporary digital technologies [25–28]. Other research concentrated on the SDR implementation of AIS, decoding, or the many options for the construction of inexpensive transponders. There have been many new types of receivers, pieces of software, and apps for chart-plotting that use smart devices developed. The adversaries are also armed with novel tools and concepts. Thus, it is vital to evaluate the assaults on modern AIS systems using the technology that is now available. The hacker community is increasingly interested in techniques that employ

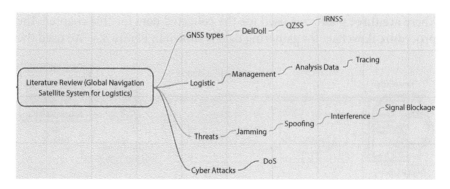

Figure 3.3 Taxonomy of GLONASS.

cyber technologies to maintain vital infrastructure; however, this out-moded way of thinking needs to be revised for these systems. Standards, laws, and security-focused organizational cultures have pushed terrestrial businesses to integrate security measures in two ways: retroactively and proactively. The organization's satellite-based systems may be easier or more advantageous to attack than its terrestrial ones. To harm an economy, one strategy may be to attack the satellites that process credit card transactions for several businesses.

The logistics business is crucial to people's daily lives, and it has expanded in importance alongside the rise of electronic commerce. Logistics is a foundational business because of its central role in the integration of data and AI into daily life. Information gleaned from the Internet of Things is revolutionary, and the rapid advancement of the intelligent logistics system has made it possible for logistics companies to better keep track of their stock, their fleet's location and movement, and the details of their products [29–32]. The robust features and expanding infrastructure of the Internet of Things technology make it a top choice for logistics companies. The Internet of Things wireless sensor network (WSN) is a self-organizing or multiple-hog mode system consisting of an equal number of sensor nodes that can monitor and perceive all types of perception object information at the location of nodes and process this information for wireless transmission to an observer. Sensor devices, data collection systems, and a wireless communication platform all come together in WSN. WSN is an innovative method of gathering and processing data. WNS is now used for warehouse condition monitoring, logistics management for hazardous materials and perishable items, and management of the cold supply chain.

3.3   Research Methods

There are three platforms used for the collected data for this chapter. The procedure flowchart for gathering data is shown in Figure 3.4. We used the

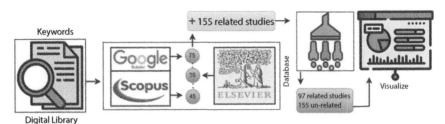

Figure 3.4 Flow chart of the data collection.

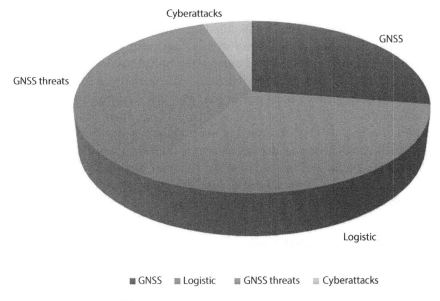

Figure 3.5 Overview of the related studies.

keyword "Global Navigation Satellite Systems, security issues in logistics." We selected these databases because they contain many research papers, book chapters and online information on numerous subjects. The overview of related studies is shown in Figure 3.5.

Four models may be drawn from the physical system of sensor nodes: sensing, communication, information analysis, and power supply. The sensing module is used to detect and collect data from the environment, digitize the data, and send it on to the information analysis module. The information analysis module, which is in charge of coordinating and dominating the other modules' modes of operation, can process and store the initial data gathered by the perception module. To achieve interaction with other sensor nodes or sink nodes, the communication module is implemented. There are four modes that the communication module can be in: sending, receiving, waiting, and sleeping [33–35]. The most power is used during the transmitting phase, whereas the least is used during the resting phase.

3.4   Global Navigation Satellite Systems

Global Navigation Satellite Systems (GNSS) provide global position and time information. These systems use satellites and ground-based receivers to locate a user's device. These systems are enhanced to improve accuracy, dependability, and availability [36–40]. Operational GNSS systems are utilised in aviation, maritime, transportation, agriculture, and military and defence applications. The control component has global nodes that upload and monitor data. These stations receive satellite signals and compare them to orbit simulations. Control centres can alter the satellite's orbit to avoid space debris. GNSS position accuracy requires this method and satellite health checks [41–43]. The user segment comprises devices that receive signals from satellites and determine where they are based on where and when at least four satellites are in orbit. This part is made up of the user's antennas, receivers, and positioning engines. These parts all work together to analyze signals and fix any timing problems.

3.4.1   Types of Global Navigation Satellite Systems

Global Navigation Satellite System (GNSS) refers to any of the satellite groups that send information about location, navigation, and time. There are six unique constellations, four major constellations and two regional constellations.

The radio frequencies in the L-band are used to send the signals from these constellations. However, each constellation can choose its frequencies and give those frequencies a different name. GNSS positioning equipment

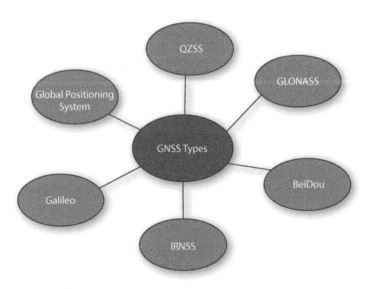

Figure 3.6 The GNSS types.

can usually pick up at least two frequencies, and more specialized equipment can pick up more L-band signals. Satellite-Based Augmentation Systems (SBAS), which offer global error corrections for better accuracy in GNSS applications, should be brought to your attention [45–47]. Many countries run their own SBAS systems, and most of the time, they are deemed independent from the typical GNSS constellations. Figure 3.6 presents the GNSS types.

3.4.2   Global Positioning System (United States)

The United States Space Force oversees the Global Positioning System (GPS) and ensures it works. It was the first constellation to be built in space [48, 49]. Its first satellite was launched in 1978, and by 1993, all its first sets of satellites were working. The year 1978 saw the launch of the constellation's first satellite.

3.4.3   GLONASS (Russia)

Now run by the Russian government's Roscosmos State Corporation for Space Activities, GLONASS was originally created in the Soviet Union as a rival to GPS in the 1970s. GLONASS has 24 satellites in orbit, with the first one being launched in 1982.

3.4.4   Galileo (European Union)

The 2011 debut of the Galileo constellation marked its relative newness. Now consisting of 26 satellites, Galileo is operated by the European Union's European Global Navigation Satellite Systems Agency; it will expand to 30 satellites by 2021.

3.4.5   BeiDou (China)

China's National Space Agency deployed the BeiDou satellite system in 2000 (CNSA). During the past two decades, BeiDou has amassed a fleet of 48 satellites.

3.4.6   IRNSS (India)

The Indian Space Research Organization (ISRO) operates another significant regional constellation called the Indian Regional Navigation Satellite System (IRNSS), which comprises eight satellites. It is also known as NavIC, which stands for "Navigation with Indian Constellation." The sphere of influence of the constellation starts in India and goes all the way to Saudi Arabia in the west, all of China in the north and east, Mozambique in the south, and Western Australia in the north.

3.5   Overview of Automatic Identification System

To reduce the risk of accidents at sea and enhance maritime security, ships and vessels use an identification tracking system called the Automatic Identification System (AIS) to communicate with one another and with land-based services. Information regarding a ship's identification, location, course, and speed can be sent and received via AIS technology using VHF radio frequencies. Concerns about marine safety, especially in congested shipping lanes and ports, prompted the IMO to create the AIS. Ships can be tracked in real time by a combination of on-shore AIS transceivers and satellite-based AIS receivers, giving ship owners a better chance of avoiding collisions [50–53]. Transmissions of AIS data occur at regular intervals, making information accessible to other ships, shore-based stations, and maritime authorities. Passenger ships and cargo ships above 300 gross tonnes that make international journeys are required to have AIS. Still, it is also widely used by smaller vessels voluntarily. AIS has been a significant advancement in maritime safety and has helped prevent collisions and improve situational awareness for ships at sea.

3.6   Discussion

The space sector has many moving pieces, shifting dynamics, and emerging concepts. With the end of the Cold War, a few countries and state-level activities took over, and they began creating costly and lengthy-lasting satellites. To limit the military capabilities of adversaries, a firm need-to-know policy was implemented to build a foundation of secrecy in research and development procedures. The emerging norms of this period are classic examples of the "Old Space" paradigm. Since then, the proliferation of consumer microelectronics, the acceleration of R&D, and the reduction in launch costs have all contributed to a newfound appreciation for space as a valuable resource for the industry. As a result of private investment, the space industry has grown (it was valued at $269 billion in [54–56], and new companies and initiatives have entered the fray. Because of the new profit-driven space economy, R&D has become more iterative and uses smaller, more agile teams, much like the technology sector rather than the aerospace or military. Businesses are becoming more daring in their use of satellites, which has resulted in cutting-edge new uses and technology. The academic community is actively working to advance New Space by showcasing cutting-edge space technologies. The STRaND-11 mission proved that smartphone electronics could be successfully integrated into satellites. Applications of satellite images and signals intelligence, such as commercial intelligence products and environmental conservation activities, have fueled a boom in investment in the Earth observation sector. Constellations of tiny satellites are being operated by companies like Planet2 and HawkEye 3603 in low Earth orbit (LEO). Another growing New Space use is global broadband services, which will help provide the internet to underserved places and create resilient networks for essential services. Revenue from satellite broadband has increased steadily over the past five years, and this trend is expected to accelerate with the launch of hundreds of thousands of satellites in constellations [57–59]. Route planning, fleet management, and other time-critical applications in the finance and energy sectors have all benefited from the continuous expansion of satellite geolocation services, which provide exact time and position data to specialized receivers. The worldwide ground equipment market has grown because of the wide range of potential GNSS applications. The value of GNSS equipment has increased steadily. With 68% of the bombs dropped in the Iraq War that began in 2003 directed by satellites, satellites play a pivotal role in modern warfare. More stringent security measures, including encryption, anti-jamming methods, and frequency hopping, must be included in these systems [60–62]. The use of commercial satellites by the United States military has grown significantly in recent wars, and this trend has been encouraged by laws approved under the George W. Bush administration [63–65]. The United States, Russia, and China each launched almost as many small satellites. The United States launched 39, Russia launched 20, and China launched 17. So, this study aims to examine the New Space period through the lenses of historic security concerns, forthcoming security issues, and foundational technologies driving the growth and reinvention of the space and satellite sector. The ability to control items as far away as satellites poses a new security issue for the hacking community.

Chapter's Contribution

Global Navigation Satellite Systems (GNSS) are critical infrastructure for various applications, including transportation, communication, and navigation. However, they are also vulnerable to cyberattacks that can cause significant disruption to these services. To ensure the security of GNSS, several cybersecurity measures can be taken:

1. Authentication: One of the most critical cybersecurity measures is authentication, which ensures that the data received by the GNSS receiver is from a legitimate source. Authentication can be achieved using cryptographic algorithms and digital signatures.
2. Encryption: Encryption is another important cybersecurity tool that helps keep GNSS transmissions safe from prying eyes. Only approved receivers in possession of the necessary encryption keys will be able to decipher the data delivered by the satellite.
3. Anti-jamming: Jamming is a common technique attackers use to disrupt GNSS signals. Anti-jamming measures, such as using directional antennas, can help mitigate this threat.

The risks of cyberattacks on GNSS can be lessened with adequate cybersecurity precautions. But it's important to remember that cybersecurity is an ongoing process, and that when new threats appear, so must the measures used to counter them. GNSS receivers are vulnerable to signal loss and erroneous data due to deliberate and inadvertent signal interference. There are several potential causes of interference, including other electrical equipment, the environment, or even intentional interference. Even though GNSS signals may span the world, there are still places where calls may be blocked, such as in urban canyons.

Completely obliterated by thick walls of noise, the GNSS is susceptible to cyberattacks, including jamming, spoofing, and hacking. Attacks of this type pose a threat to the integrity of vital infrastructure and the reliability of services that rely on GNSS signals. There are constraints on the precision that can be achieved with GNSS signals. Multipath errors, atmospheric conditions, and other variables can impact GNSS receivers and lead to inaccurate location data. Some consumers may be put off by the GNSS technology's high price tag. Even though GNSS receivers are becoming increasingly common in consumer electronics like smartphones, higher-precision receivers can be prohibitively costly and often require expert operation. To maintain the continued accuracy and reliability of GNSS signals, the infrastructure supporting them must undergo regular maintenance. For complex systems with multiple satellites and ground equipment, this upkeep may be rather costly. The advent of GNSS technology has greatly improved navigation and information retrieval, but it has also brought forth a number of new complications. To keep GNSS systems accurate, dependable, and secure, investments in research, infrastructure, and cybersecurity are necessary.

3.7 Conclusion

Protecting GNSS from cyberattacks necessitates employing appropriate cybersecurity measures. A better-protected GNSS infrastructure may be achieved by the implementation of measures including authentication and encryption, detection of jamming and spoofing, redundancy, physical protection, and routine upgrades and maintenance. To successfully implement these steps and guarantee GNSS's ongoing dependability and security, parties must collaborate. Multiple metrics may be used to assess the state of cybersecurity for GNSS in developing technologies. Possible cyber dangers and flaws in GNSS systems can be uncovered by conducting a thorough risk assessment. Assessing the possible impact of assaults on the system and its users, such as jamming, spoofing, and hacking, is part of this process. The International Electrotechnical Commission's (IEC) and the National Institute of Standards and Technology's (NIST) cybersecurity requirements should be followed by GNSS systems. Independent audits and certification methods can be used to confirm that these criteria are being met. The goal of penetration testing is to find security holes in a system by simulating an attack. This can evaluate the system's capacity to detect and respond to threats and help pinpoint any weak spots. New threats and security holes can be uncovered with the aid of constant monitoring of threat intelligence streams. Knowing this allows for the formulation and introduction of preventative strategies. To guarantee the system can successfully respond to cybersecurity issues, an incident response plan should be designed and evaluated on a regular basis. This involves figuring out who does what, how incidents are reported, and what may be done to prevent more harm. A comprehensive method that takes into account technical, operational, and organizational elements is needed to evaluate GNSS cybersecurity in cutting-edge technology.

3.8 Future Work

To guarantee the safety and dependability of the system, this method can aid in the detection of threats and vulnerabilities and the introduction of suitable countermeasures. Resilience measures, multi-factor authentication, machine learning and artificial intelligence, collaborative techniques, and international standards should all be further developed in the future as part of GNSS cybersecurity measures. By taking these steps, we can make GNSS systems safer and more reliable for use in a wide range of sectors.

References

[1] Hill, J. 2020. Maxar Stock Surges on Strong 2Q, Executives Update Legion, Telesat LEO Outlook. *Via Satellite.* Accessed July 2021. https://www.satellitetoday.com/business/2020/08/06/

[2] Huang, W., B. Männel, A. Brack, and H. Schuh. 2020. Two Methods to Determine Scale-independent GPS PCOs and GNSS-based Terrestrial Scale: Comparison and Cross-check. *GPS Solutions* 25 (1). doi:10.1007/s10291-020-01035-5.

[3] Jewett, R. 2020. FCC Grants OneWeb Market Access for 2,000-Satellite Constellation. *Via Satellite.* Accessed 10 July 2021. https://www.satellitetoday.com/broadband/2020/08/26/fcc-grants-oneweb-market-access-for-2000-satellite-constellation/

[4] Shah, I. A., Jhanjhi, N. Z., Humayun, M., & Ghosh, U. (2022). Health Care Digital Revolution during COVID-19. In *How COVID-19 Is Accelerating the Digital Revolution* (pp. 17-30). Springer, Cham.

[5] Manulis, M., Bridges, C. P., Harrison, R., Sekar, V., & Davis, A. (2021). Cyber security in new space: analysis of threats, key enabling technologies and challenges. *International Journal of Information Security, 20,* 287-311.

[6] Ujjan, R. M. A., Taj, I., & Brohi, S. N. (2022). E-Government Cybersecurity Modeling in the Context of Software-Defined Networks. In *Cybersecurity Measures for E-Government Frameworks* (pp. 1-21). IGI Global.

[7] Manesh, M. R., & Kaabouch, N. (2019). Cyber-attacks on unmanned aerial system networks: Detection, countermeasure, and future research directions. *Computers & Security, 85,* 386-401.

[8] Muzafar, S., Humayun, M., & Hussain, S. J. (2022). Emerging Cybersecurity Threats in the Eye of E-Governance in the Current Era. In *Cybersecurity Measures for E-Government Frameworks* (pp. 43-60). IGI Global.

[9] Khalil, M. I., Jhanjhi, N. Z., Humayun, M., Sivanesan, S., Masud, M., & Hossain, M. S. (2021). Hybrid smart grid with sustainable energy efficient resources for smart cities. *Sustainable Energy Technologies and Assessments, 46,* 101211.

[10] Ujjan, R. M. A., Pervez, Z., Dahal, K., Bashir, A. K., Mumtaz, R., & González, J. (2020). Towards sFlow and adaptive polling sampling for deep learning based DDoS detection in SDN. *Future Generation Computer Systems, 111,* 763-779.

[11] Kbidy, G., G. Adamski, and N. May. 2018. Design Concepts and Challenges for the Iridium NEXT Command and Control System. In *2018 Space Operations Conference*, 2708. Marseille, France, May 28–June 1.

[12] Li, B., H. Ge, M. Ge, L. Nie, Y. Shen, and H. Schuh. 2019. LEO Enhanced Global Navigation Satellite System (Legnss) for Real-time Precise Positioning Services. *Advances in Space Research* 63 (1): 73-93. doi:10.1016/j. asr.2018.08.017.

[13] Li, B., L. Nie, H. Ge, M. Ge, and L. Yang. 2017. Precise Orbit Determination of Combined GNSS and LEO Constellations with Regional Ground Stations. In *Proceedings of ION GNSS+ 2017*, 2137–2147. Portland, Oregon, September 25–29.

[14] Dawson, M., & Walker, D. (2022). Argument for Improved Security in Local Governments within the Economic Community of West African States. *Cybersecurity Measures for E-Government Frameworks*, 96-106.

[15] Li, X., F. Ma, X. Li, H. Lv, L. Bian, Z. Jiang, and X. Zhang. 2019b. LEO Constellation-augmented multi-GNSS for Rapid PPP Convergence. *Journal of Geodesy* 93 (5): 749-764. doi:10.1007/s00190-018-1195-2.

[16] Li, X., J. Wu, K. Zhang, X. Li, Y. Xiong, and Q. Zhang. 2019c. Real-Time Kinematic Precise Orbit Determination for LEO Satellites Using Zero-differenced Ambiguity Resolution. *Remote Sensing* 11 (23): 2815. doi:10.3390/rs11232815.

[17] Lu, J., G. Zhang, G. Chen, W. Gao, and C. Su. 2020. Development Status and Prospect of Satellite Navigation System. *Spacecraft Engineering* 04: 1-10.

[18] Gaur, L., Ujjan, R. M. A., & Hussain, M. (2022). The Influence of Deep Learning in Detecting Cyber Attacks on E-Government Applications. In *Cybersecurity Measures for E-Government Frameworks* (pp. 107-122). IGI Global.

[19] Ma, F., X. Zhang, X. Li, J. Cheng, F. Guo, J. Hu, and L. Pan. 2020. Hybrid Constellation Design Using a Genetic Algorithm for a LEO-based Navigation Augmentation System. GPS Solutions 24 (2): 1-14. doi:10.1007/s10291-020-00977-0

[20] Su, X. 2017. Theory and Method Research for Global Real-time Centi-meter Level Navigation System Based on High, Medium and Low Orbit Satellites. PhD diss., Wuhan University.

[21] Wang, K., and Ahmed EI-Mowafy. 2021. LEO Satellite Clock Analysis and Prediction for Positioning Applications. *Geo-spatial Information Science*: 1-20. doi:10.1080/10095020.2021.1917310.

[22] A. Almusaylim, Z., Jhanjhi, N. Z., & Alhumam, A. (2020). Detection and mitigation of RPL rank and version number attacks in the internet of things: SRPL-RP. *Sensors, 20*(21), 5997.

[23] Wang, L., D. Li, R. Chen, W. Fu, X. Shen, and H. Jiang. 2020. Low Earth Orbiter (LEO) Navigation Augmentation: Opportunities and Challenges. *Chinese Journal of Engineering Science* 22:144. doi:10.15302/j-sscae2020.02.018.

[24] Wang, L., R. Chen, B. Xu, X. Zhang, T. Li, and C. Wu. 2019. "The Challenges of LEO Based Navigation Augmentation System – Lessons Learned from Luojia-1A Satellite." In *Proceeding: China Satellite Navigation Conference (CSNC) 2019 Proceedings*, 298-310. Beijing, China: Springer Singapore.

[25] Wang, L., R. Chen, D. Li, B. Yu, and C. Wu. 2018. Quality Assessment of the LEO Navigation Augmentation Signals from Luojia-1A Satellite. *Geomatics and Information Science of Wuhan University* 43: 2191-2196.

[26] Wu, C., Y. Shu, G. Wang, and S. Li. 2020. Design and Performance Evaluation of Tianxiang-1 Navigation Enhancement Signal. *Radio Engineering* 9: 748-753.

[27] Jhanjhi, N. Z., Ahmad, M., Khan, M. A., & Hussain, M. (2022). The Impact of Cyber Attacks on E-Governance during the COVID-19 Pandemic. In *Cybersecurity Measures for E-Government Frameworks* (pp. 123-140). IGI Global.

[28] Zhang, C., J. Jin, L. Kuang, and J. Yan. 2018. LEO Constellation Design Methodology for Observing Multi-targets. *Astrodynamics* 2 (2): 121-131. doi:10.1007/s42064-017-0015-4.

[29] Novatel https://novatel.com/tech-talk/an-introduction-to-gnss/what-are-global-navigation-satellite-systems-gnss [7] Chen, P., Y. Yao, Q. Li, and W. Yao. 2017. "Modeling the Plasmasphere Based on LEO Satellites Onboard GPS Measurements." *Journal of Geophysical Research: Space Physics* 122 (1): 1221–1233.

[30] Lu, Y. Brief Introduction to the GPS and BeiDou Satellite Navigation Systems. Springer, Singapore, 2021, pp. 37-72. doi: 10.1007/978-981-16-1075-2_2.

[31] Zidan, J., E. I. Adegoke, E. Kampert, S. A. Birrell, C. R. Ford, and M. D. Higgins. GNSS Vulnerabilities and Existing Solutions: A Review of the Literature. *IEEE Access*, pp. 1–1, Feb. 2020, doi: 10.1109/access.2020.2973759.

[32]. O'Hanlon, B. W., M. L. Psiaki, T. E. Humphreys, and J. A. Bhatti. Real-Time Spoofing Detection Using Correlation Between Two Civil GPS Receiver. pp. 3584-3590, Sep. 21, 2012. http://www.ion.org/publications/abstract.cfm?jp=p&articleID=10533. Accessed: Jun. 15, 2021.

[33] O'Hanlon, B. W., M. L. Psiaki, T. E. Humphreys, and J. A. Bhatti. Real-Time Spoofing Detection in a Narrow-Band Civil GPS Receiver. pp. 2211-2220, Sep. 24, 2010. http://www.ion.org/publications/abstract.cfm?jp=p&articleID=9335. Accessed: Jun. 15, 2021.

[34] Shah, I. A., Sial, Q., Jhanjhi, N. Z., & Gaur, L. (2023). Use Cases for Digital Twin. In *Digital Twins and Healthcare: Trends, Techniques, and Challenges* (pp. 102-118). IGI Global.

[35] Yang, J., Y. J. Chen, W. Trappe, and J. Cheng. Detection and localization of multiple spoofing attackers in wireless networks. *IEEE Transactions on Parallel and Distributed Systems*, vol. 24, no. 1, pp. 44-58, 2013, doi: 10.1109/TPDS.2012.104.

[36] Daneshmand, S., A. Jafarnia-Jahromi, A. Broumandon, and G. Lachapelle. A Low-Complexity GPS Anti-Spoofing Method Using a Multi-Antenna Array. pp. 1233-1243.

[37] Hussain, M., Talpur, M. S. H., & Humayun, M. (2022). The Consequences of Integrity Attacks on E-Governance: Privacy and Security Violation. In *Cybersecurity Measures for E-Government Frameworks* (pp. 141-156). IGI Global.

[38] Tanıl, C., P. M. Jimenez, M. Raveloharison, B. Kujur, S. Khanafseh, and B. Pervan. Experimental validation of INS monitor against GNSS spoofing. In *Proceedings of the 31st International Technical Meeting of the Satellite Division of the Institute of Navigation*, ION GNSS+ 2018, Sep. 2018, pp. 2923-2937. doi: 10.33012/2018.15902.

[39] Balakrishnan, S., Ruskhan, B., Zhen, L. W., Huang, T. S., Soong, W. T. Y., & Shah, I. A. (2023). Down2Park: Finding New Ways to Park. *Journal of Survey in Fisheries Sciences*, 322-338.

[40] Tanil, C., S. Khanafseh, and B. Pervan. An INS monitor against GNSS spoofing attacks during GBAS and SBAS-assisted aircraft landing approaches. In *29th International Technical Meeting of the Satellite Division of the Institute of Navigation*, ION GNSS 2016, Sep. 2016, vol. 4, pp. 2981-2990. doi: 10.33012/2016.14779.

[41] Sun, M., Y. Qin, J. Bao, and X. Yu. GPS Spoofing Detection Based on Decision Fusion with a K-out-of-N Rule. *International Journal of Network Security*, vol. 19, no. 5, pp. 670-674, 2017, doi: 10.6633/IJNS.201709.19(5).03.

[42] Chhajed, G. J., & Garg, B. R. (2022). Applying Decision Tree for Hiding Data in Binary Images for Secure and Secret Information Flow. In *Cybersecurity Measures for E-Government Frameworks* (pp. 175-186). IGI Global.

[43] Panice, G., S. Luongo, G. Gigante, D. Pascarella, C. Di Benedetto, A. Vozella, and A. Pescapè. A SVM-based detection approach for GPS spoofing attacks to UAV. In *2017 23rd International Conference on Automation and Computing (ICAC)*, IEEE, pp. 1-11, IEEE, 2017. doi: 10.23919/IConAC.2017.8081999.

[44] Shah, I. A., Sial, Q., Jhanjhi, N. Z., & Gaur, L. (2023). The Role of the IoT and Digital Twin in the Healthcare Digitalization Process: IoT and Digital Twin in the Healthcare Digitalization Process. In *Digital Twins and Healthcare: Trends, Techniques, and Challenges* (pp. 20-34). IGI Global.

[45] Borh Borhani-Darian, P., H. Li, P. Wu, and P., Closas, P. Deep Neural Network Approach to Detect GNSS Spoofing Attacks. In *Proceedings of the 33rd International Technical Meeting of the Satellite Division of the Institute of Navigation* (ION GNSS+ 2020), pp. 3241-3252, 2020.

[46] Shafiee, E., M. R. Mosavi, and M. Moazedi. Detection of Spoofing Attack using Machine Learning based on Multi-Layer Neural Network in Single-Frequency GPS Receivers. Journal of Navigation, vol. 71, no. 1, pp. 169-188, Jan. 2018, doi: 10.1017/S0373463317000558.

[47] Neish, S. Lo, Y. H. Chen, and P. Enge. Uncoupled accelerometer based GNSS spoof detection for automobiles using statistic and wavelet based tests. In

Proceedings of the 31st International Technical Meeting of the Satellite Division of the Institute of Navigation, ION GNSS+ 2018, Sep. 2018, pp. 2938-2962. doi: 10.33012/2018.15903.

[48] Jhanjhi, N. Z., Brohi, S. N., Malik, N. A., & Humayun, M. (2020, October). Proposing a hybrid rpl protocol for rank and wormhole attack mitigation using machine learning. In *2020 2nd International Conference on Computer and Information Sciences (ICCIS)* (pp. 1-6). IEEE.

[49] Shah, I. A., Jhanjhi, N. Z., & Laraib, A. (2023). Cybersecurity and Blockchain Usage in Contemporary Business. In *Handbook of Research on Cybersecurity Issues and Challenges for Business and FinTech Applications* (pp. 49-64). IGI Global.

[50] Manickam, S., and K. O'Keefe. Using Tactical and MEMS Grade INS to Protect Against GNSS Spoofing in Automotive Applications. Proceedings of ION GNSS+2016, 2016.

[51] Ramanishka, V., Y.-T. Chen, T. Misu, and K. Saenko. Toward Driving Scene Understanding: A Dataset for Learning Driver Behavior and Causal Reasoning. *Proceedings of the IEEE Computer Society Conference on Computer Vision and Pattern Recognition*, pp. 7699–7707, Nov. 2018.

[52] Ujjan, R. M. A., Taj, I., & Brohi, S. N. (2022). E-Government Cybersecurity Modeling in the Context of Software-Defined Networks. In *Cybersecurity Measures for E-Government Frameworks* (pp. 1-21). IGI Global.

[53] Ujjan, R. M. A., Khan, N. A., & Gaur, L. (2022). E-Government Privacy and Security Challenges in the Context of Internet of Things. In *Cybersecurity Measures for E-Government Frameworks* (pp. 22-42). IGI Global.

[54] Muzafar, S., Humayun, M., & Hussain, S. J. (2022). Emerging Cybersecurity Threats in the Eye of E-Governance in the Current Era. In *Cybersecurity Measures for E-Government Frameworks* (pp. 43-60). IGI Global.

[55] Shah, I. A., Wassan, S., & Usmani, M. H. (2022). E-Government Security and Privacy Issues: Challenges and Preventive Approaches. In *Cybersecurity Measures for E-Government Frameworks* (pp. 61-76). IGI Global.

[56] Gaur, L., Ujjan, R. M. A., & Hussain, M. (2022). The Influence of Deep Learning in Detecting Cyber Attacks on E-Government Applications. In *Cybersecurity Measures for E-Government Frameworks* (pp. 107-122). IGI Global.

[57] Jhanjhi, N. Z., Ahmad, M., Khan, M. A., & Hussain, M. (2022). The Impact of Cyber Attacks on E-Governance during the COVID-19 Pandemic. In *Cybersecurity Measures for E-Government Frameworks* (pp. 123-140). IGI Global.

[58] Hussain, M., Talpur, M. S. H., & Humayun, M. (2022). The Consequences of Integrity Attacks on E-Governance: Privacy and Security Violation. In *Cybersecurity Measures for E-Government Frameworks* (pp. 141-156). IGI Global.

NAVIGATION SATELLITE SYSTEM AND LOGISTICS CHALLENGES 67

[59] Ujjan, R. M. A., Khan, N. A., & Gaur, L. (2022). E-Government Privacy and Security Challenges in the Context of Internet of Things. In *Cybersecurity Measures for E-Government Frameworks* (pp. 22-42). IGI Global.

[60] Chhajed, G. J., & Garg, B. R. (2022). Applying Decision Tree for Hiding Data in Binary Images for Secure and Secret Information Flow. In *Cybersecurity Measures for E-Government Frameworks* (pp. 175-186). IGI Global.

[61] Kok, S. H., Abdullah, A., & Jhanjhi, N. Z. (2022). Early detection of crypto-ransomware using pre-encryption detection algorithm. *Journal of King Saud University - Computer and Information Sciences, 34*(5), 1984-1999.

[62] Berrueta, E., Morato, D., Magaña, E., & Izal, M. (2022). Crypto-ransomware detection using machine learning models in file-sharing network scenarios with encrypted traffic. *Expert Systems with Applications, 209*, 118299.

[63] Singhal, V., Jain, S. S., Anand, D., Singh, A., Verma, S., Rodrigues, J. J., ... & Iwendi, C. (2020). Artificial intelligence enabled road vehicle-train collision risk assessment framework for unmanned railway level crossings. *IEEE Access, 8*, 113790-113806.

[64] Lim, M., Abdullah, A., Jhanjhi, N. Z., Khan, M. K., & Supramaniam, M. (2019). Link prediction in time-evolving criminal network with deep reinforcement learning technique. *IEEE Access, 7*, 184797-184807.

[65] Jhanjhi, N. Z., Brohi, S. N., Malik, N. A., & Humayun, M. (2020, October). Proposing a hybrid rpl protocol for rank and wormhole attack mitigation using machine learning. In *2020 2nd International Conference on Computer and Information Sciences (ICCIS)* (pp. 1-6). IEEE.

4

Importance of E-Maintenance for Railways Logistic

Areeba Laraib

Mehran University of Engineering and Technology, Shaheed Zulfiqar Ali Bhutto Campus, Khairpur Mir's, Pakistan

Abstract

It is impossible to overemphasise the significance of e-maintenance for railway logistics in today's fast-changing technological environment. E-maintenance has transformed how railways manage their maintenance procedures, ensuring maximum efficiency, safety, and cost-effectiveness. E-maintenance makes use of electronic technology and data analytics. The primary justifications for why e-maintenance is essential for railroads' logistical operations are outlined in this study. Railways can switch from conventional, time-based maintenance strategies to condition-based maintenance thanks to e-maintenance. Potential breakdowns can be identified in real time by continually monitoring the health of important components and systems via sensors and data processing, enabling preventive maintenance measures to be taken. By using a predictive strategy, railway operations are more reliably maintained, unexpected breakdowns are reduced, and service interruptions are kept to a minimum. Electronic maintenance (e-maintenance) lessens the need for physical inspections and manual interventions by enabling remote monitoring and diagnostics. Anomalies and possible problems can be found by maintenance crews without the need for on-site visits because of the quantity of data that remote sensors and monitoring systems can gather about equipment performance. Maximizing resource allocation and minimising downtime not only increases operating efficiency but also lowers maintenance expenses. E-maintenance is essential to the improvement of railway logistics. It makes data-driven decision-making, condition-based maintenance, remote monitoring, and increased safety possible. Railways may improve operational effectiveness, cut costs, and guarantee a dependable and secure transportation system for people and goods by adopting e-maintenance practices.

Email: Areebalareb.sw8@muetkhp.edu.pk

Imdad Ali Shah and Noor Zaman Jhanjhi (eds.) Cybersecurity in the Transportation Industry, (69–92) © 2024 Scrivener Publishing LLC

The primary objective of this chapter is to peer-review e-maintenance in railways and find security issues and challenges. Our recommendations are helpful for the railway industry and new researchers.

Keywords: Cloud computing, IoT, railway, logistic, security issues and challenges authorization and authentication

4.1 Introduction

In industries where maintenance is performed, locating and fixing the root of problems before they worsen is a top priority. Simultaneously, it is possible to lessen the impact of varying degrees of subjectivity when multiple people manually collect data. This simplifies things, as making the right diagnosis during maintenance is crucial to saving time and money rather than merely a diagnosis. E-maintenance allows for better and more effective maintenance work by decreasing the need for costly corrective maintenance due to unforeseen errors [1–3]. The shift in preventative maintenance toward state-based care that makes e-maintenance possible can help mitigate the hazards associated with changing functional units that arise when replacing parts at regular intervals. It can also explain why it's so important for businesses using e-maintenance to take advantage of appropriate technologies at the correct times. If this problem cannot be fixed, e-maintenance will be useless. High-quality data collection is required for accurate results in e-maintenance [4]. Large volumes of data are collected, making the systems complex, and the data are dispersed over many systems, which is a common issue with the use of computerised systems for monitoring maintenance [5]. The designs need to be flexible enough to accommodate a wide range of maintenance-related tasks, such as work orders, inventory, and parameter settings. Knowledge and capability are a company's most valuable organisational assets; education and training within the business are crucial for achieving a solid maintenance system. This is the most laborious and time-consuming section, and that fact is also addressed. The authors of [6] explain that this stage involves getting ready to begin working on e-maintenance and training to instil the necessary expertise in the appropriate individuals. In addition, concerns like "who should be trained in what and for what reason?" "who should be trained before the other?" and "in what order?" need to be addressed. The key to motivating the company to change is highlighting the positive outcomes resulting from the implementation. Figure 4.1 presents an overview of challenges of e-maintenance.

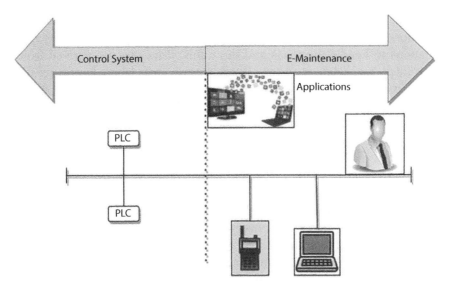

Figure 4.1 Overview of challenges of e-maintenance (This is an author contribution).

Each respondent focused on information security, referred to as "security" from here on out. Because the degree project case study takes place on the railroads, which may be seen as a subset of national security, it is natural that safety is always prioritised in all situations. There was widespread agreement among respondents that security talks are growing in frequency and importance. All aspects of the maintenance digitization project will have the same high level of security. Several respondents also expect an increase in protection from the current level, citing the controversy involving the Governmental Transport Authority and its data management as an example [7]. Respondents cited accuracy as an essential facet of security, meaning that the system itself cannot be hacked to cause harm or accidents in the plant. Second, we have security measures to keep sensitive data from falling into the wrong hands by restricting who can access our systems and why. These concerns must be considered both while information is being transmitted and when it is being stored and accessed. When sensors are linked to a safety permit, stricter regulations are implemented. The value of digitization can soon decline if access is restricted and security measures prevent information from reaching those entitled to it and can derive value from it.

Since error risks increase when information is not adequately secured, national railroads are becoming more controlled. The Governmental Railway Authority, like in every other state, is subject to the federal spending cap and distribution of duties. The Governmental Transport Authority keeps an eye on everything and must follow certain safety regulations to handle the roads and the trains. Principles are derived from this safety management system. There are two areas where laws currently need fixing: (1) when new sensors are to be installed in a plant or unit and (2) when that data is to be used. One contributor adds that because the rules are currently written for analogue components, they must be updated to account for the benefits of digital sensors [9–11]. Some respondents also mentioned that the Governmental Railway Authority has to move more quickly to make regulatory changes that will allow for the digitalization of maintenance. Because some restrictions can impede growth, one respondent also thinks there should be leeway within the regulations to test new technologies like sensors. An overview of the information source of the railway is shown in Figure 4.2.

The adaptable nature of the underlying technology makes digitalizing maintenance a viable option. Most respondents think it's important to consider the technology's usefulness and practicality first. Having reliable information delivered to key players in the most understandable way was stressed by several respondents. Many respondents also stressed the importance of the technology's ability to fix problems and open doors. They also noted the importance of ensuring that the plant's new components and systems don't create more employment than they save [8–11]. The Governmental Railway Authority faces challenges in its operations

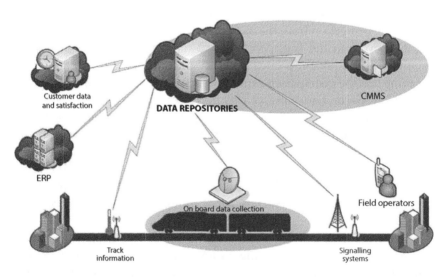

Figure 4.2 An overview of the information source of the railway [8].

since it can be difficult to track down the source of faults. Not all relevant information may be reported in the current system; furthermore, the reported information is individually interpreted when inserted into the designs. As one respondent put it, getting orders into the factory and having the correct information reach the right person is not always easy. The quality of the data obtained is crucial for digitisation to be worthwhile. Sensor selection, data analysis, and the value of standard platforms were mentioned most frequently by respondents. When asked about sensors during interviews, most people thought the interviewer was referring to the cyber-physical unit containing the sensor and its associated components [12–14]. Even though one goal of using sensors is to remove human influence from existing measures, respondents emphasised the importance of demonstrating that sensors provide greater credibility and that data produced using sensors can thus maintain a higher quality. The sensors you set up outside shouldn't require repairs more frequently than the machine they're keeping tabs on. To create value, data must be captured, but the current challenge is that nobody knows what data to record. Testing this hypothesis is crucial, but so is having the confidence to deploy the sensors and begin using them. So that the sensors can measure as precisely as possible from the get-go and then interact with qualities and functionality, it was crucial to leverage the expertise of people familiar with the unit-receiving sensors. One approach involves installing detectors in the plant at the outset and then removing them later so that the true scope of the measurement problem can be understood. If the Governmental Railway Authority and other interested parties will use the data collected by the sensors, the information they provide must be trustworthy and accurate.

The chapter focuses on the following points:

- Peer-reviewed E-maintenance Data in Railway
- E-maintenance Railway
- Cyberattacks in the IoT Environment
- Security issues and Challenges in E-maintenance Data in Railways
- Different Cyberattacks in the IoT Environment.

4.2   Literature Review

Railways are an essential part of the transportation infrastructure because they make it possible to carry people and goods across long distances. For connection and economic growth, train logistics must run smoothly and effectively. The use of e-maintenance has emerged as a game-changer in today's era of digital transformation for maintaining the dependability, safety, and cost-effectiveness of railway operations. E-maintenance is the real-time monitoring, analysis, and optimisation of maintenance processes through the integration of electronic systems, data analytics, and modern technology. With condition-based maintenance, which continuously monitors the health of vital systems and components and makes maintenance decisions based on data-driven insights, traditional time-based maintenance approaches are replaced [15–17]. Railway logistics have undergone a revolution thanks to the move towards e-maintenance, which has many advantages over traditional maintenance methods. The landscape of maintenance in railway logistics is changing as a result of the implementation of e-maintenance. It promotes a paradigm shift from time-based and reactive practices to data-driven and proactive ones. Railways may increase operational effectiveness, cut costs, and offer a dependable and secure transportation system for people and goods by adopting e-maintenance [18, 19]. E-maintenance supports data-driven decision-making. Railways may examine massive amounts of data gathered from numerous sources, including sensors, maintenance logs, and historical data, by utilising modern analytics tools. This research aids in finding patterns, trends, and correlations that can guide decisions about asset management, resource allocation, and maintenance techniques. Railways can optimise their maintenance procedures thanks to data-driven insights, which improve productivity, save costs, and extend asset lifespan. Figure 4.3 is a taxonomy of literature review.

E-maintenance needs to be updated to optimise its worth, and new ways of working are often necessary for the procurement of maintenance, which implies that there is also the prospect of strengthening their order function. To get the most out of your efforts, it's best to collaborate with other

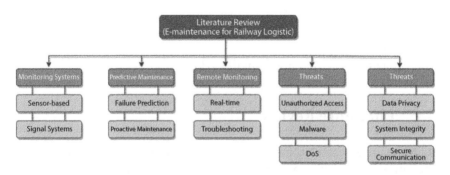

Figure 4.3 Taxonomy of literature review.

projects to process the data ownership working technique. Many of those who took part in the survey stressed the importance of always keeping in mind the value and advantage that digitalization is supposed to bring about [20–22]. Seeing where it is feasible to produce value through the new opportunities that digitization presents is a daunting task that requires attention not only to the technology but also to the strategic notion [24–27]. It's also crucial to identify potential sources of this value. This is because digitalization will only be done for implementation; doing so would yield better results. According to one respondent, one of the most significant difficulties is shifting attention from technological considerations to strategic thinking to identify areas where value may be created. An overview of security issues in the railway systems is shown in Figure 4.4.

With the advent of digitalization comes the necessity of processing and analysing the resulting mountain of data. Who should be in charge of data collection and analysis, who should have access to it, and who should own it? These were all recurring themes among respondents. Several respondents also mentioned that third parties could be employed for data collection, but the Governmental Railway Authority should be responsible for the most fundamental statistics. The Governmental Railway Authority can

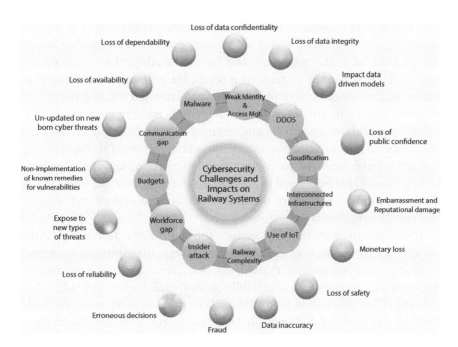

Figure 4.4 Overview of information source of railway [23].

gather and analyse data independently, making the GRA the data's rightful owner [28–30]. The analysis results are then shared with the contractors. Under this scenario, upgrades and the creation of new analytical tools are handled internally. Some of those who provided feedback stated that opening maintenance to competition needs to be clarified.

Implementing maintenance digitalization on the framework described below (which comprises two sections) necessitates an analysis of the primary capabilities and a stance on the challenges surrounding them. External aspects of regulation, oversight, and information security must always be considered when making decisions about the use and advancement of digital technology.

The management of information security is a primary concern during the digitization process. Classified information regarding the facility must be kept from falling into the wrong hands while still being available to the appropriate parties [31–34]. While it is necessary to maintain a high level of security for specific data, it is just as crucial that the data that may be made public be made public to foster progress and innovation and enable the necessary tasks. Authorised individuals must adhere to established procedures for handling sensitive data, both for the sake of internal security and public credibility. Therefore, security must be considered continuously throughout the framework's development and implementation of new technologies, methods of work, and organisational shifts. It is important to remember that rules and monitoring can have far-reaching effects on the kinds of changes that can and cannot be adopted and hence have ripple effects across the system. As a result, the rules must be adhered to but revised as necessary to ensure they remain relevant considering digital progress. Rewriting the legislation to allow tests and the insertion of digital devices without compromising security is crucial for digitalization of maintenance [35–37]. Because information is transformed throughout the transition from analogue to digital information collection, the rules governing it must also be revised to account for the new situation. Since this is the foundation for the rest of the framework, we can deduce that security and regulations impact it.

To be able to carry out digitization, the right digital technology must be chosen. By collecting data digitally rather than physically, errors resulting from subjective evaluations are reduced. It is essential to decide which sensors to use carefully so that each sensor may add value [38–40]. The information from the analysis must next be made available through standardised platforms that can receive and transmit information. Next, analysis tools must be connected to the sensors' data. This is crucial so that the appropriate information can reach the proper person at a reasonable time. The information can then be used to improve decision-making, allowing for the execution of the proper type of maintenance and the facilitation of preventative care. A shift to state-based maintenance, which can result in more effective supervision, can eventually happen with enough thorough investigation. To handle and use the new technology, new positions within the business will need to be formed due to technological advancement. Maintenance practices must be modified to take advantage of the new opportunities provided by e-maintenance [41–43]. A shift in maintenance procurement is required if novel maintenance tactics, including permit-controlled maintenance, are to be implemented. This necessitates that the company be able to do the procurement in an advantageous way for both the company and the maintenance contractors. It will also be necessary to make choices and develop plans for collecting, organising, and evaluating data. Maintenance can be co-planned with other downtime-reduction strategies because it is preventative and has a better schedule. The demand for new responsibilities and knowledge both inside and outside the organisation might increase because of the development of working techniques [44, 45]. Technology may also be developed further by identifying the need for new technology to facilitate working practices. To carry out e-maintenance, an organisation must plan and supervise the changes. For starters, it involves educating the company; it also involves cultural shifts and adopting a different way of thinking, i.e., new working methods that call for new positions. For development work, having a vision and a shared objective is beneficial. The academy and the market should work together to make this evolution as seamless as possible. To benefit from the value of e-maintenance, external parties that compete with the organisation will also need to be formed, such as the contractors that perform the maintenance themselves. The opportunity for contractors to modify their working practises and business model for the maintenance work, allowing them to realise the full potential of e-maintenance, exists if the organisation gets involved and supports entrepreneurs with the development by illustrating the significance of the product and providing incentives for change. People with the correct abilities in the proper jobs can contribute to the creation of new working techniques and technologies because organisational development is taking place. The real result of e-maintenance may be determined once these components have changed and started to work together more effectively. The technology itself is capable of continuously delivering better knowledge. This is related to operational strategies that take advantage of the knowledge that capacity rises because of decreased downtime [46, 47]. The better information produces more robust data for making decisions, which increases maintenance efficiency. With this, the shift to more preventative and, more importantly, state-controlled maintenance may happen and be effectively directed against contractors. As a result of the right kind of maintenance, the plant's service life also extends, and because of improved planning for care and increased capacity, costs are optimised. Finally, it is said that enhanced sustainability will result from ongoing work on the highlighted causes. In order to determine the state of units, less unneeded material use or travel is implemented. Economic sustainability is achieved through adequate maintenance, reducing maintenance costs while boosting plant capacity.

4.3   Overview of E-Maintenance in Railway in the Context of Security Issues

The term "e-maintenance," or "electronic maintenance," describes the use of electronic systems and cutting-edge technologies in conventional railway maintenance procedures. It uses real-time data, analytics, and remote monitoring to improve railway systems' efficiency, dependability, and safety. The potential of electronic maintenance in railway systems to enhance the optimisation of maintenance tasks, decrease downtime, and boost operational performance has attracted a lot of interest in recent years. As electronic technology has become more integrated into railway maintenance practises the term "e-maintenance" has emerged to describe these developments [48–50]. E-maintenance is the process of enhancing maintenance activities via the use of electronic technologies and data analytics to boost operational efficiency and cut costs. However, as digital technologies become more integral, railway networks will have security issues that must be resolved to protect the safety, privacy, and accessibility of vital resources. Various characteristics, including temperature, vibration, pressure, and humidity, are monitored by deploying sensor networks in railway systems. To keep tabs on the health and efficiency of vital parts and structures, these sensors are strategically installed at regular intervals. For e-maintenance to work, there must be a reliable network for sending and receiving sensor data. Some examples of this framework are Wi-Fi, cellular networks, and specialised communication channels. Predictive maintenance can be switched from conventional preventive maintenance with the use of e-maintenance. E-maintenance systems can forecast problems and plan maintenance tasks in advance of serious breakdowns by continuously monitoring the state of the equipment. With this strategy, unplanned downtime is decreased and the dependability of railway systems is increased. Railway operators can streamline maintenance processes and cut back on needless maintenance expenses by introducing e-maintenance. In order to prevent over-maintenance and increase the lifespan of assets, predictive maintenance and condition-based maintenance strategies are used. By anticipating maintenance requirements and lowering the likelihood of equipment failures that could result in accidents or service interruptions, e-maintenance increases safety.

4.3.1   Cyber Security Impact on E-Maintenance

E-maintenance has the potential to greatly enhance the effectiveness and dependability of railway systems, but its deployment is fraught with new cybersecurity risks. The rising reliance on digital technologies, networking, and data interchange raises these difficulties. Cybercriminals and other bad actors are starting to see railroad networks as tempting targets. Cyber risks and attacks, such as malware infections, ransomware attacks, phishing attempts, and denial of service (DoS) attacks, pose a real danger to e-maintenance systems. Disruption of e-maintenance system functionality, compromise of vital data, and interference with maintenance procedures are all possible outcomes of such attacks. It is critical that the data collected and analysed for upkeep be reliable and accurate. Inaccurate maintenance forecasts, poor decision-making, and even equipment breakdowns are all possible outcomes of cybersecurity breaches, including data tampering or manipulation [51–53]. The integrity of data must be checked and double-checked at every stage of its existence. Maintenance workers, third-party vendors, and contractors are just some of the many interested parties in an e-maintenance system. Insiders are a major cybersecurity concern because of the damage they may do from the inside. The availability, confidentiality, and integrity of e-maintenance systems and data are vulnerable to unauthorised access, purposeful sabotage, and carelessness on the part of employees.

Security flaws can be introduced into e-maintenance systems through their connectivity and communication architecture, which includes sensor networks, wireless networks, and data transfer mechanisms. Data breaches and unauthorised access are possible in networks with poor security due to a lack of encryption or inadequate access controls. Information regarding railway infrastructure, equipment, and operations is among the many types of sensitive data collected and processed by e-maintenance systems. Concerns about the abuse or leak of this information necessitate strict privacy and data protection measures. To protect privacy, it is essential to adhere to privacy legislation, use data anonymization methods, and implement access control systems [54–56]. Third-party manufacturers, developers, and service providers all contribute to the success of electronic maintenance systems. To ensure the entire security of e-maintenance systems, the security posture of these external entities becomes crucial. The cybersecurity of e-maintenance systems can be adversely affected by supply chain risks such as hacked or tampered components and software vulnerabilities.

4.3.2   Overview of Cyberattack in E-Maintenance

When talking about electronic systems and networks used for upkeep, a cyberattack is any form of hostile behavior. It's the practice of breaking into a computer system or piece of software in order to do something malicious, like steal data or cause a malfunction. Organizations should put in place strong security measures, such as firewalls, encryption, intrusion detection systems, routine software upgrades, personnel training on cybersecurity best practices, and proactive network activity monitoring, to reduce the danger of cyber assaults in e-maintenance.

- Botnets
  Internet-connected IoT devices are vulnerable to compromise by cybercriminal organisations, which can then employ them in coordinated attacks. Cybercriminals can take control of these devices by infecting them with malware and then using their combined processing power to launch distributed denial of service (DDoS) attacks against larger targets, send spam, steal information, or even conduct covert surveillance using IoT devices equipped with a camera or sound recording capabilities [57]. Botnets of hundreds or millions of IoT devices have also been deployed in attacks.
- Ransomware
  Ransomware is a type of malicious software that encrypts data or locks down a computer or mobile device until a ransom is paid. However, there aren't often many files, if any, kept on IoT devices. Users would most likely still be able to access their vital data even if a ransomware attack hit them on the Internet of Things (which forces the ransom payment). If cybercriminals executing IoT ransomware assaults are unsuccessful in locking out data, they may try to lock the device itself, though this is usually remedied by resetting the device or applying a patch [57] Ransomware spreads in the IoT world by focusing on mission-critical IoT devices

(such as those used in industrial settings or those on which significant corporate operations rely) and demanding a ransom be paid in a concise time frame (before a device could be properly reset).

- AI-based Attacks
  For over a decade, cybercriminals, particularly for social engineering assaults, have been utilising AI in cyberattacks. However, this trend has only taken off in recent years. There has been a recent uptick in the application of AI in the cybercrime industry. Now that cybercrime has become a thriving industry, the resources necessary to create and employ AI in cyberattacks are readily accessible for purchase on the dark web, making it possible for virtually anyone to take advantage of this technology [58]. AI systems can act like regular user traffic and avoid being caught. They can also do the repetitive tasks needed to build up IoT threats quickly.

4.4 Discussion

Many Internet of Things devices are difficult or impossible for network security systems to detect. It's difficult for a security system to readily identify dangers to an instrument if it can't even find the device. These devices and their network connections are often hidden from view by network security systems. It is essential to quickly find and keep track of any new devices that connect to an IoT network.

This is a dangerous attack because the attacker can be off a trusted network; being close enough will do. Attackers can alter every packet sent or received when they gain access to a victim's network. A wireless card-equipped device typically attempts to connect automatically to the access point with the strongest signal. In this scenario, attackers can deploy a wireless access point in the area, fool adjacent devices into joining their domain, and then manipulate all network traffic to serve their purposes [59]. Address Resolution Protocol (ARP) spoofing occurs when an attacker forges an ARP response to trick a local network into thinking that a different IP address has been assigned to a certain MAC address. The ARP cache is used by hosts whenever they need to communicate with another host using a specific IP address by first looking up the IP address in the cache and then using the MAC address that corresponds to that IP address [60]. If the address is unknown, a request is made to obtain the device's

MAC address associated with the IP address. An adversary who wishes to impersonate another host need only send back a few well-crafted packets in response to the request. Then they can eavesdrop on the conversation between the two hosts in secret. If an attacker can intercept this traffic, they can gain access to accounts within the programme that they should not have access to. Multicast DNS is similar to DNS; however, it is performed on a LAN using broadcasts like ARP, making it an easy target for spoofing attacks [61–63]. Users can trust the system to figure out the correct addresses for their devices to communicate with. Electronics that operate on trustworthy networks, such as televisions, printers, and home theatre systems, employ this protocol. When a programme requests the IP address of a certain device—a television or a computer—an attacker can quickly respond with spoofed information, telling the app to resolve to an IP address under the attacker's control. The attacker's device appears trustworthy to the victim for an extended period due to the local cache of addresses.

4.5   Cyberattacks in the Railway in the Context of IoT

The safety concern, the relevance to society, and the loss of reputation could all result from a data breach, making data extremely sensitive for company decisions and increasing competitiveness risks. Keeping this data safe is essential because if it falls into the wrong hands, it might cause serious problems. For example, a malicious actor could use the stolen information to get remote control of your assets and use them to carry out their objectives. This study focuses on an Internet of Things system installed on the rails and the train [64]. Data from the track and the vehicle itself can be collected using this technique (such as temperature, flow, position, and environment). Cybersecurity is a significant concern during data gathering; as a result, it is crucial to provide proper identification, authentication, and authorization. IBM's incident data shows that the transportation industry has been hit by many kinds of cyberattacks, including SQL injection, denial of service attacks, watering hole exploits, cross-site scripting attacks, brute force assaults, improper configuration, data breach phishing, and unknown [65]. After data gathering, it was sent to Microsoft Azure's cloud using the right data transfer protocols. The final step is to protect information while it's in transit from sensors to the cloud. This is particularly crucial because if this information fell into the wrong hands, it might cause massive disruption, danger, distrust, hazards, and catastrophic consequences.

4.6   Cyberattacks in the Railway Using IoT

Since the Internet of Things is expanding at the quickest rate of any technology, industrial engineers are naturally curious about its potential applications in the workplace. With the help of the industrial Internet of Things (IIoT), the training industry may advance without making costly new investments in infrastructure. This study focuses on an IoT system installed on the rails and the train. Data from the track and the vehicle itself can be collected using this technique. Cybersecurity is a major concern throughout the data collection process. As a result, it's vital to take care of things like identification, authentication, and authorization. Since the information being transferred is secret and its disclosure could have negative consequences at this time, As such, let's take a look at the most pressing threats that the railway industry has had to fight recently: DoS is one of the most common network threats, especially in IoT, [66] and my understanding from the literature review. The data being sent from sensors on the train track and on board has a significant risk of being subject to similar attacks. Because of the dispersed nature of distributed denial-of-service assaults (DDoS) attacks, they have become increasingly common in every industry in recent years [67–69]. Spoofed (fake) IP addresses are commonly used by attackers to conceal their identity, making it even more challenging to trace back DDoS attacks. In addition, many hosts on the internet have security flaws that attackers might use. Trains in Sweden have been running late recently due to distributed denial of service assaults. The initial attack occurred on October 11, 2017, and was directed at the Swedish Transport Administration via TDC and DGC, the country's two leading ISPs. Due to DDoS attacks, the system that alerts the train's conductor when to go and stop failed. Customers cannot make bookings or get information about traffic delays because the federal agency's email system, website, and road traffic maps are all down due to the attack. Sven Lindberg of Trafikverket claims that the hack slowed train traffic to the website, Skype, and other web-based systems because it clogged up all their servers. According to reports, manual management of railway traffic and other services was required to ensure proper operation. The website of Trafikverket, an independent government agency in charge of regulating and inspecting transportation systems, was hacked the following day. According to reports, it also affected a public transportation company in western Sweden. These two distributed denial-of-service assaults against Trafikverket demonstrate the severity of the problem that can arise without proper defences [70–75]. The Danish national rail operator DSB is another target of the DDoS attacks plaguing the railroad industry. Ticketing systems and the entire communication network have been crippled as a result of this attack. The ticketing system was the primary target of the attack, and as a result, people couldn't buy tickets anywhere in the country. Hackers also compromised the telephone system and internal mail. Social media platforms were the only means of contact with the clientele. On the evening of September 19, the source code for one of the most significant known cyberattacks, which began and centred on the IoT devices, was made public. Because of this transition to a more digitally integrated society, the railroad is becoming increasingly susceptible to cyberattacks. The introduction of IoT components like sensors and accumulators to the railway increases the technological interaction with the vehicle, which opens the door to a wide variety of potential cyber threats and attacks like hacking ECUS, spoofing GPS, altering traffic signs, injecting false bits, and altering sensor values. Using Microsoft Azure and the proper data transmission protocol, the project's next step will be to upload the gathered data to the cloud. Even at this early stage, people may have encountered various cyberattacks.

Chapter's Contribution

The railroad sector is one of many that has benefited from recent technical developments. IoT-based railway systems can significantly increase the quality of procedures and enable a more efficient, environmentally friendly train system. The results of this research have led to considerable improvements in the train system. This study targets the rail industry because of its interest in implementing information technology concepts, including cloud computing, information security, and the IoT. There is a constant flow of information into and out of the railroad business. Additionally, as technology develops, the number of contacts between robots and humans is rapidly increasing. We need to ensure this data is collected, analysed, and disseminated in a way that is safe from hackers and natural disasters. A new paradigm known as "fog computing" has emerged, free from the limitations of intelligent devices and the cloud. The integration of information technology and operational technology and the accompanying paradigm shift towards Industry 4.0 have significantly increased dependability, maintainability, operational efficiency, and capacity in complex systems like railroads. Since the IoT is growing faster than any other technology, its potential workplace uses excite industrial engineers. Industrial IoT could help the training sector develop with minimal capital expenditures. This research focuses on the Internet of Things system on the tracks and the train itself. This method helps gather information about the road and the car itself. In general, data collection raises severe concerns about cybersecurity. Therefore, ensuring proper identification, authentication, and authorization is crucial. Due to the sensitive nature of the material being conveyed and the potential implications of its exposure at this time, therefore, let's take a look at the most significant challenges the railroad business has faced as of late: the literature shows that DoS is one of the most widespread network dangers, especially in the IoT. There is a substantial danger that similar assaults will be made against the data being transmitted by sensors on the train track and board. Dispersed denial-of-service (DDoS) attacks are rising across all sectors due to their ease of implementation. Attackers often employ spoofed (false) IP addresses to hide their identities during DDoS raids, making it even more challenging to track them down. Additionally, many hosts on the internet have security weaknesses that attackers might exploit. The mechanism that notifies the train's conductor when to go and stop was disrupted by a distributed denial-of-service assault. Due to the attack, the government agency's email system, website, and road traffic maps were all down, making it impossible for customers to make reservations or obtain information on traffic delays.

The risk is great because the attacker doesn't need to be on a trustworthy network; proximity alone is enough. Hackers can tamper with every transmission if they can access a victim's network. In most cases, wireless card-enabled devices automatically try to connect to the access point with the best signal strength. When an adversary sets up a wireless access point in the vicinity, it can lure nearby devices into joining its domain and then use that domain's control over all network traffic to further its goals. Network security systems may be unable to identify many IoT devices because of their low visibility. If a security system can't locate a machine, it can't protect it from potential threats. Network security measures typically keep these gadgets and their connections to the internet out of sight. Consequently, it's critical to be able to locate and monitor any new devices that join an IoT network.

4.7   Conclusion

In today's ever-changing technological environment, e-maintenance for railway logistics is crucial. Maintenance operations on railways have become more efficient, safe, and cost-effective thanks to the implementation of electronic maintenance management systems. In order to perform e-maintenance, computers and data analytics are utilised. This study compiles the best available evidence explaining why electronic maintenance is critical to the efficient operation of railroads' supply chain management.

Electronic maintenance allows railroads to switch from time-based to condition-based upkeep. By using sensors and processing data in real-time, potential failures in vital components and systems can be identified immediately, allowing for preventative maintenance to be carried out. Better maintenance of railway operations, with fewer breakdowns and service delays, is possible with a preventative strategy. E-maintenance, also known as electronic maintenance, eliminates the need for on-site visits and human interaction by facilitating remote monitoring and diagnostics. By collecting massive volumes of data regarding equipment performance, remote sensors and monitoring systems allow maintenance professionals to see abnormalities and potential problems without physically visiting the site. Making better use of resources and reducing maintenance time can boost operational efficiency and cut expenses.

4.8   Future Work

E-maintenance is crucial to the improvement of railway logistics. Protect the e-maintenance system by allowing only authorised users access with a strong authentication approach like two-factor authentication (2FA). Set up a system of role-based access control (RBAC) that gives users different levels of access depending on their function. This limits the potential for harm from malevolent actors by limiting their access. Use encryption and other security measures to protect sensitive information contained in the e-maintenance system. Maintaining regular backups of your data might help you recover quickly from hacks or hardware issues with minimal downtime.

References

[1] Kour, R. Aljumaili, M. Karim, R. Tretten, P, eMaintenance in railways: Issues and challenges in cybersecurity. *Proceedings of the Institution of Mechanical Engineers, Part F: Journal of Rail and Rapid Transit, January 13, 2019.*

[2] Shift2Rail. Cybersecurity in the railway sector, https://shift2rail.org/project/cyrail/ 2016, accessed: 9 February 2019.

[3] Braband, J, Cybersecurity in railways: Quo Vadis. In: *International Conference on Reliability, Safety and Security of Railway Systems. 14 November 2017,* pp. 3–14. Cham: Springer.

[4] Masson, E. Gransart, C, Cybersecurity for railways – a huge challenge – Shift2Rail perspective technologies for vehicles, 4 May 2017, pp. 97–104. Cham: Springer In: *International workshop on communication*.

[5] Directive NI. Directive (EU) 2016/1148 of the European Parliament and of the Council of 6 July 2016 concerning measures for a high common level of security of network and information systems across the Union. https://eurlex.europa.eu/legalcontent/EN/TXT/PDF/?uri=CELEX:32016L1148&from=EN 2016, access: 9 February 2019.

[6] Cylus, Railway Cybersecurity, Israel. https://cylus.com/ 2018, accessed: 9 February 2019.

[7] Bloomfield, R. Bendele, M. Bishop, P, The risk assessment of ERTMS-based railway systems from a cybersecurity perspective: methodology and lessons learned. In: *International Conference on Reliability, Safety and Security of Railway Systems, 28 June 2016*, pp. 3–19. Cham: Springer.

[8] Morant, A., Galar, D., & Tamarit, J. (2012). Cloud computing for maintenance of railway signalling systems. In *International Conference on Condition Monitoring and Machinery Failure Prevention Technologies: 12/06/2012-14/06/2012* (Vol. 1, pp. 551–559).

[9] Sadeghi, A-R. Wachsmann, C. Waidner,M, Security and privacy challenges in industrial Internet of Things. *52nd ACM/EDAC/IEEE Design Automation Conference*, 2015.

[10] Ujjan, R. M. A., Pervez, Z., & Dahal, K. (2018, June). Suspicious traffic detection in SDN with collaborative techniques of snort and deep neural networks. In *2018 IEEE 20th International Conference on High Performance Computing and Communications; IEEE 16th International Conference on Smart City; IEEE 4th International Conference on Data Science and Systems (HPCC/SmartCity/DSS)* (pp. 915–920). IEEE.

[11] Kumar, T., Pandey, B., Mussavi, S. H. A., & Zaman, N. (2015). CTHS based energy efficient thermal aware image ALU design on FPGA. *Wireless Personal Communications*, 85, 671–696.

[12] Ujjan, R. M. A., Pervez, Z., Dahal, K., Bashir, A. K., Mumtaz, R., & González, J. (2020). Towards sFlow and adaptive polling sampling for deep learning based DDoS detection in SDN. *Future Generation Computer Systems, 111*, 763–779.

[13] Srinivasan, K., Garg, L., Datta, D., Alaboudi, A. A., Jhanjhi, N. Z., Agarwal, R., & Thomas, A. G. (2021). Performance comparison of deep cnn models for detecting driver's distraction. *CMC-Computers, Materials & Continua, 68*(3), 4109–4124.

[14] Shah, I. A., Habeeb, R. A. A., Rajper, S., & Laraib, A. (2022). The Influence of Cybersecurity Attacks on E-Governance. In *Cybersecurity Measures for E-Government Frameworks* (pp. 77–95). IGI Global.

[15] Anam, S. Abbas, H. Saleem, K, Cloud-Assisted IoT-Based SCADA Systems Security: A Review of the State of the Art and Future Challenges. Special

Section on the Plethora of Research in Internet of Things (IoT), 2016. *IEEE Access*, Vol. 4, March 31, 2016, pp. 1375–1384.

[16] Shafiq, M., Ashraf, H., Ullah, A., Masud, M., Azeem, M., Jhanjhi, N., & Humayun, M. (2021). Robust cluster-based routing protocol for IoT-assisted smart devices in WSN. *Computers, Materials & Continua*, 67(3), 3505–3521.

[17] K, Karimi. G, Atkinson, What the Internet of Things (IoT) Needs to Become a Reality. *White Paper, FreeScale and ARM*, 2013.

[18] Lim, M., Abdullah, A., & Jhanjhi, N. Z. (2021). Performance optimization of criminal network hidden link prediction model with deep einforcement learning. *Journal of King Saud University - Computer and Information Sciences*, 33(10), 1202–1210.

[19] Zhao, K. Ge, L. A survey on the internet of things security. *Ninth international conference on Computational Intelligence and Security (CIS)*, 2013.

[20] Kumar, T., Pandey, B., Mussavi, S. H. A., & Zaman, N. (2015). CTHS based energy efficient thermal aware image ALU design on FPGA. *Wireless Personal Communications*, 85, 671–696.

[21] C, Kolias. G, Kambourakis. A, Stavrou. J, Voas. DDoS in the IoT: Mirai and other botnets. *Computer*, 50(7), pp. 80–84, 2017.

[22] Shah, I. A., Jhanjhi, N. Z., Humayun, M., & Ghosh, U. (2022). Health Care Digital Revolution during COVID-19. In *How COVID-19 Is Accelerating the Digital Revolution* (pp. 17–30). Springer, Cham.

[23] Khan, H. (2019). What Are the Security Challenges Concerning Maintenance Data in the Railway Industry. Master's thesis, Luleå University of Technology.

[24] Ujjan, R. M. A., Hussain, K., & Brohi, S. N. (2022). The Impact of Blockchain Technology on Advanced Security Measures for E-Government. In *Cybersecurity Measures for E-Government Frameworks* (pp. 157–174). IGI Global.

[25] Singh, A. Maneesh, S. Overview of Security issues in Cloud Computing. *International Journal of Advanced Computer Research* (ISSN (print): 2249-7277 ISSN (online): 2277-7970) Volume 2, March 2012.

[26] Chhajed, G. J., & Garg, B. R. (2022). Applying Decision Tree for Hiding Data in Binary Images for Secure and Secret Information Flow. In *Cybersecurity Measures for E-Government Frameworks* (pp. 175–186). IGI Global.

[27] Shafiq, M., Ashraf, H., Ullah, A., Masud, M., Azeem, M., Jhanjhi, N. Z., & Humayun, M. (2021). Robust Cluster-Based Routing Protocol for IoT-Assisted Smart Devices in WSN. *Computers, Materials & Continua*, 67(3).

[28] Lim, M., Abdullah, A., & Jhanjhi, N. Z. (2021). Performance optimization of criminal network hidden link prediction model with deep reinforcement learning. *Journal of King Saud University - Computer and Information Sciences*, 33(10), 1202–1210.

[29] https://www.techrepublic.com/article/microsoft-cloud-cybersecurity-attacks-up-300-in-last-yearreport-says/, accessed: 3 March 2019.

[30] Hussain, M., Talpur, M. S. H., & Humayun, M. (2022). The Consequences of Integrity Attacks on E-Governance: Privacy and Security Violation. In

Cybersecurity Measures for E-Government Frameworks (pp. 141–156). IGI Global.

[31] Jhanjhi, N. Z., Ahmad, M., Khan, M. A., & Hussain, M. (2022). The Impact of Cyber Attacks on E-Governance during the COVID-19 Pandemic. In *Cybersecurity Measures for E-Government Frameworks* (pp. 123–140). IGI Global.

[32] Shah, I. A., Jhanjhi, N. Z., Humayun, M., & Ghosh, U. (2022). Impact of COVID-19 on Higher and Post-secondary Education Systems. In *How COVID-19 Is Accelerating the Digital Revolution* (pp. 71–83). Springer, Cham.

[33] Harrell, Brian, Why the Ukraine power grid attacks should raise alarm, *CSO*, March 6, 2017. https://www.csoonline.com/article/560467/why-the-ukraine-power-grid-attacks-should-raise-alarm.html. accessed: 6 March 2019.

[34] AlertLogic,"Targeted attacks andopportunistic hacks, state of cloud security report spring 2013", available at https://www.alertlogic.com/alert-logic-releases-2013-state-of-cloud-securityreport,accessed:16 February 2019.

[35] P, Mell. T, Grance. The NIST definition of cloud computing, Special Publication 800-145, National Institute of Standards and Technology, 2011.

[36] E, Chickowski. Sony Still Digging Its Way Out of Breach Investigation. 02 Apr 2013, accessed: 9 March 2019.

[37] Q, Jing. A. V, Vasilakos. J, Wan. J, Lu. D, Qiu. Security of the Internet of Things: perspectives and challenge. *Wireless Networks*, 2014.

[38] S. T, Zargar. J, Joshi. Tipper, D. A Survey of Defense Mechanisms against Distributed Denial of Service (DDoS) Flooding Attacks. *IEEE Communications Surveys & Tutorials*, 11 February 2013.

[39] Gaur, L., Ujjan, R. M. A., & Hussain, M. (2022). The Influence of Deep Learning in Detecting Cyber Attacks on E-Government Applications. In *Cybersecurity Measures for E-Government Frameworks* (pp. 107–122). IGI Global.

[41] Shah, I. A. (2022). Cybersecurity Issues and Challenges for E-Government during COVID-19: A Review. *Cybersecurity Measures for E-Government Frameworks*, 187-222.

[42] Gibson G, Timlin A, Curran S, Wattis J. The scope for qualitative methods in research and clinical trials in dementia. *Age Ageing.* 2004; 33:422–6. [PubMed] [Google Scholar]

[43] Miles, M. and Huberman, M. *An expanded sourcebook – Qualitative Data Analysis*, 2nd ed., Sage Publications, Thousand Oaks, CA, USA; 1994.

[44] Adeyemo, V. E., Abdullah, A., JhanJhi, N. Z., Supramaniam, M., & Balogun, A. O. (2019). Ensemble and deep-learning methods for two-class and multi-attack anomaly intrusion detection: an empirical study. *International Journal of Advanced Computer Science and Applications*, 10(9).

[45] Kok, S. H., Abdullah, A., & Jhanjhi, N. Z. (2022). Early detection of crypto-ransomware using pre-encryption detection algorithm. *Journal of King Saud University - Computer and Information Sciences*, 34(5), 1984–1999.

[46] Lindgren, R., Henfridsson, O., and Schultze, U. (2004): Design Principles for Competence Management Systems: A Synthesis of an Action Research Study. *MIS Quarterly*, 28(3), pp 435–472.

[47] https://www.pinterest.com/pin/173177548148377796/ accessed: 2 April 2019.47

[48] Abowitz, D. A., & Toole, T. M. Mixed Method Research: Fundamental Issues of Design, Validity, and Reliability in Construction Research. *Journal of Construction Engineering and Management*; 2010.

[49] Chakrabartty, S. N. Best Split-Half and Maximum Reliability. *IOSR Journal of Research & Method in Education*; 2013.

[50] Brett, S. Generalizability in qualitative research: misunderstandings, opportunities and recommendations for the sport and exercise sciences, *Qualitative Research in Sport, Exercise and Health*; 2017.

[51] Shah, I. A., Wassan, S., & Usmani, M. H. (2022). E-Government Security and Privacy Issues: Challenges and Preventive Approaches. In *Cybersecurity Measures for E-Government Frameworks* (pp. 61–76). IGI Global.

[52] Ujjan, R. M. A., Taj, I., & Brohi, S. N. (2022). E-Government Cybersecurity Modeling in the Context of Software-Defined Networks. In *Cybersecurity Measures for E-Government Frameworks* (pp. 1–21). IGI Global.

[53] Shah, I. A. (2022). Cybersecurity Issues and Challenges for E-Government during COVID-19: A Review. *Cybersecurity Measures for E-Government Frameworks*, 187-222.

[54] Dawson, M., & Walker, D. (2022). Argument for Improved Security in Local Governments Within the Economic Community of West African States. *Cybersecurity Measures for E-Government Frameworks*, 96–106.

[55] Phogat, S. & Gupta, A. K.2017. Identification of problems in maintenance operations and comparison with manufacturing operations: A review, *Journal of Quality in Maintenance Engineering*, vol. 23, no. 2, pp. 226–238.

[56] Ujjan, R. M. A., Pervez, Z., Dahal, K., Bashir, A. K., Mumtaz, R., & González, J. (2020). Towards sFlow and adaptive polling sampling for deep learning based DDoS detection in SDN. *Future Generation Computer Systems*, *111*, 763–779.

[57] Muzafar, S., Humayun, M., & Hussain, S. J. (2022). Emerging Cybersecurity Threats in the Eye of E-Governance in the Current Era. In *Cybersecurity Measures for E-Government Frameworks* (pp. 43–60). IGI Global.

[58] Ujjan, R. M. A., Khan, N. A., & Gaur, L. (2022). E-Government Privacy and Security Challenges in the Context of Internet of Things. In *Cybersecurity Measures for E-Government Frameworks* (pp. 22–42). IGI Global.

[59] Kiran, S. R. A., Rajper, S., Shaikh, R. A., Shah, I. A., & Danwar, S. H. (2021). Categorization of CVE Based on Vulnerability Software by Using Machine Learning Techniques. *International Journal*, *10*(3).

[60] Umrani, S., Rajper, S., Talpur, S. H., Shah, I. A., & Shujrah, A. (2020). Games based learning: A case of learning physics using Angry Birds. *Indian Journal of Science and Technology*, *13*(36), 3778–3784.

[61] Shah, I. A., Sial, Q., Jhanjhi, N. Z., & Gaur, L. (2023). Use Cases for Digital Twin. In *Digital Twins and Healthcare: Trends, Techniques, and Challenges* (pp. 102–118). IGI Global.

[62] Alabdulkarim, A. A., Ball, P.D. & Tiwari, A. (2014). Influence of resources on maintenance operations with different asset monitoring levels: A simulation approach, *Business Process Management Journal*, vol. 20, no. 2, pp. 195–212.

[63] Ujjan, R. M. A., Pervez, Z., & Dahal, K. (2018, June). Suspicious traffic detection in SDN with collaborative techniques of snort and deep neural networks. In *2018 IEEE 20th International Conference on High Performance Computing and Communications; IEEE 16th International Conference on Smart City; IEEE 4th International Conference on Data Science and Systems (HPCC/SmartCity/DSS)* (pp. 915–920). IEEE.

[64] Shah, I. A., Jhanjhi, N. Z., & Laraib, A. (2023). Cybersecurity and Blockchain Usage in Contemporary Business. In *Handbook of Research on Cybersecurity Issues and Challenges for Business and FinTech Applications* (pp. 49–64). IGI Global.

[65] S Umrani, S Rajper, SH Talpur, IA Shah, A Shujrah - *Indian Journal of Science and Technology*, 2020.

[66] Patidar, L., Soni, V.K. & Soni, P.K. (2017). Maintenance strategies and their combine impact on manufacturing performance, *International Journal of Mechanical and Production Engineering Research and Development*, vol. 7, no. 1, pp. 13–22.

[67] Shah, I. A., Sial, Q., Jhanjhi, N. Z., & Gaur, L. (2023). The Role of the IoT and Digital Twin in the Healthcare Digitalization Process: IoT and Digital Twin in the Healthcare Digitalization Process. In *Digital Twins and Healthcare: Trends, Techniques, and Challenges* (pp. 20-34). IGI Global.

[68] Narayan, V. (2012). Business performance and maintenance: How are safety, quality, reliability, productivity and maintenance related? *Journal of Quality in Maintenance Engineering*, vol. 18, no. 2, pp. 183–195.

[69] Velmurugan, R.S. & T. Dhingra. (2015). Maintenance strategy selection and its impact in maintenance function: A conceptual framework, *International Journal of Operations and Production Management*, vol. 35, no. 12, pp. 1622–1661.

[70] Mishra, R.P., Kodali, R.B., Gupta, G. & Mundra, N. (2015). Development of a framework for implementation of world-class maintenance systems using interpretive structural modeling approach, *Procedia CIRP*, vol. 26, pp. 424–429.

[71] Nazeri, V. & Naderikia, R. (2017). A new fuzzy approach to identify the critical risk factors in maintenance management, *International Journal of Advanced Manufacturing Technology*, vol. 92, nos. 9–12, pp. 3749–3783.

[72] Adhikari, P.P & Buderath, M. (2016). A Framework for Aircraft Maintenance Strategy including CBM, European Conference of the Prognostics and Health Management Society 2016, pp. 1–10. [10] Zilka, M. 2014. Methodology for Selecting the Appropriate, Maintenance Systems, pp. 209–216.

[73] Selcuk, S. (2017). Predictive maintenance, its implementation and latest trends, Proceedings of the Institution of Mechanical Engineering. *Part B Journal of Engineering Manufacture*, vol. 231, no. 9, pp. 1670–1679.

[74] Shah, I. A., Jhanjhi, N. Z., Amsaad, F., & Razaque, A. (2022). The Role of Cutting-Edge Technologies in Industry 4.0. In *Cyber Security Applications for Industry 4.0* (pp. 97–109). Chapman and Hall/CRC.

[75] Alaswad, S. & Xiang, Y. (2017). A review on condition-based maintenance optimization models for stochastically deteriorating system, *Reliability Engineering and System Safety*, vol. 157, pp. 54–63.

5

Privacy and Security Challenges in Unmanned Aerial Vehicles (UAVs)

Imdad Ali Shah

School of Computing Science, Taylor's University, Kuala Lumpur, Selangor, Malaysia

Abstract

An unauthorized person's use of sensitive information is referred to as a human privacy breach, also known as a privacy violation or breach. It takes place when a person's privacy rights are breached, exposing or compromising their private information. Technology's most crucial goal is removing obstacles and supporting human life. An example of a technology created in this area is the unmanned aerial vehicle (UAV). It becomes more apparent when performing duties that endanger people's health and safety. UAVs can also be used to accomplish tasks that would be impossible for humans to complete correctly and that are not easy to reach. Every new technology has both benefits and drawbacks. Some of its drawbacks include the requirement for energy, range restrictions, problems with command and control, hardware and software limitations, and weak environmental resilience. In recent years, UAVs have been used for logistics and military operations and also for illegal and unauthorized information collection, intelligence studies, attacks, and destruction. Cyberattacks on the UAV's parts, systems, and missions also have ulterior motives in addition to these. Attacks against coordination information and communication systems are of particular concern. In this chapter, we discuss UAV system components, features, an introduction, and security concerns for UAV systems. The steps to protect yourself from threats and attacks are then enumerated. These include evaluating UAV software, hardware, and transmission systems for vulnerabilities and risks, and using data encryption to ensure transmission security. Our recommendation helps new researchers and concerned companies.

Keywords: UAV systems, cyberattacks, vulnerabilities, UAS software and hardware

Email: shahsyedimdadali@gmail.com

Imdad Ali Shah and Noor Zaman Jhanjhi (eds.) Cybersecurity in the Transportation Industry, (93–116) © 2024 Scrivener Publishing LLC

5.1   Introduction

One of the essential purposes of technology is to facilitate human existence by removing barriers. The unmanned aerial vehicle (UAV) is one product of this technology field. Reconnaissance, observation, research, search, control, transportation, and logistics are just a few of the many military and civilian uses for UAVs today. This is especially true when dealing with tasks that could endanger other people's lives. UAVs can also be used to reach and do jobs that are too high or too far away for humans to safely and effectively carry out.

UAVs have increased in various civilian and military applications due to the increasing technological capabilities of automated systems. Besides their primary use in military operations, UAVs are now widely deployed in other fields, such as animal monitoring, weather research, and catastrophe assessment. Similarly, UAVs are predicted to play a significant role in the development of smart cities in the future [1–5]. Due to the volume and variety of data carried by UAVs, they constitute a tempting target for cyber-criminals. However, UAVs' cybersecurity has not been thoroughly considered during their development. So, UAVs are more likely to be targets of cybercrime. Communication between UAVs and control stations, as well as the modules responsible for their operation, could introduce security flaws. Since UAVs frequently transport sensitive information that enemies could exploit, communication security stands out as particularly crucial to the success of UAVs. Recent reports also include incidents of GPS spoofing, session hijacking, and hacked surveillance systems. Figure 5.1 presents the Tractica Unmanned Aerial Vehicle Sales Report.

Innovations in the Internet of Things Unmanned Aerial Vehicle Technology Rapid and low-cost UAV deployment has led to widespread acceptance of these aircraft. A UAV can serve not only as a reconnaissance tool but also as a communication hub. Compared to a satellite communication platform, it has fewer moving parts, more throughput, and less delay in transmission. As a supporting framework, it ensures secure and reliable data transfer for users on the ground through dependable wireless connectivity [7–10]. When operating independently, the available energy source constrains the flight range and distance. However, its communication dependability is low, and it is susceptible to several network attacks. Considering this, the future of UAV communication may lie in forming networks comprised of numerous UAVs to increase reliability and act as relay nodes for other networks. Figure 5.2 shows the threats that can be presented to UAVs.

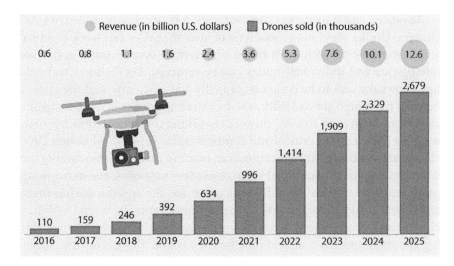

Figure 5.1 The tractica unmanned aerial vehicle sales report [6].

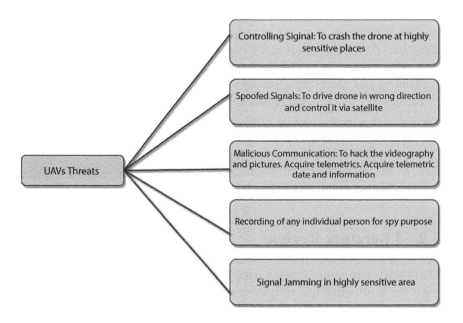

Figure 5.2 Threats that can be presented to UAVs.

Advanced and transparent communication networks are crucial to UAV clusters. Unlike previous generations of aircraft, UAVs can work together and communicate with each other. The system demonstrates collective intelligence and individual nodes can be replaced. UAV cluster technology allows the task to be completed rapidly and efficiently, and the system benefits from high survivability and decentralized control. There is significant room for growth in UAV cluster networking communication, but first, we must solve certain critical and complex issues [11–15]. Although UAV cluster networking communication is an efficient means of overcoming the coverage gaps in conventional cellular wireless networks, the networking mode must be chosen carefully to account for the specific environment and operational parameters. When the communication between UAVs in a cluster works, the amount of data being transmitted increases dramatically, but the static spectrum allocation efficiency is low. This harms the cluster system's overall performance. Increases in transmission power can improve communication dependability, but they also make it easier for snoops to collect high-quality eavesdropping signals, compromising the transmitted data's security. Additionally, as models continue to get more diverse and smaller, limitations in power supply and endurance will pose significant difficulties for UAVs, affecting the viability of their long-term performance in a wide variety of roles. All the topics—communications security, energy availability, and spectrum allocation—deserve additional research.

The chapter focuses on the following points:

- Peer-reviewed Unmanned Aerial Vehicle
- Cyberattacks and cybersecurity measures in UAVs
- Security issues and challenges in UAVs
- Vulnerabilities and threats in UAVs.

5.2   Literature Review

Many scientists and engineers have been focusing their efforts in recent years on improving the autonomy and durability of Unmanned Aerial Vehicles (UAVs). UAVs can be broken down into two classes: rotary-wing and fixed-wing aircraft [16–18]. Due to their reliance on batteries for power, UAVs are limited in their mission scope when flight autonomy is required [19, 20]. In civilian settings, it is preferred that the UAV fly itself. Here, it's important to note that to conduct autonomous flights, avionics will need to be updated. To enhance a UAV's performance in autonomous flying, the authors suggested a small UAV and autopilot system that could be used in tandem. In-depth state-space models of the UAV for various flight conditions present the linearized versions of the underlying mathematical equations. An autopilot hierarchy using proportional-integral-derivative (PID) controllers is investigated and tested in a closed-loop environment. Figure 5.3 presents the taxonomy of the literature review.

Self-driving cars are unquestionably the future of the auto business. Cyber-physical systems (CPS) bring the physical and digital worlds closer by connecting sensors and actuators via wireless communication networks. One everyday use of CPS is in autonomous vehicles (AVs), which can improve transportation networks' safety, efficiency, and sustainability. The ability to direct the movement of AVs along a predetermined path is critical to their success. For the car to travel along the targeted path safely and comfortably, it determines the appropriate steering wheel angle based on the current state of the vehicle. The lateral offset and the heading inaccuracy should be minimized using the controls [21–25]. Controlling the path being tracked reliably and securely is crucial. Figure 5.4 presents UAVs in detail.

A knowledge curve is established by applying the fuzzy monitoring system, allowing for precise regulation of a wide range of velocities and courses [26–29]. The techniques produce satisfactory regulating effects in similar contexts. However, most of the present work does not adequately consider vehicles' nonlinearities and malicious disturbances, which might reduce control performance or cause instability [30–34]. Nonlinear features inside the vehicle model are considered by the model predictive and active control (MPC) approach, which can also limit the state variables

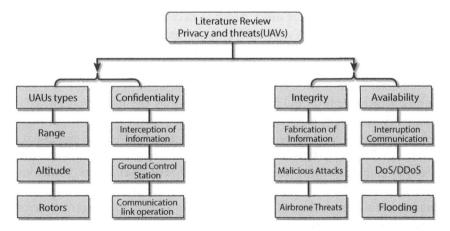

Figure 5.3 The taxonomy of the literature review.

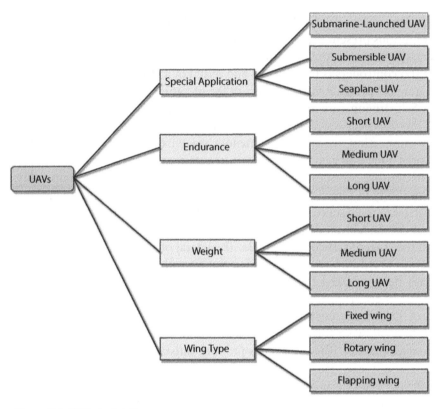

Figure 5.4 UAVs in detail.

and control variables for maximum efficiency while solving multi-constrained optimal problems. Disturbances are used to estimate the body's location and orientation, which is necessary for AV path-tracking control to be realized. AVs use GPS, LiDAR, cameras, and other sensors for localization and perception. Most modern navigation techniques [35–41] rely on multisensory fusion technology to obtain high-precision directional data. In addition, AVs can now communicate with each other and infrastructure units on the road to form platoons and increase traffic efficiency. Accordingly, it is crucial to ensure the precision of in-car sensors to achieve risk-free driving. While autonomous vehicles have the potential to revolutionize transportation, their sensors may be designed without security in mind, leaving car systems vulnerable to cyberattacks. Malicious interference with AVs has the potential to produce critical safety issues and lead to accidents, posing a physical hazard to users or passengers. Several research projects have shown that sensors can be used to launch attacks against AVs. For instance, GPS spoofing creates or modifies GPS signals to trick a target device or receiver. As mentioned, LiDAR spoofing attacks can use processed point cloud data to either introduce virtual impediments or remove real-world obstacles from a scene. Sensor data never reaches its intended recipient when a denial-of-service attack is launched.

The term "cyberterrorism," which refers to illegal attacks or threats of attacks via networks, computers, and the data contained therein, is a portmanteau of the words "cyber" and "terrorism." Social or political goals may motivate those behind these acts, which aim to scare or pressure authorities or the populace. Terrorists who use the internet to threaten lives or cause material damage to infrastructure are known as "cyber terrorists." The global sea transport business has played an essential part in the efficient distribution and conveyance of goods worldwide since the advent of COVID-19 [42–44]. Commercial ships transport the world's energy, food, raw materials, and all manufactured components and goods, accounting for over 80% of global trade, according to the United Nations Conference on Trade and Development (UNCTAD) [38]. Also included are medical supplies, which are in high demand everywhere and necessary for stabilizing the current crisis. The maritime industry's plea to governments worldwide to facilitate the continued flow of maritime trade by reducing commercial ships' access to ports and replacing crew members on ships worldwide is an important consideration that cannot be ignored here. Maintaining regular shipping and allowing cross-border transportation is crucial during global crises [39]. Another critical part is ensuring that landlocked nations have unimpeded access to food and medicine via the seaports of neighbouring states. The global economy could be negatively impacted by trade restrictions, which could cause disruptions to firms and disrupt supply chains. State leaders should listen to the maritime industry's plea to keep maritime trade flowing in the recent virtual G20 Leaders Summit on COVID-19. Because of its outsized effect on businesses worldwide and its potential to halt the supply chain sector, the pandemic has been dubbed a "black swan," the consequences of which have yet to be fully quantified. Systems that combine digital and physical components are called "cyber-physical" systems (CPS). When we talk about the "cyber dimension," we're referring to computers and other forms of electronic communication. Physical components include both organic and inorganic matter, as well as artificial components like sensors and actuators. Cyber-physical systems relate to computing and communication infrastructures that operate in tandem with the real world. CPS are defined as "hybrid networked cyber and engineered physical elements co-designed to generate adaptive and predictive systems for increased performance," as stated. Security, availability, responsiveness, stability, effectiveness, efficiency, longevity, and confidentiality are all examples of performance indicators. [45–47] found that CPS and IoT are similar since they employ the same basic architecture, and they also classified CPS and explained some of the differences between them. There is a lot of integration and coordination between the IoT's physical and computational parts in a cyber-physical system. There are many parallels and distinctions between cyber-physical systems, the Internet of Things, and wireless sensor networks. They're intertwined and built on the same foundational level. Technology such as networks, communication, and secure computing devices, things, and digital machines are accessible to all three of them thanks to the internet. With their newfound ability to automatically exchange data across a network and their assigned unique identifiers, devices are becoming increasingly useful.

5.3   Methodology

There are four platforms used for the collected data for this chapter, the procedure flowchart for gathering data is shown in Figure 5.5. We used the keyword "UAV, Privacy and Security Issues." We selected these databases because they contain many research papers, book chapters and online information on numerous subjects.

5.4   Evaluation of UAV Cybersecurity Issues and Challenges

Thanks to advances, the modern world has witnessed many revolutionary changes. This has been shown to produce more reliable, comprehensible, and cost-effective results in our daily lives. In addition, people are

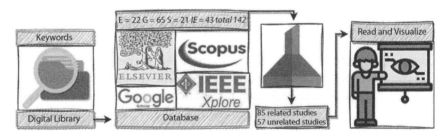

Figure 5.5 Flow chart of data collection.

constantly coming up with new ways to interact with friends and family. In addition to their widespread military use, unmanned aerial vehicles (UAVs) have found general application in various civilian and business settings. China's Unmanned Aerial Vehicle Industry (CUAVI) predicts a CNY 80 billion medium-sized drone industry by 2025 [48], while the FAA estimates that there are presently 3 million drones in the air over the United States. This number will expand fourfold by the end of 2022. The versatility of drones makes them attractive for a growing number of industries and uses, including live event broadcasting, aerial film shoots, and package delivery. These drones are frequently used for transportation because of their low cost of upkeep, ability to take off and land vertically, hovering capability, and a high degree of mobility. These drones are a good option for surveillance and rescue operations [49], and they are often equipped with computer vision and Internet of Things (IoT)-like functions, especially for drone swarming. But there are a few key factors linked to UAV security concerns. Figure 5.6 presents UAV types.

Even though the Iranian military's jamming of an American drone's control signals is documented here, it remains challenging to design an unbreakable security control module for UAVs. Since cameras were less sophisticated at the time, it was recommended that they be used in this manner to increase visibility. Several of them were also utilized in the hunt for terrorists during the Afghanistan War. These drones were once only

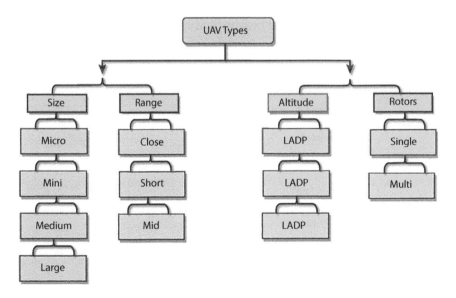

Figure 5.6 Types of UAVs.

used for military purposes, but they are now the preferred option for many civilian uses, including package delivery by Amazon. Agriculture, construction site inspection and emergency rescue operations are just a few of the other areas where they have been put to use. In the early 1910s, the United States of America began the production of pilotless aircraft with a range of approximately one kilometre. The United States began building high-tech UAV programmes like the N2C-2 drone and the OQ-2 communications plane during World War II. Still, these efforts were costly and prone to failure. In the late 1980s, the United States began research and development on high-tech drones, and the country already has several excellent micro-UAVs. Media companies are increasingly turning to drones for cinematic and photographic aerial shots. Security and privacy concerns have become more nuanced and pressing as drone use has rapidly expanded. For safety reasons, passive and aggressive attacks are more likely to be carried out in national airspace where UAVs are allowed. Below, we break down UAV security concerns into four groups: sensor, hardware, software, and communication. Then, we look at the attacks and the defences that have been developed thus far. An overview of cyberattacks and defences against them is shown in Figure 5.7.

Problems with the sensors are critical to the operation of uncrewed aerial vehicles because they allow the vehicles to collect information about their surroundings. Due to their delicate nature, these records must be shielded from prying eyes. Compromised UAV sensors could lead to system failure in hostile environments. We then detail various sensor-level threats, weaknesses, and assaults that could be launched against UAVs.

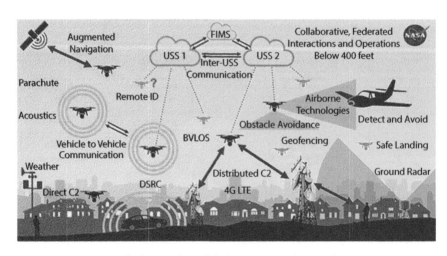

Figure 5.7 Overview of cyberattacks and defences against them [50].

- Vulnerabilities and Threats
  Unmanned aerial vehicles rely heavily on their sensors. All sorts of sensors, including cameras, global positioning systems, and accelerometers, are built into them. As a result, accurate sensor readings are crucial to their functioning. These sensors, however, deal with sensitive data that a hostile operator could exploit to jeopardize the flight. When used for civilian purposes, GPS signals, for instance, lack encryption and authentication. To exploit this weakness, an adversary must only fake a GPS signal to trick the user. The attacker aims to compromise the UAV system by using real-time data from the onboard sensors [51–53]. The flight controller is vulnerable to this flaw because it does not verify the validity of sensor inputs.

- Sensor-based Attacks
  Jamming GPS signals, injecting false data into sensors, and attacking through the senses themselves are all examples of attacks that rely on the data collected by those devices. The satellite signal is picked up by the GPS receiver and transmitted to the GCS in real time during flight missions. Doing so exposes the UAV to probable hijacking because the pilot will lose control. Subverting external sensors like electro-optical and infrared detectors requires injecting bogus sensor data readings into the flight controller. The stability of the UAV is disrupted because of this assault. Attackers who get access to UAVs can tamper with the sensor readings or the onboard flight controller system, both allowing for injecting fake sensor data. Otherwise, he can send bogus signals to the sensors and take down the UAV in the air. The authors present an attack against UAVs that involves faking their GPS signals [54]. The drone's maritime capabilities are compromised due to the GPS spoofing attack—attempts to exploit the senses. The sensory channels used by UAVs provide a target for cyberattacks.

- Countermeasures for Sensor-based Attacks
  As an alternative, some methods use ML-based IDS to spot common and uncommon attacks that target sensors. These systems mine UAVs' internal components, like flight logs and sensor readings, for training data [55]. However, due to the UAVs' restricted energy and computational resources, the actual implementation is difficult. In addition, we

point out that anti-GPS spoofing techniques can be easily included in the Flight Controller to provide a reliable hijacking detection solution [56]. To protect against assaults on any of the senses, various countermeasures have been developed. The currently available literature provides sensor-type dependent solutions. The correctness of GPS coordinates can be verified, for example, through a collaborative data attestation methodology or by implementing anti-GPS-spoofing tools. UAVs can avoid collecting erroneous sensor data thanks to cross-verification, which involves collecting readings from multiple sensors. However, we must also take into account the fundamental limitations of the proposed defences against sensor-based attacks. Computational costs may rise, for instance, if practical safeguards against GPS jamming assaults are implemented. In addition, with so many channels available, providing a different set of sensors for each one would be inefficient.

5.5   Security and Privacy Requirements

There are numerous security concerns brought up by UAVs' widespread use in civilian settings. For this reason, many safeguards are required to prevent UAVs from being exposed, disrupted, modified, or destroyed. For a safe UAV flight, we list the following important privacy and security measures to make sure these things happen: An overview of security requirements is shown in Figure 5.8.

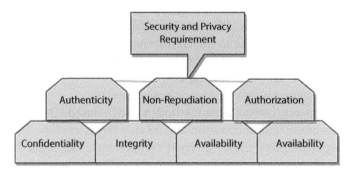

Figure 5.8 Overview of security requirements.

- Confidentiality
  Sensitive information about the flight mission, like telemetry data and control directives, must be kept secret at all costs, making it imperative that UAVs and the GCS transmit the minimum amount of data necessary to carry out their missions. We should create robust cryptography solutions to stop the enemy from gaining access to this data.

- Integrity
  Maintaining unaltered data is crucial. It is essential for a flight's mission success and keeps bad guys from spoofing your network. Altering the UAV system's behaviour through tampering could render the mission unsuccessful. Therefore, all communications must be encrypted and checked for authenticity. Using authenticated encryption algorithms [18], we can guarantee this condition.

- Availability
  There can be no deliberate or accidental downtime for UAVs. Those with permission must have access to all the facilities necessary to carry out a flight mission. In addition, the availability of the UAV system is being threatened by conventional Denial of Service (DoS) attacks, so defence against these attacks is essential. Fortunately, an Intrusion Detection System (IDS) can protect against these kinds of assaults.

- Authenticity
  Authentication is a crucial part of making sure the various parts of the AUV can talk to each other safely. It enables the identification and validation of UAVs participating in the flight mission. By authenticating every UAV, we guarantee that only reliable ones participate in the flight mission. As a bonus, the authentication prevents malicious actors from faking legitimate nodes inside the UAV network.

- Non-Repudiation
  Users' actions (such as data transmission and reception) within UAV Net7 FOR cannot be denied. Unless we do this, we may have to deal with questions of responsibility if our mission is unsuccessful. With this feature, the user's actions can't be blocked. In addition, non-repudiation techniques should be built into the UAV system, such as a digital signature for all communications.

- Authorization
  The UAV system's data exchange must be kept private and accessible only by authorized users. It should be noted that the UAV network has strict rules against any activity by unauthorized users. In addition, the UAV system should detail the resources a given user has access to. Policies must be in place to regulate who gets access to what resources.

5.6 Discussion

Using "unmanned aerial vehicle" as a search term returns many academic articles. Within the last seven years, advances in technology have been made for unmanned aerial vehicles (UAVs) and multi-UAV systems, marking a preliminary stage of progress in this area. The vast majority of those above are merely experimental hypotheses or thoughts that lack substantial quantitative data and practical applications to the present issues. Some of the major studies that follow propose solutions to various problems with data security, mutability, and networking that show originality and usefulness. The studies' conclusions are conditional on various system conditions and external elements, such as weather, labour, and attacks. For the reasons stated in [57] and the results of practical experiments of a specific length, UAV applications are currently more effective than traditional security measures. Significant data security efforts are being made to protect data networking and communication. Cybersecurity threats and tactics and creative problem-solving play a role in reducing the impact of cyberattacks, risks, and vulnerabilities. Although steps may be taken to lessen the impact of cyberattacks, there is not foolproof method of eliminating all potential threats to a network's security. Researchers used cutting-edge network security approaches like machine learning-based intrusion detection systems. Although attacks can be mitigated, there does not appear to be a foolproof method for eliminating such network security holes [58–61].

The examination of the frameworks has considered both performance metrics and security features. Regarding UAVs, safety and security are essential considerations due to their reliance on cellular networks and limited processing power. They could be at risk of intrusion attempts, compromising the confidentiality and integrity of the collected information. Something else may be brought in to replace it, or it could be stolen. This necessitates the development of novel techniques that can be implemented on board to protect passengers' confidentiality while they are in transit. Further research and development are needed for recent technologies like blockchain technology and physical layer protection to achieve the required security level with the necessary quality and dependability. Optical wireless communications (OWCs) have proven worth in 4G, 5G, and beyond 5G mobile networks. Its use is widespread in UAV communication and will likely be implemented in the forthcoming 6G mobile network. However, a few problems still require fixing with this technology. An Intrusion Detection System with Unmanned Aerial Vehicles Real-time network traffic analysis is required to detect intrusions against UAVs in flight. To this end, it is helpful to utilize an IDS for drones, which can identify various intrusions like those that modify signals, malware, attack routing, and message forgery [62–64]. Attack pattern identification also relies heavily on the evolution of anomaly detection frameworks to monitor intrusive activity. In addition to IDS, honeypots and honeynets can be used to protect the aircraft and its mission further. A downside of expanding one's informational horizons is that it may increase one's communication and processing costs. Since there is currently a compromise between security and performance, developing such solutions takes time and effort. Lightweight intrusion detection systems are required for monitoring UAV communications and threat detection. Some systems do this by analyzing the flight's behaviour for signs of anomalies or incursions. Unfortunately, this does not ensure the UAV's flight pattern will not be disrupted by cyberattacks.

Chapter's Contribution

The removal of obstacles is one of the primary goals of technology. One product of this type of technology is the unmanned aerial vehicle (UAV). There are various military and civilian applications for UAVs, including surveillance, observation, research, search, control, transportation, and logistics. This is especially important to keep in mind when performing any tasks that could put the lives of others in jeopardy. Also, UAVs can be utilized to accomplish tasks that are too high or too far away for humans to do effectively and securely. As the capabilities of automated systems have improved, UAVs have found significant employment in a wide range of military and civilian contexts. UAVs are not just used for military purposes; they are also frequently used in disciplines including animal monitoring, meteorology, and disaster assessment. Future smart city development is also expected to involve UAVs. UAVs are enticing to cybercriminals because of the wealth of information they transport. Nevertheless, cybersecurity is not being fully considered in the construction of UAVs. As a result, UAVs are more likely to become victims of cybercrime. Security flaws could be introduced by the modules responsible for the operation of UAVs and the communication between UAVs and control stations.

Communication security is critical to the success of UAVs because of the sensitive information they transport and the potential for abuse by foes. Wi-Fi-based attacks, including eavesdropping, information injection, denial-of-service, and distributed DoS, threaten the privacy of UAV communications. There have been recent allegations of GPS spoofing, session hijacking, and hacked surveillance systems.

Sensing devices are crucial components of unmanned aircraft systems. They have numerous built-in sensors, including cameras, GPS, and accelerometers. Hence, reliable sensor readings are essential to their operation. Yet, these sensors process private information that a malicious operator could use to endanger the flight. GPS signals aren't encrypted or authenticated for recreational reasons. An attacker can exploit this vulnerability by sending a spoof GPS signal to the user's device. The attacker hopes to hack the UAV system via analysis of sensor data in real-time. This vulnerability exists in the flight controller because it does not correctly validate sensor inputs. Infecting the UAV's sensors with malware is another way it might be compromised. As sensory-channel attacks are plausible in realistic settings.

Jamming GPS signals, inserting fake data into sensors, and attacking through the senses are all examples of attacks that rely on the data collected by those devices. When in flight, the GPS receiver picks up the satellite signal and sends it to the GCS in real time. When an adversary disrupts a UAV's access to GPS signals, the UAV becomes disoriented. If the pilot loses control, the UAV is vulnerable to being hijacked. It is necessary to insert false sensor data readings into the flight controller to fool external sensors such as electro-optical and infrared detectors. The attack causes instabilities in the UAV.

In light of the general threat that UAVs pose to national security, in-depth system threat analysis is meant to help the designers and users of the system identify potential vulnerabilities and implement suitable countermeasures and recovery procedures. Since most data regarding the existing protections for UAV systems are classified, it is currently hard to determine which threats could have the most impact. Several of these threats will be worked on in the future, and mission data will be used to represent them more accurately in simulations. Similarly destructive to UAVs, this form of attack involves using malicious software or code to keep tabs on what's happening on a network and perhaps delete data and files. This assault has a significant impact that is not confined to a single system but rather rapidly escalates. It enables hackers to exert remote control over systems. Malware software installed within the system is the most effective defence against such dangerous attacks.

5.7   Conclusion

One of technology's most crucial goals is removing obstacles and supporting human life. An example of a technology created in this area is the unmanned aerial vehicle (UAV). Today, UAVs are widely used for various military and non-military tasks, such as surveys, observation, research, search, control, transportation, and logistics. It becomes more apparent when performing duties that endanger people's health and safety. UAVs can also be used to accomplish tasks that would be impossible for humans to complete correctly and that are not easy to reach. Attacks against the hardware and software of UAVs, which are being used more frequently in line with evolving societal norms and technological advancements, are also on the rise. Attacks against coordination information and communication systems are of particular concern. When UAV systems are attacked, lives can be lost and property can be destroyed. The elimination of obstacles is one of the primary goals of technology. One product of this branch of technology that facilitates navigation by skipping over obstructions is the UAV. One of the technologies developed in this area is the UAV. Reconnaissance, observation, research, search, control, transportation, and logistics are just few of the common uses of UAVs in both civilian and military settings. This is especially important to remember when performing actions that could risk the lives of others. Unmanned aerial vehicles (UAVs) can also be employed to carry out jobs that are either dangerous or too inaccessible for humans to handle safely. There has been a growth in attacks on the hardware and software of UAVs since their use has increased in tandem with shifting cultural norms and technological developments. It is especially worrying when coordinated information and communication networks are attacked.

5.8   Future Work

Cyberattacks against UAV systems can take several forms, including attacks on data transmission links, spoofing of GPS coordinates (known as a "GPS scam"), brute-force authentication, attacks on software vulnerabilities, and attacks on hardware ports and protocols. Casualties and property damage have resulted from attacks on UAV systems. Delays in completion, data breaches failed completion, and reputational harm are other forms of damage. A downside of expanding one's informational horizons is that it may increase one's communication and processing costs. Since there is currently a compromise between security and performance, developing such solutions takes time and effort. Lightweight intrusion detection systems are required for monitoring UAV communications and threat detection. Several systems use the flight's behavioural profile to identify anomalies and potential threats.

References

[1] Wenxuan Zheng, Honglun Wang, Hongxia Ji, Jianfa Wu, UAV formation flight and collision warning with centralized control of ground control station, in: *2019 IEEE International Conference on Unmanned Systems (ICUS)*, IEEE, 2019, pp. 103–108.

[2] Vu Phi Tran, Fendy Santoso, Matt Garratt, Sreenatha Anavatti, Distributed Artificial neural networks-based adaptive strictly negative imaginary formation controller for unmanned aerial vehicles in time-varying environments, *IEEE Trans. Ind. Inf.* (2020).

[3] Nicoletta Bloise, Stefano Primatesta, Roberto Antonini, Gian Piero Fici, Marco Gaspardone, Giorgio Guglieri, Alessandro Rizzo, A survey of unmanned aircraft system technologies to enable safe operations in urban areas, in: *2019 International Conference on Unmanned Aircraft Systems (ICUAS)*, IEEE, 2019, pp. 433–442.

[4] Nahina Islam, Md Mamunur Rashid, Faezeh Pasandideh, Biplob Ray, Steven Moore, Rajan Kadel, A review of applications and communication technologies for Internet of Things (IoT) and Unmanned Aerial Vehicle (UAV) based sustainable smart farming, *Sustainability* 13 (4) (2021) 1821.

[5] David Nodland, Hassan Zargarzadeh, Sarangapani Jagannathan, Neural network-based optimal adaptive output feedback control of a helicopter UAV, *IEEE Trans. Neural Netw. Learn. Syst.* 24 (7) (2013) 1061–1073.

[6] Asif Ali Laghari, Awais Khan Jumani, Rashid Ali Laghari, Haque Nawaz, Unmanned aerial vehicles: A review, *Cognitive Robotics*, Volume 3, 2023.

[7] Shah, I. A., Jhanjhi, N. Z., Humayun, M., & Ghosh, U. (2022). Impact of COVID-19 on Higher and Post-secondary Education Systems. In *How COVID-19 Is Accelerating the Digital Revolution* (pp. 71-83). Springer, Cham.

[8] Rajesh Mahadevappa, T. Virupaksha, L.N. Raghavendra, A practical approach to enhance the flight endurance of a fixed-wing UAV, in: *Proceedings of the National Aerospace Propulsion Conference*, Singapore, Springer, 2020, pp. 297–309.

[9] Navid Ali Khan, Noor Zaman Jhanjhi, Sarfraz Nawaz Brohi, Anand Nayyar, Emerging use of UAV's: secure communication protocol issues and challenges, in: *Drones in Smart-Cities*, Elsevier, 2020, pp. 37–55.

[10] Omar I.Dallal Bashi, W.Z. Hasan, N. Azis, S. Shafie, Hiroaki Wagatsuma, Unmanned aerial vehicle quadcopter: a review, *J. Comput. Theor. Nanosci.* 14 (12) (2017) 5663–5675.

[11] Aakif Mairaj, Asif I. Baba, Ahmad Y. Javaid, Application specific drone simulators: recent advances and challenges, *Simul. Modell. Pract. Theory* 94 (2019) 100–117.

[12] Alireza Malehmir, Lars Dynesius, Kent Paulusson, Alex Paulusson, Henrik Johansson, Mehrdad Bastani, Mats Wedmark, Paul Marsden, The potential of rotary-wing UAV-based magnetic surveys for mineral exploration: a case study from central Sweden, *Lead. Edge* 36 (7) (2017) 552–557.

[13] Telmo Adão, Jonáš Hruška, Luís Pádua, José Bessa, Emanuel Peres, Raul Morais, Joaquim João Sousa, Hyperspectral imaging: a review on UAV-based sensors, data processing and applications for agriculture and forestry, *Remote Sens.* 9 (11) (2017) 1110.

[14] Kai Daniel, Christian Wietfeld, Using Public Network Infrastructures for UAV Remote Sensing in Civilian Security Operations, Dortmund University (Germany FR), 2011.

[15] Ramon A.Suarez Fernandez, Jose Luis Sanchez-Lopez, Carlos Sampedro, Hriday Bavle, Martin Molina, Pascual Campoy, Natural user interfaces for human-drone multi-modal interaction, in: *2016 International Conference on Unmanned Aircraft Systems (ICUAS)*, IEEE, 2016, pp. 1013–1022.

[16] S. Sudhakar, Varadarajan Vijayakumar, C. Sathiya Kumar, V. Priya, Logesh Ravi, V. Subramaniyaswamy, Unmanned Aerial Vehicle (UAV) based Forest Fire Detection and monitoring for reducing false alarms in forest-fires, *Comput. Commun.* 149 (2020) 1–16.

[17] Zhipeng Zhou, Javier Irizarry, Ying Lu, A multidimensional framework for unmanned aerial system applications in construction project management, *J. Manage. Eng.* 34 (3) (2018) 04018004.

[18] Riccardo Costanzi, Davide Fenucci, Vincenzo Manzari, Michele Micheli, Luca Morlando, Daniele Terracciano, Andrea Caiti, Mirko Stifani, Alessandra Tesei, Interoperability among unmanned maritime vehicles: review and first in-field experimentation, *Front. Robotics AI* 7 (2020).

[19] Jafet Morales, Gerson Rodriguez, Grant Huang, David Akopian, Toward UAV control via cellular networks: delay profiles, delay modeling, and a case study within the 5-mile range, *IEEE Trans. Aerosp. Electron. Syst.* 56 (5) (2020) 4132–4151.

[20] Michael Warren, Melissa Greeff, Bhavit Patel, Jack Collier, Angela P. Schoellig, Timothy D. Barfoot, There's no place like home: visual teach and repeat for emergency return of multirotor UAVs during GPS failure, *IEEE Robotics Autom. Lett.* 4 (1) (2018) 161–168.

[21] Konstantinos Kanistras, Kimon P. Valavanis, Matthew J. Rutherford, The history of circulation control, in: *Foundations of Circulation Control Based Small-Scale Unmanned Aircraft*, Springer, Cham, 2018, pp. 19–25.

[22] Sudhir Kumar Chaturvedi, Raj Sekhar, Saikat Banerjee, Hutanshu Kamal, Comparative review study of military and civilian unmanned aerial vehicles (uavs), *Incas Bull.* 11 (3) (2019) 183–198.

[23] Imad Jawhar, Nader Mohamed, Jameela Al-Jaroodi, Dharma P. Agrawal, Sheng Zhang, Communication and networking of UAV-based systems: classification and associated architectures, *J. Netw. Comput. Appl.* 84 (2017) 93–108.

[24] Baohua Shao, Mark S. Leeson, PaFiR: particle Filter Routing–A predictive relaying scheme for UAV-assisted IoT communications in future innovated networks, Internet Things (2019) 100077.

[25] Asif Ali Laghari, M. Sulleman Memon, Agha Sheraz Pathan, RFID based toll deduction system, *IJ Inform.n Technol. Comput. Sci.* 4 (2012) 40–46.

[26] Heda, Giriraj, Sayan Mandal, and S.N. Omkar. "Design, analysis and development of engine mount for a hybrid unmanned aerial vehicle." In *7th International Engineering Symposium - IES 2018*, Kumamoto University, Japan, March 2018.

[27] Zhenyu Na, Jun Wang, Chungang Liu, Mingxiang Guan, Zihe Gao, Join trajectory optimization and communication design for UAV-enabled OFDM networks, *Ad. Hoc. Netw.* 98 (2020) 102031.

[28] Ali Arshad Nasir, Hoang Duong Tuan, Trung Q. Duong, H. Vincent Poor, UAV-enabled communication using NOMA, *IEEE Trans. Commun.* 67 (7) (2019) 5126–5138.

[29] Yan Sun, Dongfang Xu, Derrick Wing Kwan Ng, Linglong Dai, Robert Schober, Optimal 3D-trajectory design and resource allocation for solar-powered UAV communication systems, *IEEE Trans. Commun.* 67 (6) (2019) 4281–4298.

[30] Tsao, K. Y., Girdler, T., & Vassilakis, V. G. (2022). A survey of cyber security threats and solutions for UAV communications and flying ad-hoc networks. *Ad Hoc Networks, 133*, 102894.

[31] Francisco Fabra, Willian Zamora, Julio Sangüesa, Carlos T. Calafate, Juan-Carlos Cano, Pietro Manzoni, A distributed approach for collision avoidance between multirotor UAVs following planned missions, *Sensors* 19 (10) (2019) 2404.

[32] Shah, I. A., Jhanjhi, N. Z., Humayun, M., & Ghosh, U. (2022). Health Care Digital Revolution During COVID-19. In *How COVID-19 Is Accelerating the Digital Revolution* (pp. 17–30). Springer, Cham.

[33] Haque Nawaz, Husnain Mansoor Ali, Asif Ali Laghari, UAV communication networks issues: a review, *Arch. Comput. Meth. Eng.* (2020) 1–21.

[34] Robert Reid, Andrew Cann, Calum Meiklejohn, Liam Poli, Adrian Boeing, Thomas Braunl, Cooperative multi-robot navigation, exploration, mapping and object detection with ROS, in: 2013 IEEE Intelligent Vehicles Symposium (IV), IEEE, 2013, pp. 1083–1088.

[35] Mekonen H. Halefom, Tailoring an Airworthiness Document to Unmanned Aircraft Systems: A Case Study of MIL-HDBK-516C, Virginia Tech, 2020.

[36] Jithin Jagannath, Anu Jagannath, Sean Furman, Tyler Gwin, Deep Learning and Reinforcement Learning For Autonomous Unmanned Aerial Systems: Roadmap for Theory to Deployment, arXiv preprint, 2020.

[36] Ujjan, R. M. A., Pervez, Z., & Dahal, K. (2018, June). Suspicious traffic detection in SDN with collaborative techniques of snort and deep neural networks. In *2018 IEEE 20th International Conference on High Performance Computing and Communications; IEEE 16th International Conference on Smart City; IEEE 4th International Conference on Data Science and Systems (HPCC/SmartCity/DSS)* (pp. 915–920). IEEE.

[37] Mustafa Demir, Nathan J. McNeese, Nancy J. Cooke, Team communication behaviors of the human-automation teaming, in: 2016 IEEE International Multi-Disciplinary Conference on Cognitive Methods in Situation Awareness and Decision Support (CogSIMA), IEEE, 2016, pp. 28–34.

[38] M. Grasso, A. Renga, G. Fasano, M.D. Graziano, M. Grassi, A. Moccia, Design of an end-to-end demonstration mission of a Formation-Flying Synthetic Aperture Radar (FF-SAR) based on microsatellites, *Adv. Space Res.* (2020).

[39] Shah, I. A., Wassan, S., & Usmani, M. H. (2022). E-Government Security and Privacy Issues: Challenges and Preventive Approaches. In *Cybersecurity Measures for E-Government Frameworks* (pp. 61–76). IGI Global.

[40] Ujjan, R. M. A., Pervez, Z., & Dahal, K. (2018, June). Suspicious traffic detection in SDN with collaborative techniques of snort and deep neural networks. In *2018 IEEE 20th International Conference on High Performance Computing and Communications; IEEE 16th International Conference on Smart City; IEEE 4th International Conference on Data Science and Systems (HPCC/SmartCity/DSS)* (pp. 915–920). IEEE.

[41] Shah, I. A. (2022). Cybersecurity Issues and Challenges for E-Government During COVID-19: A Review. *Cybersecurity Measures for E-Government Frameworks*, 187–222.

[42] Ujjan, R. M. A., Pervez, Z., Dahal, K., Bashir, A. K., Mumtaz, R., & González, J. (2020). Towards sFlow and adaptive polling sampling for deep learning based DDoS detection in SDN. *Future Generation Computer Systems, 111*, 763–779.

[43] Norbert Haala, Michael Cramer, Florian Weimer, Martin Trittler, Performance test on UAV-based photogrammetric data collection, Int. Arch. Photogramm. *Remote Sens. Spat. Inf. Sci.* 38 (6) (2011).

[44] Shah, I. A., Jhanjhi, N. Z., Amsaad, F., & Razaque, A. (2022). The Role of Cutting-Edge Technologies in Industry 4.0. In *Cyber Security Applications for Industry 4.0* (pp. 97–109). Chapman and Hall/CRC.

[45] Mason Itkin, Mihui Kim, H. Sø/1SOPS widel, UAV-Based Remote Sens. 1 (1) (2018) 191.

[46] Kok, S. H., Abdullah, A., & Jhanjhi, N. Z. (2022). Early detection of crypto-ransomware using pre-encryption detection algorithm. *Journal of King Saud University - Computer and Information Sciences*, 34(5), 1984–1999.

[47] Ujjan, R. M. A., Pervez, Z., & Dahal, K. (2018, June). Suspicious traffic detection in SDN with collaborative techniques of snort and deep neural networks. In *2018 IEEE 20th International Conference on High Performance Computing and Communications; IEEE 16th International Conference on Smart City; IEEE 4th International Conference on Data Science and Systems (HPCC/SmartCity/DSS)* (pp. 915–920). IEEE.

[48] Ujjan, R. M. A., Pervez, Z., Dahal, K., Bashir, A. K., Mumtaz, R., & González, J. (2020). Towards sFlow and adaptive polling sampling for deep learning based DDoS detection in SDN. *Future Generation Computer Systems, 111,* 763–779.

[49] Shah, I. A., Sial, Q., Jhanjhi, N. Z., & Gaur, L. (2023). Use Cases for Digital Twin. In *Digital Twins and Healthcare: Trends, Techniques, and Challenges* (pp. 102–118). IGI Global.

[50] Altawy, R., & Youssef, A. M. (2016). Security, privacy, and safety aspects of civilian drones: A survey. *ACM Transactions on Cyber-Physical Systems, 1*(2), 1–25.

[51] Ujjan, R. M. A., Pervez, Z., Dahal, K., Bashir, A. K., Mumtaz, R., & González, J. (2020). Towards sFlow and adaptive polling sampling for deep learning based DDoS detection in SDN. *Future Generation Computer Systems, 111,* 763–779.

[52] Shah, I. A., Jhanjhi, N. Z., & Laraib, A. (2023). Cybersecurity and Blockchain Usage in Contemporary Business. In *Handbook of Research on Cybersecurity Issues and Challenges for Business and FinTech Applications* (pp. 49–64). IGI Global.

[53] Ujjan, R. M. A., Pervez, Z., & Dahal, K. (2018, June). Suspicious traffic detection in SDN with collaborative techniques of snort and deep neural networks. In *2018 IEEE 20th International Conference on High Performance Computing and Communications; IEEE 16th International Conference on Smart City; IEEE 4th International Conference on Data Science and Systems (HPCC/SmartCity/DSS)* (pp. 915–920). IEEE.

[54] Torsten Mack, Peter Kunz, Mechanically Steered and Horizontally Polarized Antenna For Aerial vehicles, and Associated Systems and Methods, U.S. Patent Application, 2020 16/859 filed September 17.

[55] Huang Yao, Rongjun Qin, Xiaoyu Chen, Unmanned aerial vehicle for remote sensing applications—A review, *Remote Sens.* 11 (12) (2019) 1443.

[56] Mochamad Mobed Bachtiar, Fernando Ardilla, Abdi Alghifara Felinanda, Android Application Design as Ground Control Station (GCS) and waypoint navigation in Unmanned Aerial Vehicle (UAV), in: *2019 International Electronics Symposium (IES)*, IEEE, 2019, pp. 299–306.

[57] Shuo Wan, Jiaxun Lu, Pingyi Fan, Khaled B. Letaief, Towards big data processing in iot: path planning and resource management of UAV base stations in mobile-edge computing system, *IEEE Internet Things J.* (2019).

[58] Shah, I. A., Jhanjhi, N. Z., Amsaad, F., & Razaque, A. (2022). The Role of Cutting-Edge Technologies in Industry 4.0. In *Cyber Security Applications for Industry 4.0* (pp. 97–109). Chapman and Hall/CRC.

[59] Muhammad Naveed, Sameer Qazi, QoE analysis of real-time video streaming over 4G-LTE for UAV-based surveillance applications, in: *International Conference on Intelligent Technologies and Applications*, Singapore, Springer, 2019, pp. 443–458.

[60] M. Raja, Gaurav Asthana, Ajay Singh, Ashna Singhal, Pallavi Lakra, Design of accurate navigation system by integrating INS and GPS modules, *INCAS Bull.* 11 (4) (2019) 139–154.

[61] Víctor González-Jaramillo, Andreas Fries, Jörg Bendix, AGB estimation in a tropical mountain forest (TMF) by means of RGB and multispectral images using an unmanned aerial vehicle (UAV), *Remote Sens.* 11 (12) (2019) 1413.

[62] Eleftherios Lygouras, Antonios Gasteratos, Konstantinos tarchanidis, and athanasios mitropoulos. ROLFER: a fully autonomous aerial rescue support system, *Microprocess. & Microsyst.* 61 (2018) 32–42.

[63] Klaus Schneider-Zapp, Manuel Cubero-Castan, Dai Shi, Christoph Strecha, A new method to determine multi-angular reflectance factor from lightweight multispectral cameras with sky sensor in a target-less workflow applicable to UAV, *Remote Sens. Environ.* 229 (2019) 60–68.

[64] Shah, I. A., Sial, Q., Jhanjhi, N. Z., & Gaur, L. (2023). The Role of the IoT and Digital Twin in the Healthcare Digitalization Process: IoT and Digital Twin in the Healthcare Digitalization Process. In *Digital Twins and Healthcare: Trends, Techniques, and Challenges* (pp. 20–34). IGI Global.

6

Intelligent Transportation Systems (ITS): Opportunities and Security Challenges

Areeba Laraib[1]* and Raja Majid Ali Ujjan[2]

[1]Mehran University of Engineering and Technology, Shaheed Zulfiqar Ali Bhutto
Campus, Khairpur Mir's, Pakistan
[2]School of Computing, Engineering & Physical Sciences, University, Paisley Scotland

Abstract

The idea of a smart city, which converts urban areas into digital communities and improves the quality of life for its residents in every respect, necessitates incorporating an intelligent transport system. The ease with which city residents can get around is a significant issue. This is true whether the trip is for leisure, necessity, or any combination. By implementing an intelligent transportation system (ITS), the city can become even more progressive with the help of its residents. The purpose of an ITS is to reduce traffic congestion and maximise travel time. It's useful since it gives riders additional insight into travel time, stops along the way, and seating availability ahead of time. This makes commuters' trips more pleasant and safer while reducing travel time. Glasgow, Scotland, is a prime instance of this type of metropolis. City dwellers who take the bus to work each day can use the Intelligent Transport System to find out when their bus will arrive at their stop, how full it is, how long it will take to get where they need to go, where it is now, where it will be next, and how many other people will be riding with them.

Intelligence integration is gaining prominence in the transportation sector. While attacks on transportation infrastructure have been relatively rare, the increased connectivity of vehicles raises the risk of cyberattacks, underscoring the need to protect private and public transportation systems with secure Intelligent Transportation Systems. The safety and efficiency of transportation depend on the integrity of these systems. Implementing measures to address the system's flaws, shield it from outside interference, and reduce its susceptibility to harm can prevent or lessen an attack on an ITS. The need for movement among humans is ancient. Typically, when people think of mobility, they envision transportation networks

*Corresponding author: Areebalareb.sw8@muetkhp.edu.pk

Imdad Ali Shah and Noor Zaman Jhanjhi (eds.) Cybersecurity in the Transportation Industry,
(117–142) © 2024 Scrivener Publishing LLC

that allow for the conveyance of people and goods. The importance of transportation to human survival, progress, and civilization is widely acknowledged. The primary object of this chapter is to peer-view the ITS emerging technologies and their security issues and challenges. Our study results help new researchers and concerned companies.

Keywords: IoT, artificial intelligence, ITS, and emerging technology

6.1 Introduction

Intelligent Transportation Systems (ITS) are defined by the Federal Highway Administration (FHWA) of the United States Department of Transportation (USDOT) as the incorporation of cutting-edge communications technologies into the nation's transportation network and individual vehicles to boost national productivity. Information and electronic technology used in ITS include wireless and wired communication forms [1–3]. Information and communication technology has a significant role in traffic control and transportation management systems. To increase the reliability, efficiency, and sustainability of transportation networks, lessen the impact of traffic congestion on drivers' daily commutes and improve the quality of life for those who use these systems, it is essential to implement intelligence into transportation and traffic management systems. Intelligent Transportation Systems are the product of the merging of computational intelligence, data, and communication networks to increase the reliability, efficiency, and sustainability of transportation networks, lessen the impact of traffic congestion on drivers' daily commutes and improve the quality of life for those who use these systems. It is essential to implement intelligence into transportation and traffic management systems. Every new infrastructure added to our transportation and traffic control systems is another potential entry point for hackers [4, 5]. Therefore, it is much more crucial to safeguard the ITS. The term "cybersecurity" refers to a set of practices that can be implemented in many contexts. Considering the devastation that might result from such attacks, it is essential to have a solid defence in place, one that can fix the system's flaws, repel the outsiders who want to harm them and lessen the chances of an attack. This paper's contribution reviews the difficulties and potential remedies associated with safeguarding ICT infrastructures. According to our examination of the available literature, studies of cybersecurity risks to ITS are few and far between. In this survey, we will go deeper into the problems with ITS security and how we may fix them [6]. While there is no single vulnerability that may be exploited to compromise ITS security, there is a wide variety of attack vectors that must be addressed individually. An overview of the global intelligent transportation system marking size is shown in Figure 6.1.

Vehicles with in-vehicle connectivity can share the latest data on traffic conditions. Through the deployment of ITS, traffic accidents, delays, and congestion can all be reduced [8–11]. ITS contributes significantly to a country's economy by facilitating more effective time management and lowering per capita fuel usage. Research into intelligent transport system stations (ITS-Ss) that use wireless communication to improve traffic flow, safety, and efficiency is a rapidly expanding field. The vehicle ad hoc network (VANET) is an integral part of intelligent transportation systems. Vehicle Area Networks rely on Intelligent Transportation System technologies to relay accurate data on where and how fast vehicles are travelling, their directions and the state of the roads they're on. There are more cars on the road and more accidents because drivers aren't taking the responsibility of being on the road seriously. Congestion, accidents, and travel delays can all be mitigated by making productive use of technology in transportation networks for the greater good of society. Congestion, traffic bottlenecks, and accidents can all be mitigated with the help of ITS, which has been implemented for the greater good of humanity. The usefulness of ITS extends to many fields. Advanced driver assistance systems (ADAS), advanced traveller information systems (ATIS), and advanced traffic management systems (ATMS) are the primary buckets into which ITS applications fall [12–16]. Cooperating collision alerts, slow vehicle

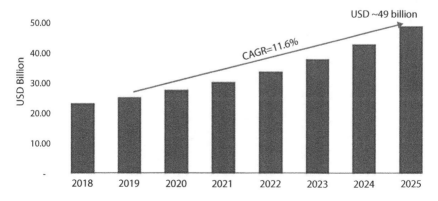

Figure 6.1 Overview of the global intelligent transportation system marking size from 2018 to 2025, adapted from [7].

indicators, lane change messages, speed controls, reverse parking aids, and junction collision warnings are all examples of ADAS uses. Trip matching, route planning, online reservations, electronic shopping locally, and public transportation information are all examples of ATIS applications. ITS may be conceptualized as a sub-type of IoT; its development can make use of the same strategies and designs. Figure 6.2 demonstrates the way the majority of IoT applications' frameworks are structured. Use in ITS is possible as well.

Four layers make up the proposed architecture, each of which is in charge of a separate IoT function. Each layer's functionality is increased when these guidelines are applied to ITS. Intelligent transportation technologies, particularly vehicle ad hoc network (VANET) systems, put transportation providers at greater risk from a cybersecurity perspective because of their interconnected nature. These systems frequently function together, connect equipment, or different information systems, and provide access to diverse networks like the internet [17]. Networks linked together are more likely to be the target of cyberattacks and invasions. These assaults have the potential to cause severe damage. To keep these systems safe, it's essential to do a thorough risk analysis and then put into practice effective procedures that are tailored to high-stakes settings without sacrificing usability or responsiveness in the here and now. The security of ITSs is a growing concern as these systems have crucial applications for human road safety. Because these networks rely on vehicle communications, they are susceptible to the same issues as other wireless systems. ITS security is complex because it involves many moving parts (applications, communication architectures, and protocols). To ensure this safety, we must determine what threats could be levelled against the ITS and then design appropriate countermeasures.

The chapter focuses on the following points:

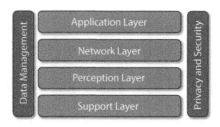

Figure 6.2 Descriptions of Internet of Things (IoT) architecture.

- Peer-reviewed the Intelligent Transportation System (ITS)
- Security issues and challenges in ITS
- Data collection and data transmission
- Data analysis and traveller information.

6.2   Literature Review

New traffic control methods have been developed because of technical progress in response to the growing number and density of cars on the roads. These technological innovations are being applied to vehicular transportation via Intelligent Transportation Systems. Data is gathered from vehicles' and buildings' installed sensors and other equipment. The data can be used to enhance the current transportation networks. Increasing transportation system safety, traffic efficiency, and value-added applications is the goal. Data is utilised to make roads safer and lessen the impact of collisions that cannot be avoided [18, 19]. Traffic efficiency applications aim to ease congestion and speed up vehicle travel times. Infotainment, destination details, route planning, and internet connectivity are all examples of valuable extras. Vehicles and roadside infrastructure must be able to communicate wirelessly with one another for ITS to function [20]. There is a great deal of activity and variety in the several subfields of research that make up the topic of intelligent transportation systems. Vehicle and transportation system management technologies keep getting better and better.

Since new transportation technologies are constantly being developed and introduced, ITS security is becoming increasingly important. Attackers can more easily disrupt the ITS because of flaws in the underlying technologies. Its cutting-edge services are used by various transportation systems and traffic management agencies to create more efficient and effective transportation networks [21]. Attacks on ITS can have severe consequences for urban transportation networks, making them essential to developing smart cities. Personal automobiles also benefit from ITS for added security and comfort. The importance of ITS, which incorporates a wide variety of applications, continues to rise for both private and public transportation networks. Improvements in traffic flow, traffic management, and transportation-related environmental impacts are all possible thanks to the data processed and shared by these programmes [22–24]. Information about a person's vehicle can be shared with other drivers and with nearby or far-off infrastructure thanks to the use of technology installed in their automobile. Figure 6.3 presents the taxonomy of the literature review of ITS.

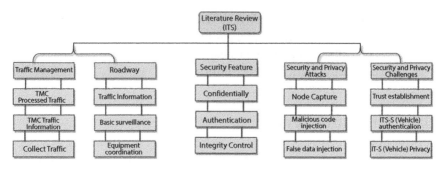

Figure 6.3 The taxonomy of the literature review ITS.

The technology used to repair automobiles has advanced in tandem with the advancements made to the automobiles themselves. As transportation technology advances and evolves, ensuring the safety of all this equipment in private vehicles and public transportation systems becomes more crucial. The current body of knowledge mostly ignores the cybersecurity implications of intelligent transportation systems in favour of exploring their potential uses [25]. The vulnerability of these ITS to attack has not been thoroughly studied. Cybersecurity within ITS has been the subject of recent literature reviews. In this study, we will compare various approaches to enforcing internal security. A preliminary investigation has been conducted into the nature of cyber assaults against ITS and the methods for protecting against them. Figure 6.4 presents an overview of technologies in ITS.

Electric vehicles (EVs) are gaining popularity because they are a practical and environmentally friendly means of transportation. It's a known fact

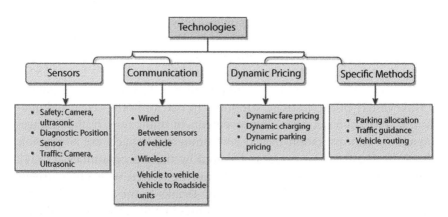

Figure 6.4 Overview of technologies in ITS.

that the emissions of carbon dioxide into the environment are increased using conventional automobiles powered by internal combustion engines. If the electricity used to charge EVs comes from renewable sources rather than generators that rely on fossil fuels, then the vehicles' impact on CO2 emissions will be greatly reduced [26–30]. More infrastructure and innovative technologies, such as efficient charging stations, are required for the long-term development of EVs. The useful CS for EVs in general, include but are not limited to power price forecasting and EV charging station placement.

The goal is to lessen the time and money spent on charging electric vehicles kept at workplaces and schools (Das, Bhattacharya, and). We are enthusiastic about the prospect of repurposing retired EV batteries as BESS to secure cost-effective electricity and enable the usage of renewable energy sources at EV charging stations. But the transportation and grid networks will be impacted by charging many EVs. As a result, studying how people make appointments and pay is essential [31–37]. Recent studies have focused on the scheduling process independent of the grid system and transport data. The former is often intended for a solitary automobile. The latter, though, will accommodate a fleet of cars. The busiest time of year for charging electric vehicles (EVs) might vary with the seasons. Different EVs have different charging capabilities. Point out that traffic congestion is likely to emerge because of the concentration of EVs in the CS. Demand variability and the intermittency of renewable energy sources like solar and wind necessitate optimization of the charging scheduling approach in terms of a time frame if grid congestion and poor service are to be avoided. The authors developed a method for scheduling electric vehicle charging that is efficient and practical. Charging scheduling in EVs is a fascinating subject due to the higher charging time required by the batteries and the physical and power limits of CSs. Smart scheduling, which uses the Artificial Bee Colony (ABC) algorithm, is useful for optimising resource utilisation and satisfying user needs simultaneously [38]. Various meta-heuristics, such as the Memetic Algorithm, have been developed to address these issues. This research introduces a new electric car charging coordination paradigm: the autonomous stochastic charging control scheme (ASCCS).

6.3 Evaluation of the Intelligence Transportation System

Saving lives, time, money, and the environment are just some of the many goals of Intelligent Transportation Systems (ITS), which is the implementation of cutting-edge and futuristic transportation technologies. All forms of transportation, from cars and trains to planes and ships, are included in this umbrella term. However, the focus of this article is limited to the danger posed by cyberattacks on connected cars, autonomous vehicles, and intelligent roads because of the more significant publicity, the more immediate impact, and the potentially disastrous consequences such assaults would have on public safety.

Integrated ITS applications are highly complex, and their design and deployment necessitate a strategic framework to foresee future investments. Technical features of ITS may be visualised by designers and planners thanks to the ITS framework architecture, which also lays out the necessary legal and business foundation. This process guarantees that the final ITS rollout is well-thought-out, compatible with other systems, and able to deliver on the expectations of its stakeholders and users regarding performance and behaviour [39–41]. The entire ecosystem may be more easily managed, maintained, and expanded with the support of an ITS framework design. Multiple applications can coordinate with one another even on a global scale if they conform to a standard ITS framework architecture. European ITS Framework Architecture, National ITS Architecture in the United States, and ITS System Architecture in Japan are the three

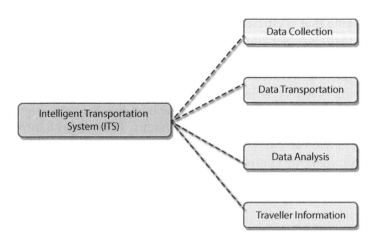

Figure 6.5 Overview of ITS working.

most important ITS frameworks now under development worldwide. Although ITS is still a young study area, it has been rapidly evolving thanks to the introduction of novel concepts and technologies. While intelligent vehicles are a vital part of ITS, there are other components of ITS, and other details of ITS have been given less consideration. This section presents a high-level summary of ITS, including an explanation of its main elements and a survey of its enabling technologies. Figure 6.5 presents an overview of ITS working.

6.3.1 Data Collection

Data collection and real-time monitoring are essential for strategic planning. Information from various hardware sources forms the foundation for future ITS operations. This includes Automatic Vehicle Identifiers, Automatic Vehicle Locators based on Global Positioning System technology, sensors, cameras, etc. Hardware often keeps tabs on things like traffic volumes, the whereabouts of vehicles, how heavy each car is, how long each trip takes, how often it is delayed, and so on [42]. Connected to the servers housed in the data centre, these pieces of hardware store and process massive amounts of data.

6.3.2 Data Transmission

The success of any ITS installation hinges on the ability to communicate information quickly and effectively; therefore, this component of ITS involves sending data gathered in the field to TMC, which will then evaluate the data and provide the results to travellers. Travellers can receive updates about traffic conditions via the Internet, SMS, or in-vehicle displays [43]. Dedicated short-range communications (DSRC) employ radio, whereas Continuous Air Interface Long and Medium Range (CAILM) employ cellular connectivity and infrared links.

6.3.3 Data Analysis

In subsequent stages, TMC processes the gathered and received data. These procedures include checking for and fixing errors, cleaning and synthesising data, and using an adaptive logic analysis. Inconsistencies in data are identified and corrected using specialised software. The information is then combined and processed in several ways. To provide users with relevant information, this repaired aggregate data is processed further to predict traffic scenarios.

6.3.4   Traveler Information

A Travel Advisory System (TAS) aims to provide the user with relevant transportation information. This technology may access information about traffic conditions, road closures, detours, and construction in real time. To get this information out to the public, electronic tools like variable message signs, highway advisory radio, the internet, short messaging service (SMS), and automated cell phones are used. The growing number of cars can be attributed to the rapid pace at which metropolitan areas develop. In turn, combining the two puts tremendous pressure on cities to improve their traffic systems to ensure that the city continues functioning smoothly and efficiently. The only option available is to implement an intelligent transport system [44]. Citizens' safety and comfort are improved, while city administrators' workload is reduced, thanks to ITS.

6.4   Importance of Intelligent Transportation System

The ability to recognise potential dangers is crucial for Information and Communications Technologies (ICTs). Potential threats to ITS are discussed, including those from foreign intelligence, and criminal gangs. Nation-states' software espionage tools and viruses are tailored to their specific purposes. The purpose of such an assault is to steal intellectual property or acquire a competitive edge. During wartime, for instance, an enemy nation may attempt to penetrate a country's ITS network and steal sensitive information. It is possible for the state to have direct control of hacking teams and resources or to contract them out to third parties to preserve plausible deniability. Groups of criminals are using various methods to hack into ITS with the intention of making money through dishonest means. The purpose of hacktivists is to bring attention to a political cause by targeting ITS networks. Hacking highway message boards to promote a political message is possible. By attacking ITS, cyberterrorists hope to cause widespread destruction of property and spread fear and panic. When insiders attack the company, they work for or have worked for in the past, and they often do so in a way that works against their own interests. There isn't just one reason for these attacks [45–49]. Operators with bad motives may launch attacks on ITS for several reasons, including evading fees and penalties, avoiding congestion, and undermining competitors' work. Disasters of untouched nature are likewise a potential hazard to ITS. The infrastructure of ITS is vulnerable to breakdowns caused by natural occurrences. An overview of smart mobility is shown in Figure 6.6.

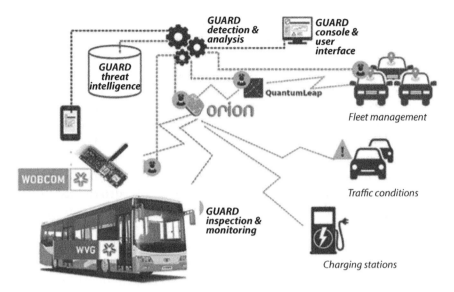

Figure 6.6 Overview of smart mobility [50].

The WOBCOM city infrastructure hosts the cloud apps in the cases under consideration. By connecting to the buses' IBIS-Bus, the Internet of Things device may gather route data, pinpoint bus stops, and estimate the number of passengers based on the signal strength of nearby wireless (Wi-Fi) devices. LoRaWAN network information is also provided, and it can act on commands from the management app.

Typically, financial gain is the driving force behind cyberattacks. When an assault occurs on its system, however, it has a much more noticeable and far-reaching effect than on a typical computer network. Having an audience can be a powerful incentive. Possible motivations for these attacks include, but are not limited to, ransom demands, theft of sensitive information, information warfare, system gaming and theft, and even vengeance and terrorism. There are various ways to obtain this data, including physical, wireless, and network attacks. Threats may come from a single or several entry points. In the event of a ransomware attack, both data and infrastructure may be encrypted. If you want the decryption key, you'll have to pay a ransom [51–53]. A hacker with access to a connected car might theoretically hold it hostage until a ransom is paid. These vehicles' security may be compromised. Many different things can be done with stolen information. Most likely, data thieves are nation-states and unscrupulous competitors. The motivation for data theft is financial gain. A denial-of-service attack on the ITS infrastructure is an example of information warfare.

The resulting system crashes lead to traffic mayhem. Additionally, political statements, protests, and practical jokes can be shared using this medium. The risk is that this will damage the company's image and bottom line [54]. Confusion in traffic can result from the transmission of a bogus V2V message. This exploit can be used to launch a V2V information-poisoning assault. GPS transmitters, receivers, and spoofing of GPS signals can also be compromised through map hacking. Vehicle theft is a form of system gaming. Some people use ITS services without paying for them. Hackers can divert autonomous vehicles to an alternative destination to conceal the delivery of illegal goods or evade detection. Hackers have demonstrated the ability to direct autonomous automobiles to a predetermined place, where they can steal valuables, vehicle components, and the entire vehicle or abduct the occupants. Employing an ITS system allows users to avoid incurring service fees. A mobile infrared transmitter (MIRT) can remotely activate a computer-controlled traffic light. It's possible to hack into a competitor's car and render it useless, thwarting the competition. Hackers can set up a scenario in which a compromised vehicle is given higher priority than other vehicles on the road, forcing autonomous vehicles to move over. To scam unwary riders, fraudsters can submit fake orders for rideshares. The Taxonomy of ITS privacy issues is shown in Figure 6.7.

One of the most dangerous and lethal attack vectors against ITS is using revenge and terrorism as a paradigm. Threat actors can use vulnerabilities in driving features to manufacture weapons. There is a high degree of difficulty in predicting and defending against these attacks. The common goal of hackers who target ITS infrastructure is to access other parts of the ITS ecosystem via the target system [55–57]. If an attacker breaches the ITS infrastructure, they can access any component of the ITS ecosystem that uses the same network (whether it's the internet or a virtual private network). Without much trouble, you can get into the inner workings of the network. Scanning an encrypted or closed network can reveal its topology. File deletion is a common method of compromising an ITS device or system. Credentials and settings can be restored by installing the necessary firmware. The data is intercepted and spoofed to the backend servers in a man-in-the-middle attack that uses exposed wires or connections. Data on a device could be stolen or compromised if tampered with. Malware can be introduced using a removable storage device [58-60]. The controller and the backend servers are vulnerable to receiving invalid commands. turning an ITS appliance into a secure portal to the company network. Flaws in the code can be used as an entry point for malicious attacks. The misuse of authority by trusted operators is another vector through which devices

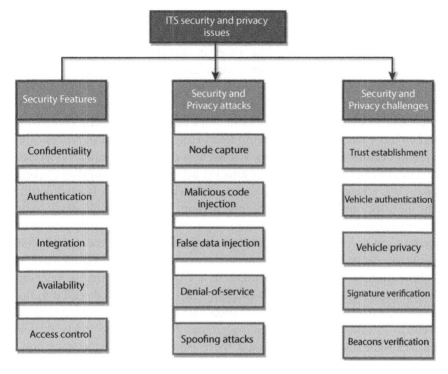

Figure 6.7 The taxonomy of ITS privacy issues and challenges.

can be compromised. When it comes to information technology, wireless attacks are among the most concerning threats that may be made against an ITS system [61–63].

One of the most widespread methods of web hacking is known as "structured query language" (SQL) injection. Using a legitimate user session is what is meant by "session hijacking." A hacker can spoof or hijack a computer system by manipulating the name server to return a false IP address. Malware can enter a network through "watering holes" by infecting popular sites that users frequently visit. To perform a Pass the Hash attack, an attacker must obtain legitimate credentials from a victim and then use them elsewhere on the same network. A pass-the-ticket attack is used to move laterally within a network. The controller and backend server could receive invalid commands [64, 65]. Devices equipped with ITS technology can be repurposed as secure portals into the business's internal network. It is possible for trusted operators to abuse their position and cause harm to the systems or devices under their control. The company's network may be breached through a contractor's computer system. The security of vehicular ad hoc networks (VANETs) can be compromised, posing a risk to drivers on the road.

Sybil attacks are among the most damaging kinds of cyberattacks because they are often hard to spot. Typically, they include a car that seems to be in two places at once. It is unclear whether or not the data collected from this car is originating from a single source. This is a tool used by attackers to manipulate networks in ways favourable to their objectives. When more data requests are submitted to a system than it can process, the system crashes due to overload, known as a distributed denial-of-service assault. In a black hole attack, the attacker acts as a conduit for data packets [66]. The attacker drops the data packets, which causes a breakdown in the network's ability to exchange information. For a wormhole attack to be successful, it requires two or more compromised cars to participate in as many routing requests as possible by falsely claiming to know the quickest route to a desired location. Cars or RSUs (roadside units) can launch a false information attack on other vehicles in a VANET by creating or relaying bogus data. A malicious vehicle can generate bogus data and send it to the VANET. Attackers can use fake location data broadcast by moving targets. Vehicle location data becomes inaccurate, compromising safety-related applications and systems. Because these packets are being sent to non-existent cars, they are being lost. Using deceptive driving circumstances to trick sensors is dangerous [67]. An adversary can trick in-vehicle sensors. By storing and rebroadcasting messages later, when they are no longer valid, a replay attack can fool other computers in the network. This kind of attack attempts to replicate the exact conditions that existed during the initial transmission. An attacker can passively eavesdrop on vehicle communications or track their whereabouts by monitoring the network. Attack vehicles act as interceptors, reading and analysing intercepted communications [68, 69]. Data is collected about the vehicles and communication methods to be used in future assaults. The prevalence of ITS attacks is growing. Select cyberattack vectors can be assessed to determine the danger of such attacks.

6.5   Discussion

Ultimately safeguarding the complex, ITS environment is an arduous task. While it's true that cyberattacks and breaches will occur eventually, ITS operators should build prevention and recovery measures into their routine procedures. The latency criteria for data transmission must be met. This should be carried out using lightweight cryptographic techniques with low overhead. Key security features for ITS ecosystems include confidentiality and authentication. Rapid detection and constant remediation of security holes are essential. Protected information must be protected from being leaked, and security breaches must be managed. The only way to stop attacks is to close all possible entry points [70, 71]. After an attack on the ITS ecosystem, it is necessary to bolster defences and prevent future accidents. Tools like breach detection systems (BDS), anti-malware software, and phishing filters can also be implemented. Security solutions such as intrusion prevention and detection systems, vulnerability scanning, patch management, and the Shodan web application scanner are also available [72]. By dividing a network into smaller, more manageable pieces, network segmentation can ease traffic, boost network security, and reduce the likelihood of breakdowns. By separating the ITS controllers onto their network, lateral movement concerns are mitigated, and network security is bolstered. Using firewalls, incoming and outgoing data traffic may be monitored and managed. This regulation is implemented via a set of rules that are applied to the screen. We can pinpoint the apps and hosts likely to generate or request malicious traffic. Modern unified threat management gateways and next-generation firewalls consolidate several security functions into a single machine. Low-traffic devices in a network can be better understood by analysing traffic at line speed. Data can be scanned with anti-malware software [73].

To eliminate malware, it must first be identified, then inhibited, and finally eliminated. Malware is identified in three ways: by heuristics, specialised signatures, and generic signatures. One of the most common ways to spread infections is by spear-phishing, which highlights the significance of anti-phishing solutions. Anti-phishing software will examine incoming messages for signs of spam or phishing and filter them out. Message sandboxes, which are a feature of anti-phishing technologies, can be used to detect and block malicious attachments [74, 75]. A breach detection system (BDS) will alert administrators when a system is under attack or threat. BDS can evaluate and detect complex attacks, but it cannot stop them. Various protocols allow for the study of traffic patterns in networks. Infected websites can be pinpointed. Emulation-sandboxing is a technique for simulating the behaviour and effects of malicious files. IPS and IDS are watching the network for any suspicious activity. Intrusion detection systems are inactive systems that generate a report after an attack. If IPS detects a malicious event, it will discard the packet. Most assaults on ITS applications and systems can be thwarted with the help of digital signature algorithms. When digital signatures are not sufficient to prevent an attack, encryption might be employed instead. Data can be encrypted

Figure 6.8 Overview of ITS service [76].

and decrypted using encryption technology. An overview of Intelligent Transportation Systems is shown in Figure 6.8.

The use of encrypted network communication is effective in protecting against man-in-the-middle (MitM) attacks. Patch management software can be physical or virtual, and it is used to keep servers, workstations, and other systems up to date. The system has had its security patched and updated. Scanners for security flaws in computer systems, networks, and software are called vulnerability scanners. Vulnerabilities in the system that have not been fixed are discovered during the scanning process. IT administrators can set security holes once they have been discovered. Connected gadgets on the internet can be scanned with Shodan. This tool is used to obtain OSINT (open-source intelligence). As a result of the data acquired by Shodan, unprotected cyber assets with unpatched vulnerabilities can be located. Shodan can be used by ITS operators to check for unprotected devices and systems over the internet. When a vehicle is equipped with data fusion software, its true condition can be determined. It can also provide details on the area immediately surrounding the car. All data collected is analysed and provided. Depending on the data that is still accessible in the vehicle, attackers can be recognised and countered. Corroboration or refutation of observations made by a compromised vehicle may be provided by cooperating neighbouring vehicles or elements inside the infrastructure. Attacks can be detected with the aid of additional sources of information. Anomaly detection during cyberattacks may be aided by these data fusion techniques.

As a kind of authentication, biometrics makes use of one's unique physiological and behavioural traits. Then, these features are checked mechanically. A key component of future safety will be biometric systems. Simply put, a biometric system is an automatic setup. To gather data, the system takes note of many attributes [77–80]. The data is then passed around the system, stored, and processed. The question of whether to grant access is resolved. Biometrics can be used to strengthen the overall security of the ITS system by making impersonation much harder to pull off. Biometrics offers a way to strengthen the ITS's security and reduce potential threats.

Safeguarding ITS can be aided by suggested policy changes. Rather than trying to integrate incompatible ITS frameworks, countries that share land borders should collaborate so that their ITS systems can function together. Awareness campaigns that alert end-users of the threats they may face in ITS environments can be developed and implemented with the support of increased international cooperation, information sharing, and cybersecurity expertise. Cybersecurity risks and responses can be discussed openly. Updating current communication protocols is preferable to creating new ones because of the savings in time and money. To manage ITS communications, several different protocols are required.

Chapter's Contribution
It can be difficult to implement the policy suggestion of coordinating ITS frameworks when people are hesitant to work together and share data. Reasons for this include the opportunity cost of repairing damaged reputations, competitive pressures, and potential financial losses from cybercrime. It's possible that information can't be shared because crucial infrastructure or safeguards haven't been set up. Underinvestment in cybersecurity is another problem that needs fixing. Countermeasures for cybersecurity are not appropriately evaluated. The difference between effective and ineffective cybersecurity measures needs to be better understood, and there needs to be more awareness and information about both. The transition from older ITS systems to newer, networked ones is laborious. They need to improve security results from efficient communication and information sharing. Understanding the various cyber risks and developing strategies to protect ITS systems can be challenging. Cybersecurity measures may be put in place, but they will only be as successful as they may be if users have a firm grasp of how to operate the software. Cyberattacks are becoming more sophisticated and entering deeper into the ITS environment; however, countermeasures can be effective to prevent and resolve these attacks if adopted. More study is required to assess biometrics' efficacy in preventing cyberattacks and to identify best practices for implementing

biometrics in ITS ecosystems. Threat analysis during the formative stages of vehicle automation system development requires a more comprehensive assessment of ITS. The research process needs to be flexible enough to accommodate multiple points of view and provide for the anticipation of a wide array of potential dangers. The ITS ecosystem requires an evaluation of security vectors that strike a balance between security, convenience, and functionality.

6.6   Conclusion

An intelligent transport system is essential to a smart city, which transforms traditional metropolitan areas into digital communities and enhances the quality of life for its citizens in every imaginable way. The accessibility of a city is a crucial factor. Whether taking a trip for pleasure, business or some combination thereof, that holds. The town may advance even further with the support of its citizens by installing an intelligent transportation system. Congestion is minimised, and travel times are extended thanks to ITS. It's helpful since it gives passengers more information on the route, the stops along the way, and the availability of seats. It lessens the stress and danger of commuting while speeding up travel. The Scottish city of Glasgow is a classic example of this type of modern megacity. City dwellers who rely on public transportation to get them to and from work each day can use the Intelligent Transport System to track their bus's location in real time, see how full it is, calculate how long it will take to get where they need to go and see how many other people will be riding with them. The transportation industry is one of the most visible examples of the rise of intelligence integration. While transportation infrastructure attacks have been uncommon, rising vehicle connectivity increases the potential for cyberattacks, highlighting the need for secure, intelligent transportation systems to defend public and commercial transportation networks. When these infrastructures are working correctly, transportation is both safe and efficient. An attack on an ITS can be prevented or mitigated by fixing the system's vulnerabilities, protecting it from outside meddling, and making it less vulnerable to harm. Humans have always had a fundamental need to be on the go. Modern conceptions of mobility frequently centre on transportation systems that facilitate the movement of people and things. The importance of transportation to human life, progress, and civilization is widely accepted. It ensures that people can reach their places of employment, medical care, schools, and other critical social resources. It's crucial to the economy since it facilitates interaction between buyers and suppliers.

Transportation and the infrastructure it supports are vital to the survival of today's global and metropolitan economies.

6.7   Future Work

More and better forms of transportation are essential to advancing society and the economy. ITS ecosystems are changing, as are the threats to them. A wide range of enhancements is possible. Enhancing security that is better geared toward avoiding and eradicating assaults is essential. Earlier sections emphasised the importance of addressing the numerous issues with the existing models used by ITS ecosystems. More investigation is required to evaluate solutions tailored to the various ITS systems and uses. More study of collaborative systems is necessary to discover cyber risks and create countermeasures. When it comes to its future cybersecurity, biometric technologies are essential.

References

[1] J. Zhang, F. Wang, K. Wang, W. Lin, X. Xu, and C. Chen. Data-driven intelligent transportation systems: A survey. *IEEE Transactions on Intelligent Transportation Systems* 12, no. 4 (2011): 1624-1639.

[2] K. Qureshi, and A. Abdullah. A survey on intelligent transportation systems. *Middle-East Journal of Scientific Research* 15, no. 5 (2013): 629-642.

[3] A.S. Elmaghraby, and M. M. Losavio (2014). Cyber security challenges in Smart Cities: Safety, security and privacy. *Journal of Advanced Research*, 5(4), 491-497.

[4] M.A. Javed, B. Hamida, and W. Znaidi, (2016). Security in intelligent transport systems for smart cities: From theory to practice. *Sensors*, 16(6), 879.

[5] A. Vaibhav, D. Shukla, S. Das, S. Sahana, and P. Johri. Security challenges, authentication, application and trust models for vehicular ad hoc network-a survey. *IJ Wireless and Microwave Technologies* 3 (2017): 36-48.

[6] Guerrero-ibanez, J. A., Zeadally, S., & Contreras-Castillo, J. (2015). Integration challenges of intelligent transportation systems with connected vehicle, cloud computing, and internet of things technologies. *IEEE Wireless Communications*, 22(6), 122-128.

[7] Kołodziej, J., Hopmann, C., Coppa, G., Grzonka, D., & Widłak, A. (2022). Intelligent Transportation Systems–Models, Challenges, Security Aspects. In *Cybersecurity of Digital Service Chains: Challenges, Methodologies, and Tools* (pp. 56-82). Cham: Springer International Publishing.

[8] E. Bubeníková, M. Franeková, and P. Holečko, P. (2013, October). Security increasing trends in intelligent transportation systems utilising modern image processing methods. In *International Conference on Transport Systems Telematics* (pp. 353-360). Springer, Berlin, Heidelberg.

[9] M. Alam, J. Ferreira, and Fonseca, J. (2016). Introduction to intelligent transportation systems. In *Intelligent Transportation Systems* (pp. 1-17). Springer International Publishing.

[10] S. Chakraborty, and S. Ramesh. (2016, January). Technologies for Safe and Intelligent Transportation Systems. In *VLSI Design and 2016 15th International Conference on Embedded Systems (VLSID), 2016 29th International Conference on* (pp. 56-58). IEEE.

[11] R. Blanes, R. A. Paton, and I. Docherty. (2015, January). Public Value of Intelligent Transportation System. In *System Sciences (HICSS), 2015 48th Hawaii International Conference on* (pp. 1389-1399). IEEE.

[12] K. Dellios, D. Papanikas, and D. Polemi. (2015). Information Security Compliance over Intelligent Transport Systems: Is IT Possible? *IEEE Security & Privacy*, 13(3), 9-15.

[13] M. Franeková and P. Lüley. (2013, October). Security of digital signature schemes for Car-to-Car communications within intelligent transportation systems. In *International Conference on Transport Systems Telematics* (pp. 258-267). Springer, Berlin, Heidelberg.

[14] K. Kelarestaghi, K. Heaslip, M. Khalilikhah, A. Fuentes, and V. Fessmann. Intelligent transportation system security: hacked message signs. *SAE International Journal of Transportation Cybersecurity and Privacy* 1, no. 11-01-02- 0004 (2018): 75-90.

[15] Alam, M., Ferreira, J., & Fonseca, J. (2016). Introduction to intelligent transportation systems. In *Intelligent Transportation Systems* (pp. 1-17). Springer International Publishing.

[16] E. Bubenikova, J. Durech, and M. Franekova. (2014, May). Security solutions of intelligent transportation system's applications with using VANET networks. In *Control Conference (ICCC), 2014 15th International Carpathian* (pp. 63-68). IEEE.

[17] J. H. Lee, and Ernst, T. (2011, November). Security issues of IPv6 communications in cooperative intelligent transportation systems (poster). In *Vehicular Networking Conference (VNC)*, 2011 IEEE (pp. 284-290). IEEE.

[18] Petit, J. (2015). Potential cyber attacks on automated vehicles, *IEEE Transitions on Intelligent Transportation Systems*, 16(2), 546-556.

[19] S. Kumar and B. Xu. A Machine Learning Based Approach to Detect Malicious Fast Flux Networks. In *2018 IEEE Symposium Series on Computational Intelligence (SSCI)*, pp. 1676-1683. IEEE, 2018.

[20] D. Eastman and S. Kumar, A Simulation Study to Detect Attacks on Internet of Things. In *2017 IEEE 15th Intl Conf on Dependable, Autonomous and Secure Computing, 15th Intl Conf on Pervasive Intelligence and Computing, 3rd Intl Conf on Big Data Intelligence and Computing and Cyber Science and*

Technology Congress (DASC/PiCom/DataCom/CyberSciTech) (pp. 645-650). IEEE.

[21] Shah, I. A., Sial, Q., Jhanjhi, N. Z., & Gaur, L. (2023). The Role of the IoT and Digital Twin in the Healthcare Digitalization Process: IoT and Digital Twin in the Healthcare Digitalization Process. In *Digital Twins and Healthcare: Trends, Techniques, and Challenges* (pp. 20-34). IGI Global.

[22] S. Kumar, and B. Xu. Vulnerability assessment for security in aviation cyber-physical systems. In *2017 IEEE 4th International Conference on Cyber Security and Cloud Computing (CSCloud)*, pp. 145-150. IEEE, 2017.

[23] J. Chelladhurai, P. Chelliah, and S. Kumar. Securing docker containers from denial of service (dos) attacks. In *2016 IEEE International Conference on Services Computing (SCC)*, pp. 856-859. IEEE, 2016.

[24] S. Kumar, B. Bhargava, R. Macêdo, and G. Mani. Securing iot-based cyber-physical human systems against collaborative attacks. In *2017 IEEE International Congress on Internet of Things (ICIOT)*, pp. 9-16. IEEE, 2017.

[25] Shah, I. A., Jhanjhi, N. Z., Humayun, M., & Ghosh, U. (2022). Health Care Digital Revolution During COVID-19. In *How COVID-19 Is Accelerating the Digital Revolution* (pp. 17-30). Springer, Cham.

[26] geospatialworlds: https://www.geospatialworld.net/blogs/what-is-intelligent-transport-system-and-how-it-works/

[27] S. Kumar, T. Vealey, and H. Srivastava. Security in internet of things: Challenges, solutions and future directions." In *2016 49th Hawaii International Conference on System Sciences (HICSS)*, pp. 5772-5781. IEEE, 2016.

[28] S. Srinivasan, S, and S. P. Alampalayam. Intrusion Detection Algorithm for MANET. *International Journal of Information Security and Privacy (IJISP)* 5, no. 3 (2011): 36-49.

[29] S. Kumar, Classification and review of security schemes in mobile computing. *Wireless Sensor Network* 2, no. 06 (2010): 419.

[30] S.P. Alampalayam, and S. Srinivasan. Intrusion recovery framework for tactical mobile ad hoc networks. *International Journal of Computer Science and Network* Security 9, no. 9 (2009): 1-10.

[31] IBM, Smarter Cities, 2017. [Online]. Available: https://www. ibm.com/smarterplanet/us/en/smarter cities/overview/

[32] B. Telecom, BT CityVerve Portal, 2017. [Online]. Available: https://portal. bt-hypercat.com/

[33] S. de Luca, R. D. Pace, A. D. Febbraro, and N. Sacco, Transportation Systems with Connected and Non-Connected Vehicles: Optimal Traffic Control, in *2017 5th IEEE International Conference on Models and Technologies for Intelligent Transportation Systems (MT-ITS). Naples, Italy*: IEEE, June 2017, pp. 13-18.

[34] Ujjan, R. M. A., Pervez, Z., & Dahal, K. (2018, June). Suspicious traffic detection in SDN with collaborative techniques of snort and deep neural networks. In *2018 IEEE 20th* International Conference on High Performance Computing and Communications; *IEEE 16th International Conference on*

Smart City; IEEE 4th International Conference on Data Science and Systems (HPCC/SmartCity/DSS) (pp. 915-920). IEEE.

[35] H. Qin and C. Yu, A Road Network Connectivity Aware Routing Protocol for Vehicular Ad Hoc Networks, in *2017 IEEE International Conference on Vehicular Electronics and Safety (ICVES)*. *Vienna, Austria*: IEEE, June 2017, pp. 57-62.

[36] M. Alam, J. Ferreira, and J. Fonseca, Introduction to Intelligent Transportation Systems, in *Intelligent Transportation Systems*. Springer, 2016, pp. 1-17.

[37] A. Munir, Safety Assessment and Design of Dependable Cybercars: For today and the future, *IEEE Consumer Electronics Magazine*, vol. 6, no. 2, pp. 69-77, April 2017.

[38] K. B. Kelarestaghi, K. Heaslip, and R. Gerdes, Vehicle Security: Risk Assessment in Transportation, arXiv preprint arXiv:1804.07381, 2018.

[39] L. Figueiredo, I. Jesus, J. A. T. Machado, J. R. Ferreira, and J. L. M. de Carvalho, Towards the development of intelligent transportation systems, in *ITSC 2001 IEEE Intelligent Transportation Systems*, Aug 2001, pp. 1206-1211.

[40] J. B. Kenney, "Dedicated Short-Range Communications (DSRC) Standards in the United States," *Proceedings of the IEEE*, vol. 99, no. 7, pp. 1162-1182, July 2011.

[41] SAE, Dedicated Short Range Communications (DSRC) Message Set Dictionary, 2016. [Online]. Available: https://www.sae.org/ standards/content/j2735 201603/

[42] K. M. Bayarou, E-Safety Vehicle Intrusion Protected Applications, 2008. [Online]. Available: https://www. evita-project.org/index.html

[43] T. Wollinger, OVERSEE - Open Vehicular Secure Platform, 2010. [Online]. Available: https://www.oversee-project.com/ index.html

[44] J. M. d. Fuentes, A. I. González-Tablas, and A. Ribagorda, Overview of Security Issues in Vehicular Ad-Hoc Networks, 2010.

[45] L. He and W. T. Zhu, Mitigating DoS Attacks against SignatureBased Authentication in VANETs, in *2012 IEEE International Conference on Computer Science and Automation Engineering (CSAE)*. *Zhangjiajie, China*: IEEE, May 2012, pp. 261-265.

[46] B. Poudel and A. Munir, Design and Evaluation of a Reconfigurable ECU Architecture for Secure and Dependable Automotive CPS, *IEEE Transactions on Dependable and Secure Computing*, 2018.

[47] Shah, I. A., Wassan, S., & Usmani, M. H. (2022). E-Government Security and Privacy Issues: Challenges and Preventive Approaches. In *Cybersecurity Measures for E-Government Frameworks* (pp. 61-76). IGI Global.

[48] Kumar, T., Pandey, B., Mussavi, S. H. A., & Zaman, N. (2015). CTHS based energy efficient thermal aware image ALU design on FPGA. *Wireless Personal Communications*, 85, 671-696.

[49] Dawson, M., & Walker, D. (2022). Argument for Improved Security in Local Governments within the Economic Community of West African States. *Cybersecurity Measures for E-Government Frameworks*, 96-106.

[50] Kołodziej, J., Hopmann, C., Coppa, G., Grzonka, D., & Widlak, A. (2022). Intelligent Transportation Systems–Models, Challenges, Security Aspects. In *Cybersecurity of Digital Service Chains: Challenges, Methodologies, and Tools* (pp. 56-82). Cham: Springer International Publishing.

[51] Kok, S. H., Abdullah, A., & Jhanjhi, N. Z. (2022). Early detection of crypto-ransomware using pre-encryption detection algorithm. *Journal of King Saud University-Computer and Information Sciences, 34*(5), 1984-1999.

[52] Ujjan, R. M. A., Khan, N. A., & Gaur, L. (2022). E-Government Privacy and Security Challenges in the Context of Internet of Things. In *Cybersecurity Measures for E-Government Frameworks* (pp. 22-42). IGI Global.

[53] Shah, I. A., Jhanjhi, N. Z., Amsaad, F., & Razaque, A. (2022). The Role of Cutting-Edge Technologies in Industry 4.0. In *Cyber Security Applications for Industry 4.0* (pp. 97-109). Chapman and Hall/CRC.

[54] Shafiq, M., Ashraf, H., Ullah, A., Masud, M., Azeem, M., Jhanjhi, N., & Humayun, M. (2021). Robust cluster-based routing protocol for IoT-assisted smart devices in WSN. *Computers, Materials & Continua, 67*(3), 3505-3521.

[55] Muzafar, S., Humayun, M., & Hussain, S. J. (2022). Emerging Cybersecurity Threats in the Eye of E-Governance in the Current Era. In *Cybersecurity Measures for E-Government Frameworks* (pp. 43-60). IGI Global.

[56] Lim, M., Abdullah, A., & Jhanjhi, N. Z. (2021). Performance optimization of criminal network hidden link prediction model with deep reinforcement learning. *Journal of King Saud University - Computer and Information Sciences, 33*(10), 1202-1210.

[57] Adeyemo, V. E., Abdullah, A., JhanJhi, N. Z., Supramaniam, M., & Balogun, A. O. (2019). Ensemble and deep-learning methods for two-class and multi-attack anomaly intrusion detection: an empirical study. *International Journal of Advanced Computer Science and Applications, 10*(9).

[58] Kok, S. H., Abdullah, A., & Jhanjhi, N. Z. (2022). Early detection of crypto-ransomware using pre-encryption detection algorithm. *Journal of King Saud University - Computer and Information Sciences, 34*(5), 1984-1999.

[59] Jhanjhi, N. Z., Ahmad, M., Khan, M. A., & Hussain, M. (2022). The Impact of Cyber Attacks on E-Governance During the COVID-19 Pandemic. In *Cybersecurity Measures for E-Government Frameworks* (pp. 123-140). IGI Global.

[60] Revazov A.M., Lezhnev M.A. The impact of accidents at the facilities of pipeline transport of oil and petroleum products on the environment. *Environmental protection in oil and gas complex.* 2021. N 6 (303), p. 12-17 (in Russian). DOI: 10.33285/2411-7013-2021-6(303)-12-17

[61] Verma, S., Kaur, S., Rawat, D. B., Xi, C., Alex, L. T., & Jhanjhi, N. Z. (2021). Intelligent framework using IoT-based WSNs for wildfire detection. *IEEE Access, 9*, 48185-48196.

[62] Hussain, S. J., Ahmed, U., Liaquat, H., Mir, S., Jhanjhi, N. Z., & Humayun, M. (2019, April). IMIAD: intelligent malware identification for android

platform. In *2019 International Conference on Computer and Information Sciences (ICCIS)* (pp. 1-6). IEEE.

[63] Gaur, L., Afaq, A., Solanki, A., Singh, G., Sharma, S., Jhanjhi, N. Z., ... & Le, D. N. (2021). Capitalizing on big data and revolutionary 5G technology: Extracting and visualizing ratings and reviews of global chain hotels. *Computers and Electrical Engineering, 95*, 107374.

[64] Qian Chen, Lili Zuo, Changchun Wu et al. Short-term supply reliability assessment of a gas pipeline system under demand variations. *Reliability Engineering & System Safety.* 2020. Vol. 202. N 107004. DOI: 10.1016/j.ress.2020.107004

[65] Gaur, L., Singh, G., Solanki, A., Jhanjhi, N. Z., Bhatia, U., Sharma, S., ... & Kim, W. (2021). Disposition of youth in predicting sustainable development goals using the neuro-fuzzy and random forest algorithms. *Human-Centric Computing and Information Sciences, 11*, NA.

[66] Gaur, L., Ujjan, R. M. A., & Hussain, M. (2022). The Influence of Deep Learning in Detecting Cyber Attacks on E-Government Applications. In *Cybersecurity Measures for E-Government Frameworks* (pp. 107-122). IGI Global.

[67] Wasim M., Djukic M.B. External corrosion of oil and gas pipelines: A review of failure mechanisms and predictive preventions. *Journal of Natural Gas Science and Engineering.* 2022. Vol. 100. N 104467. DOI: 10.1016/j.jngse.2022.104467

[68] Stubelj I.R., Ruschmann H., Wold K., Gomnaes J.O. Pipeline Predictive Analitics Trough On-Line Remote Corrosion Monitoring. *Corrosion* 2019, 24-28 March 2019, Nashville, Tennessee, USA. N NACE-2019-12899.

[69] Brünenberg K., Vogt D., Ihring M. Additional Functionalities of Model Based Leak Detection Systems to Improve Pipeline Safety and Efficiency. *Pipeline Technology Journal.* 2020. Iss. 1, pp. 38-44.

[70] Ghorbani B., Ziabasharhagh M., Amidpour M. A hybrid artificial neural network and genetic algorithm for predicting viscosity of Iranian crude oils. *Journal of Natural Gas Science and Engineering.* 2014. Vol. 18, pp. 312-323. DOI: 10.1016/j.jngse.2014.03.011

[71] Hankun Wang, Yunfei Xu, Bowen Shi *et al.* Optimization and intelligent control for operation parameters of multiphase mixture transportation pipeline in oilfield: A case study. *Journal of Pipeline Science and Engineering.* 2021. Vol. 1. Iss. 4, pp. 367-378. DOI: 10.1016/j.jpse.2021.07.002

[72] Suzhen Li, Chen Wei, Xinghua Peng. Safety Monitoring of Buried Pipeline with Socket Joints Subjected to Ground Deformation Using MEMS Inclinometers. *Journal of Pipeline Systems Engineering and Practice.* 2019. Vol. 10. Iss. 2. N 04019008. DOI: 10.1061/(ASCE)PS.1949-1204.0000380

[73] Tao Zhang, Hua Bai, Shuyu Sun. Intelligent Natural Gas and Hydrogen Pipeline Dispatching Using the Coupled Thermodynamics-Informed Neural Network and Compressor Boolean Neural Network. *Processes.* 2022. Vol. 10. N 2. DOI: 10.3390/pr10020428

[74] Kraidi L., Shah R., Matipa W., Borthwick F. An investigation of mitigating the safety and security risks allied with oil and gas pipeline projects. *Journal of Pipeline Science and Engineering.* 2021. Vol. 1. Iss. 3, pp. 349-359. DOI: 10.1016/j.jpse.2021.08.002

[75] Li Xin, Bai Mingzhou, He Bohu *et al.* Safety analysis of landslide in pipeline area through field monitoring. *Journal of Testing and Evaluation.* 2022. Vol. 50. Iss. 6. DOI: 10.1520/JTE20200751

[76] Ujjan, R. M. A., Pervez, Z., Dahal, K., Bashir, A. K., Mumtaz, R., & González, J. (2020). Towards sFlow and adaptive polling sampling for deep learning based DDoS detection in SDN. *Future Generation Computer Systems, 111,* 763-779.

[77] Mohd Nazmi bin Mohd Ali Napiah, Hambali bin Chik. Revolutionising Pipeline Safety: Intelligent Weldment Inspection Decision Support System. *Pipeline Technology Journal.* 2019. Vol. 2, pp. 38-42. 20. Grazhdankin A.I., Pecherkin A.S., Samuseva E.A. *et al.* On the background levels of emergency hazards at hazardous production facilities. *Occupational Safety in Industry.* 2019. N 10, pp. 50-56 (in Russian).

[78] Revazov A.M., Savushkina V.N. Improving methods of trunk pipelines anti-terrorist security. *Proceedings of Gubkin University.* 2019. N 4 (297), pp. 127-137 (in Russian). DOI: 10.33285/2073-9028-2019-4(297)-127-137

[79] Belostotsky M.A., Kunlin Li, Korolenok A.M., Korolenok V.A. Formation of intelligent repair management system on the linear part of main oil pipelines. *Science & Technologies: Oil and Oil Products Pipeline Transportation.* 2022. Vol. 12. N 4, pp. 368-375 (in Russian). DOI: 10.28999/2541-9595-2022-12-4-368-375

[80] Shah, I. A. (2022). Cybersecurity Issues and Challenges for E-Government during COVID-19: A Review. *Cybersecurity Measures for E-Government Frameworks,* 187-222.

7

IoT-Based Railway Logistics: Security Issues and Challenges

N.Z. Jhanjhi[1]*, Loveleen Gaur[2] and Imran Taj[3]

*[1]School of Computing Science, Taylor's University, Kuala Lumpur,
Selangor, Malaysia*
[2]Amity University Noida, Noida, Uttar Pradesh, India
*[3]BC Public Service, Ministry of Attorney General, Information System Branch,
Victoria, Canada*

Abstract

In order to improve and optimise logistical operations, the railway sector is integrating Internet of Things (IoT) technology and systems. Real-time data is collected, sent, and analysed throughout the railway logistics process via linked equipment, sensors, data analytics, and communication networks. Various parts and systems of the rail infrastructure are outfitted with IoT sensors and devices for IoT-based railway logistics. These sensors can keep watch on and record data on the train's whereabouts, its speed, the temperature, the state of the cargo, and any necessary repairs. A central management system or cloud-based system will subsequently get the collected data for analysis and decision-making. IoT-based railway logistics promises to improve efficiency, safety, and dependability in railway logistics operations by using real-time data, connections, and intelligent decision-making skills. By boosting customer happiness, lowering costs, and improving operational efficiency, it has the potential to completely change the railway sector.

To secure the integrity, confidentiality, and availability of data and systems, a number of security concerns and difficulties related to railway logistics must be addressed. These include security flaws on the internet: Railway logistics IoT systems and devices are vulnerable to cybersecurity risks such as malware, hacking, and unauthorised access. These devices can serve as entry points for cyberattacks since they are networked and connected to the internet, which might interrupt operations, compromise data, or endanger users' safety. Railway logistics IoT devices produce and send a large quantity of data, including train movements,

*Corresponding author: noorzaman.jhanjhi@taylors.edu.my

Imdad Ali Shah and Noor Zaman Jhanjhi (eds.) Cybersecurity in the Transportation Industry,
(143–164) © 2024 Scrivener Publishing LLC

freight details, and maintenance logs. It is essential to protect this data and maintain privacy and prevent unauthorised entry. Both IoT devices and railway infrastructure are susceptible to physical assaults, vandalism, and manipulation. Critical components are physically accessed by unauthorised people. A possible point of vulnerability is the connection of IoT devices to the underlying network infrastructure. Strong security practices and methods must be put in place to handle these security issues. The primary object of this chapter is to focus on IoT-based railway logistics and security issues and challenges. Our studies will help the railway industry and new researchers.

Keywords: IoT, railway applications, railway transportation, logistics, security issues and challenges

7.1   Introduction

The Internet of Things (IoT) has emerged as a game-changing technology with the potential to completely change a number of sectors, including transportation. IoT-based solutions may significantly improve the customer experience, increase efficiency, and reduce costs in the railway logistics industry in particular. To maintain the integrity, confidentiality, and availability of crucial systems and data, however, a number of security difficulties and challenges have emerged with the emergence of IoT in railway logistics, necessitating careful thought and rigorous solutions [1]. Unauthorised access to linked systems and equipment is one of the main issues with IoT-based railway logistics. The deployment of a large number of IoT devices throughout railway networks, each of which presents a possible entry point, makes it crucial to ensure effective access controls and authentication systems [2]. If robust security measures aren't put in place, unauthorised persons may obtain access to crucial infrastructure, posing a serious threat to public safety. IoT devices frequently have little computational power, which leaves them open to a number of security flaws. Manufacturers might not give security top priority while developing products, which results in poor quality. Figure 7.1 shows that the number of IoT-connected devices is increasing every year.

Data transmission between devices and backend systems is impossible without reliable network connectivity in the railway logistics IoT environment. However, the network may be vulnerable to eavesdropping, data manipulation, and denial of service (DoS) assaults if communication routes and encryption protocols are not sufficiently secure. Safeguards against these dangers must include both a secure network infrastructure and the use of robust encryption methods [3–5]. Typically spanning many

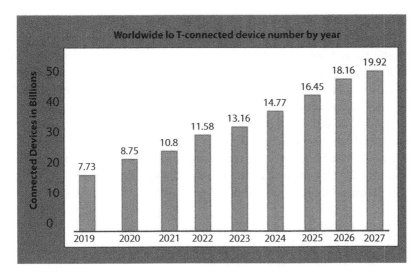

Figure 7.1 The number of IoT-connected devices is increasing every year.

locations and including a plethora of equipment and systems, railway logistics networks are enormous and intricate. Consistent monitoring and reaction to security incidents, as well as the management of access restrictions, offer substantial problems for securing such a massive IoT implementation. Often, outdated systems in railway infrastructure were not created with IoT connection. These older systems may not have the proper security safeguards, therefore integrating them with IoT technology might increase security concerns [6–11]. It is extremely difficult to retrofit security features into current systems without affecting operations. Figure 7.2 presents the top cybersecurity demand.

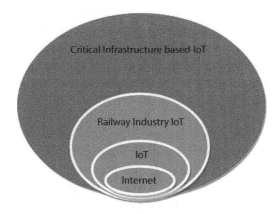

Figure 7.2 The top cybersecurity demand [5].

India's current conventional rail system is about 68,000 kilometres long and is used for passenger and freight transportation. Ten cities in India have metro systems, with a total of around 515 km of track in use and another 620 km in the planning stages. For the following five years, planners aim to add another 600 kilometres of metro lines. At present, high-speed rail is not available in India [12–15]. But in 2015, India and Japan struck a deal to build a high-speed rail route connecting Ahmedabad and Mumbai, which is scheduled to open in 2023. The feasibility of seven additional high-speed lines is being considered right now. When finished, they would link the cities that make up the Golden Quadrilateral.

The chapter focuses on the following points:

- Peer-reviewed Railway Transportation and IoT
- Sustainable railway management and operations
- Security issues and challenges
- IoT applications.

7.2   Literature Review

IoT (Internet of Things) gadgets are indispensable now more than ever. As more and more objects are connected to a worldwide network, the IoT is expanding at a rapid rate. It is important that only authorised personnel have access to the data and apps stored in many IoT devices. These applications are computer programmes that operate in real time or near real time to prevent failure, and they assess and anticipate the future based on consumption data using AI algorithms. IoT security should extend beyond the device itself. There are several vulnerabilities and inadequate security measures in IoT devices [16–19]. There is a widespread belief that the makers of IoT devices do not put user safety and privacy first. Nonetheless, despite the security concerns, IoT adoption continues to grow. Users and security professionals alike must therefore acquire knowledge of it to improve safety. Further contributing to the expansion of the railway cybersecurity market is the rising prevalence of the Internet of Things, artificial intelligence (AI), automated technology on trains, and government regulation for implementing security solutions. The global market has shown a significant decline because of the widespread COVID-19 pandemic, which has weakened the economy [20–22]. Markets were affected by lockdowns, which limited people's ability to travel to other parts of the country, and by societal norms that encouraged people to keep their distance from

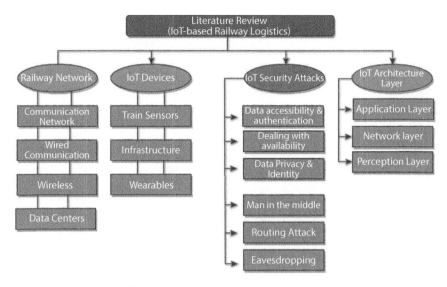

Figure 7.3 Taxonomy of literature review.

one another. Dependence on labour, supply chain performance, working capital management, regulatory and policy changes, and liquidity and solvency management are the primary risk factors for sector participants. Figure 7.3 is a Taxonomy of Literature Review.

Transportation of people and commodities across India's vast land, as well as the integration of markets and the connection of communities, have been greatly facilitated by the country's railway system. Since 2000, passenger rail travel in India has grown by about 200%, and freight rail travel has increased by 150%. However, the country still has a huge need for transportation that is not being met [23–25]. When comparing India and Europe, the average daily distance travelled by an individual in India by private road car is about 3 kilometres, while in Europe, it is about 17.5 kilometres. There will be more growth in train travel in India than in any other country. Figure 7.4 presents an overview of the size of the railway cybersecurity market.

One of their many plans of action is to adopt cutting-edge methods of communication; this will help them to serve their customers better and adapt to the ever-shifting demands of the market. Early in the 1990s, when existing standards and the ability to provide rail services were considered, the groundwork was laid for the current generation of European railway communications technology.

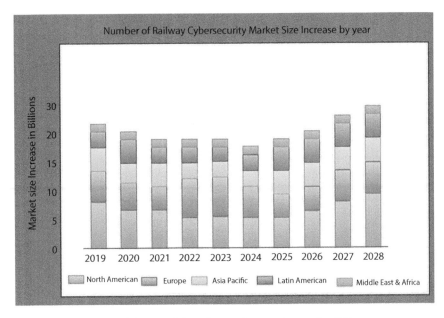

Figure 7.4 Overview of the size of the railway cybersecurity market [31].

7.3   Evaluation of IoT in Railway Transportation

With a CAGR of 15.14% between 2020 and 2026, the intelligent rail industry based on the Internet of Things is expected to rise from a projected $15.85 billion in 2020 to $36.58 billion by 2026. The demand for better urban connection, the proliferation of Internet of Things–based technologies and services, and a renewed commitment to cutting emissions are all factors that might drive rapid expansion in the railway industry. Current forecasts predict a 150–250% rise in freight traffic and a 200–300% increase in passenger traffic [26–29]. IoT rail applications are projected to grow in value to $30 billion. Some of the most crucial Internet of Things–based applications that have seen widespread usage in the railway sector are discussed in further detail in the following parts of the document. When axle counters are put on railroad tracks, they can find cars and estimate how many axles are entering and leaving traces. No vehicles should be allowed to pass through this section unless they have the same number of axles coming in as going, like an oncoming train. As a result, axle counters are crucial for maintaining a fast train. Additionally, temperature sensors provide post-ride temperature monitoring of the sensor's installation sites. Suppose the measured temperature rises over a certain limit. In that case, the train will be halted at the next station to prevent damage to passengers, freight, and the environment from sparks and overheating. The use of temperature sensors can help prevent accidents brought on by overheating bearings. Fibre optic sensing (FOS) allows for accurate trackside environment monitoring [30–33]. The FOS may detect several different things, such as landslide-caused track bottlenecks, faulty point machine diagnostics, derailed trains, stolen cables, and even flat tyres. In order to make FOS possible, a fibre optic cable needs to be installed in the cable duct that now runs beside the railroad. The sensor equipment at the cable duct can be linked to a line up to 40 kilometres in length. Detection unit sensors can employ detectable changes in light intensity to identify events and sound alarms. Figure 7.5 presents an overview of railway IoT security.

7.3.1   Role of IoT Applications

With the help of the Internet of Things (IoT), which connects common devices to the internet so they may exchange data, disruptive technology has evolved. Various businesses now have access to a wide range of IoT applications because of this connectivity and data exchange. IoT has the potential to completely change the way we interact with the world around us, from smart homes to industrial automation. In this introduction, we'll look at a few of the most important IoT applications and their potential effects on various industries. Smart home automation is one of the most well-known IoT applications. To create a seamless and intelligent home environment, IoT devices like smart thermostats, lighting systems, security

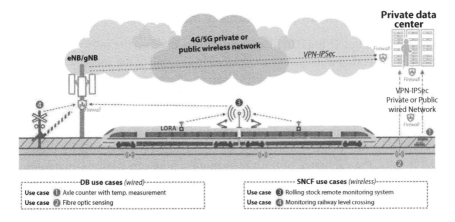

Figure 7.5 Overview of railway IoT security [52].

cameras, and voice assistants can be connected. Through voice commands or mobile applications, users may remotely manage and monitor these devices, improving convenience, energy efficiency, and home security. IoT is essential for building sustainable and intelligent cities. Cities may obtain real-time data on traffic patterns, air quality, trash management, energy usage, and other topics by incorporating IoT devices and sensors into urban infrastructure. Through programmes like smart transportation, effective energy management, and improved public services, cities can use this data to make well-informed decisions, allocate resources efficiently, and enhance the quality of life for their citizens.

Comfort, little friction, and low noise have made maglev trains popular. Maglev trains employ IoT apps. The IoT increased maglev train and passenger safety. A database stores all the data. Proprietary diagnostics and monitoring software analyses and displays data to suitable employees. The right people can analyse data and assess a maglev train's condition [34–37]. Staff might use a specialised suspension control approach to improve maglev train magnetic suspension system performance. This survey looked at the current and future trends and research needs related to the use of IoT in railway operations. It also looked at the development of IoT technologies, problems with IoT implementation, IoT solutions for making level crossings safer, and more. In this study, researchers looked at the most recent research in the field by using the content analysis method, which is a standard way to do systematic reviews of the relevant literature [38]. We also looked at a few publications that discussed how future technologies like 6G and 7G may enhance railway administration and guarantee the long-term viability of operations in the next few years.

7.3.2   IoT Applications for Railway Management

Many Internet of Things (IoT) applications focused on the railway industry have been created in recent years. looked into some of the possible benefits of implementing IoT in the training sector. The research suggested tracking software that could be used in real time to check on the condition of the items as they travelled by train. Research has assessed the feasibility of implementing the Internet of Things in China's railway network. Train monitoring and location, automatic fee collecting, early warning for potential threats, the exchange of train information between stations, managing freight, and overseeing a warehouse are only some of the many uses mentioned for IoT-based technology. Look at how different Internet of Things technologies may keep bullet trains running smoothly [39–42]. It was suggested that the Internet of Things may be used to detect problems with trains in real time and send out warnings as necessary. Internet of Things technology might also gather and process the necessary data to guarantee adequate train maintenance throughout the train's operational lifetime. The research showed that IoT might reduce the time and effort spent on maintenance as well as the probability of failure [43]. Improving China's rail transportation services requires better information perception, processing, and sharing. The use of IoT-based technology may benefit railway information integration. Research suggests an IoT-based system with the following layers. The use of smart IoT devices would boost the economic advantages of safety by eliminating freight theft, fire dangers, improper maintenance monitoring, and improper inventory management. The growth of the IoT, as pointed out by Shi and Wang, may have a beneficial effect on railway data transmission [44–47]. While IoT has clear benefits for railway safety monitoring, widespread adoption of such technology may take some time.

Researchers have examined the difficulties brought on by Beijing's massive passenger influx in the subway system (China). To improve mass passenger rail transit, the research recommended a system based on the Internet of Things that would rely on data sharing, real-time sensing, and analytical reasoning. The capacity needed to accommodate high volumes of passengers may be reliably predicted using the suggested technique, which can help manage rail transit more efficiently. Research indicated that integrating the primary components of railway transportation systems is crucial to their future growth [48–51]. The proposed approach is thought to be capable of efficiently processing large amounts of data over a broad range. A communication paradigm for improving railway services was proposed; this model was given the acronym "RIoT" (Rail Internet of Things). There were several parts to the RIoT system, including trains, tracks, stops, passengers, and a command hub. Low adhesion might be a serious problem for railroads since it can reduce acceleration and braking efficiency, which was highlighted in the paper along with possible security threats for the RIoT and offered solutions. The research suggested a new Internet of Things–based technology for a low-cost, high-resolution rail moisture monitoring system. In addition, theoretical analysis and experimental results confirmed that the proposed low-cost sensor outperformed the already available, more expensive sensors [52–55].

A new system was proposed based on the Internet of Things to improve train traveller service and comfort. Using Bluetooth Low Energy, the system was able to pinpoint the precise locations of train staff members at all times. An autonomous train stop mechanism was based on a multi-objective optimization algorithm. Possible cybersecurity problems arising from the Internet of Things were also mentioned. Safety concerns as autonomous cars approach level crossings were highlighted. It was mentioned that autonomous vehicle perception sensors, vehicle-to-everything communications, and train-tracking technologies might make it easier for cars to navigate through level crossings safely. The oncoming train and the roadside equipment at level crossings can share information via dedicated short-range communications (DSRC) [56, 57]. To further ensure no collisions between autonomous cars and oncoming trains, the roadside equipment can broadcast the information to the autonomous vehicles in the area of a certain level crossing.

We looked at a strategy that may be used to spot obstructions on train tracks and in their immediate surroundings. There were two primary components utilised to keep an eye on the items and gather information. The initial component was the Internet of Things system that tracks and records information about things near train lines. The second component was the radar and processing software used to depict the interval between the device and the objects. The lack of automation at many level crossings in Tanzania has been highlighted as a source of delays and increased accident risk. Mechanisms based on the Internet of Things were developed, that could function automatically and with little to no human intervention. A study concluded that the suggested approach effectively increased safety at level crossings and fostered efficient train travel. An Internet of Things-based automatic vehicle detection system was proposed by [58–60]. The research thoroughly examined several obstacles and problems associated with autonomous vehicle recognition at level crossings. Improved traffic control and fewer accidents are possible outcomes of the proposed vehicle identification system for use at level crossings. A novel Internet of Things (IoT)-based system was developed that uses many sensors and may be used in railway upkeep. In an accident, the IoT system might help mitigate the damage or avoid it entirely.

The potential for hacker assaults on the planned system has been raised. For this reason, we switched to using one-time passwords. The research recommended using force-sensitive resistor detectors at pedestrian crossings to ensure their automated protection. In an emergency, the suggested technology could contact the nearest command centre. In addition, sonar sensors were implemented to determine what could be in the path of an oncoming train. The degree of crossing circumstances is expected to be successfully monitored using the proposed IoT technology [61]. The Internet of Things is only one of several technologies that have been explored as possible solutions for driverless trains. Concerns about level-crossing safety were highlighted. It was suggested that cutting-edge Internet of

Things technology will eliminate collisions between autonomous vehicles and trains, boosting the security of level crossings even more.

7.4   Railway Security Issues and Challenges

IoT-based Railway logistics has the power to transform the transportation industry by increasing operational effectiveness and promoting customer satisfaction. IoT technology integration does, however, bring with it security concerns and difficulties that need to be carefully addressed. Railway logistics stakeholders may reduce the risks and create a safe and resilient IoT environment by putting in place strong security measures, such as access limits, encryption protocols, and frequent vulnerability assessments. For complete security to be established, cooperation between industry players, technology suppliers, and regulators is essential [62–64]. Acts of terrorism and sabotage against railroads can result in fatalities, destruction of infrastructure, and interruption of transportation services, among other serious repercussions. The requirement for strong security measures, including perimeter defence, surveillance systems, access controls, and the incorporation of explosive detection technology, is emphasised by research. Safety for passengers must be a priority for train operators. According to research, it can be difficult to control busy platforms, prohibit unauthorised entry to secured areas, and identify and counter potential threats like individuals carrying hazardous items or concealing weapons. As potential remedies, improved screening procedures, video analytics, and situational awareness are suggested. Figure 7.6 presents the cyber threats.

Railways are a target for theft and other illegal acts because they transport valuable and delicate commodities. The literature talks about issues with cargo security, including supply chain vulnerabilities, tracking and monitoring systems, and preventing unauthorised entry to cargo containers. Real-time monitoring tools, safe container locking systems, and secure transportation lanes are some of the solutions suggested. The railway industry faces new security risks as more and more IoT devices are adopted. There is a rise in the attack surface and potential entry points due to the proliferation of devices like sensors, actuators, and surveillance cameras [65–67]. The literature recommends that in order to reduce the security concerns associated with the Internet of Things, the user implements security procedures such as device authentication, secure communication protocols, and routine firmware updates.

Data-driven decision-making algorithms improve railroad operations, dependability, maintenance, and passenger experience. Yet, the intricacy

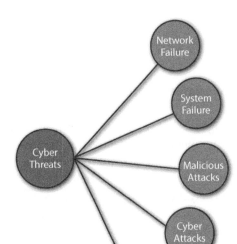

Figure 7.6 The cyber threats.

of train transportation systems presents several problems. Numerous writers are investigating these elements and suggesting new study avenues. Digitalization allowed cybercriminals to commit more crimes. The most crucial railway infrastructure threats, problems, weaknesses, and dangers have been covered in the literature. The report also offers cybersecurity strategies to improve data protection. One study [68] gave a history of the most significant railroad cybersecurity events and emphasised the major concerns, such as the growing usage of cloud and IoT technology and the capacity to defend against cyberattacks. Comparably, it gave useful information on transportation infrastructure difficulties and technology. Although the essay was written over a decade ago, most of the technology is still relevant. Numerous papers have examined train communication networks, network deployment requirements and the most applicable technology. These studies suggests various areas where AI, big data, and sensors might transform the railway business and give a security analysis and suggestions for the European Rail Traffic Management System (ERTMS). The scientists say an intelligent monitoring system and position-aware smart antennas would thwart these threats. One study examines WSNs for railways using wireless technology [69]. It discusses radio technology's prospects and difficulties. The article also discusses operational non-safety services and railway safety services. Industrial cyberattacks are getting more sophisticated and common. For instance, SIEM infiltration can cause significant problems. It is essential to identify abnormal behaviour in various systems to improve incident detection. Train stations are one of the most congested city areas, making security and privacy difficult. In unmanaged public places, real-time pedestrian tracking poses significant computing, object identification, and privacy concerns.

7.5 Discussion

It was mentioned that reducing emissions may be accomplished by improving train schedules, using energy storage devices, implementing innovative metering practices, and improving rail routes. Researchers looked at current Internet of Things green sustainability technologies used by the Malaysian rail sector and the Internet of Things was cited as a critical factor in the increased operational efficiency, heightened automation, and enhanced passenger experience of rail transportation networks. Yet, further thought is needed to handle green and sustainable development targets properly. The report recommended policies and procedures to promote the environmentally friendly and long-term growth of Malaysia's railway sector. Objects in the environment may be sensed, monitored, and tracked with the help of the IoT, which can contribute to a more eco-friendly and sustainable way of living. To illustrate, the European Union's goal of lowering emissions of greenhouse gases is highly ambitious. The pollution levels in various city regions may be measured using IoT apps. IoT devices may gather data on pollution levels and make that information public, allowing for the implementation of long-term remedies in problem regions. Many difficulties with putting G-IoT into practice were also explored in the research. The use of ML and IoT in modern transportation networks was the subject of an in-depth study [70]. The study found that AI and IoT might aid in optimising travel routes. With better planning, we can reduce the pollution caused by cars and trucks on our roads and rails and lessen the amount of time spent in traffic. Timely arrivals may also be facilitated by AI and IoT applications. Integration of IoT, edge computing, and the smart grid were all discussion topics. Applications for the Internet of Things have impacted many facets of our lives, revolutionising industries and improving our daily lives. The potential of IoT is endless and is still growing, ranging from connected cities to automated factories and smart homes. There are prospects for increased productivity, efficiency, and decision-making across industries thanks to the capacity to link and

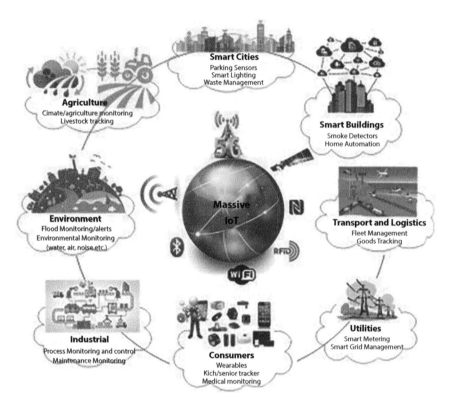

Figure 7.7 The technologies required to actualize IoT [64].

collect data from various devices and things. The potential for IoT applications to revolutionise businesses and influence the future is enormous as
technology develops. The technologies required to actualize IoT are presented in Figure 7.7.

Chapter's Contribution

The Internet of Things has a lot of potential in the railway industry and
beyond because it can work in an embedded mode, collect real-time data,
estimate physical parameters, help make decisions based on the data collected, and use several different networks. This potential extends beyond
the railway industry. The purpose of this research is to conduct an in-depth
investigation of the numerous Internet of Things (IoT) resources that have
the potential to improve railroad administration, maintenance, video
monitoring, and safety at grade separations. The need for various forms of
transportation is quickly expanding all over the world. It is anticipated that
by the year 2050, both passenger and freight traffic will have increased by

a factor of two due to the current pace of expansion. Its expansion is a sign of societal and economic progress. Yet, it comes with the consequences of greater energy demand and increased CO2 emissions and other air pollutants. A rise in the utilisation of rail transportation may slow down this growth. Rail travel has proven feasible and handy as the world's population continues to cluster in cities. High-speed rail may be an alternative to flying for shorter distances. In contrast, conventional rail and freight rail can be used as a supplement to other forms of transportation to offer efficient mobility. Internet of Things applications are quickly becoming essential to people's lives. The internet is a potent instrument that continually allows for improvements to be made to the standard of living in many places worldwide. Everything, at any time and in any location, can communicate with the internet to deliver specific services or information to anyone connected to it via any network. A phenomenon of this kind is the basis for the Internet of Things. As a result of the development of technologies for the next generation, it is projected that the expansion of IoT-based technologies will occur at a rate that is far quicker than in the past. These technologies can allow Internet of Things applications to function more safely, faster, and be more dependable than could be imagined. The Internet of Things has seen widespread adoption across many industries, including commercial, educational, and industrial settings as well as transport, infrastructure, and smart cities.

7.6   Conclusion

In order to improve and optimise logistical operations, the railway sector is integrating Internet of Things (IoT) technology and systems. Real-time data is collected, sent, and analysed throughout the railway logistics process via linked equipment, sensors, data analytics, and communication networks. Various parts and systems of the rail infrastructure are outfitted with IoT sensors and devices for IoT-based railway logistics. These sensors can keep watch on and record data on the train's whereabouts, its speed, the temperature, the state of the cargo, and any necessary repairs. A central management system or cloud-based system will subsequently get the collected data for analysis and decision-making. IoT-based railway logistics promises to improve efficiency, safety, and dependability in railway logistics operations by using real-time data, connections, and intelligent decision-making skills. By boosting customer happiness, lowering costs, and improving operational efficiency, it has the potential to completely change the railway sector.

There are several challenges brought about by the complexity of rail transportation networks. Many authors are investigating these components and offer suggestions for new research directions. The advent of digital technology facilitated the proliferation of online crime. At a compound annual growth rate of 15.14%, it is anticipated that the market value of IoT-based smart railways will expand from $15.85 billion in 2020 to $36.58 billion in 2026. This represents an increase from the current market value of $15.85 billion. The rising need for urban connections, the expansion of IoT-based solutions and applications, and a greater emphasis on reducing pollution levels will probably be the primary drivers of the increased growth in railroads. The COVID-19 epidemic has significantly influenced the transportation system that uses trains. The number of people using public rail transportation systems fell significantly, particularly during the periods in which COVID-19 led to lockdowns. In public rail transport systems and other types of transit systems, there is always a reason to be concerned about the possibility of the transmission of airborne infections. Future research may investigate the viability of employing a variety of Internet of Things technologies and contact tracing techniques to curtail the spread of infectious diseases, thereby enhancing the resistance of rail transportation systems to epidemics in the foreseeable future.

7.7   Future Work

IoT-based Railway logistics has the power to transform the transportation industry by increasing operational effectiveness and promoting customer satisfaction. IoT technology integration does, however, bring with it security concerns and difficulties that need to be carefully addressed. Railway logistics stakeholders may reduce the risks and create a safe and resilient IoT environment by putting in place strong security measures, such as access limits, encryption protocols, and frequent vulnerability assessments. For complete security to be established, cooperation between industry players, technology suppliers, and regulators is essential.

References

[1] Abioye, O.F., Dulebenets, M.A., Pasha, J., Kavoosi, M., Moses, R., Sobanjo, J., Ozguven, E.E., 2020. Accident and hazard prediction models for highway–rail grade crossings: a state-of-the-practice review for the USA. *Railway Eng. Sci.* 28 (3), 251–274.

[2] Abosata, N., Al-Rubaye, S., Inalhan, G., Emmanouilidis, C., 2021. Internet of things for system integrity: a comprehensive survey on security, attacks and countermeasures for industrial applications. *Sensors* 21 (11), 3654. Aboti, C.D., 2020. Studies of challenges to mitigating cyber risks in iot-based commercial aviation. *Int. J. Sci. Res. Develop.* 7, 133–139.

[3] Adebiyi, O.O., Cruz, M., 2018. Green sustainability development for industry internet of things in railway transportation industry. *Int. J. Trend Sci. Res. Develop.* 3 (1), 203–208.

[4] Adeel, A., Gogate, M., Farooq, S., Ieracitano, C., Dashtipour, K., Larijani, H., Hussain, A., 2019. A survey on the role of wireless sensor networks and IoT in disaster management. In *Geological disaster monitoring based on sensor networks* (pp. 57–66). Springer, Singapore.

[5] Yaacoub, E., Alsharoa, A., Ghazzai, H., & Alouini, M. S. (2021). Seven challenges for communication in modern railway systems. *Frontiers in Communications and Networks, 1,* 8.

[6] Adil, M., Khan, M.K., 2021. Emerging IoT applications in sustainable smart cities for COVID-19: network security and data preservation challenges with future directions. *Sustain. Cities Soc.*, 103311.

[7] Ahmed, E., Yaqoob, I., Hashem, I.A.T., Khan, I., Ahmed, A.I.A., Imran, M., Vasilakos, A. V., 2017. The role of big data analytics in Internet of Things. *Comput. Netw.* 129, 459–471.

[8] Ai, B., Guan, K., Rupp, M., Kurner, T., Cheng, X., Yin, X.F., Wang, Q., Ma, G.Y., Li, Y., Xiong, L., Ding, J.W., 2015. Future railway services-oriented mobile communications network. *IEEE Commun. Mag.* 53 (10), 78–85.

[9] Ai, B., Molisch, A.F., Rupp, M., Zhong, Z.D., 2020. 5G key technologies for smart railways. *Proc. IEEE* 108 (6), 856–893.

[10] Akyildiz, I.F., Kak, A., Nie, S., 2020. 6G and beyond: the future of wireless communications systems. *IEEE Access* 8, 133995–134030.

[11] AL Enterprise.com, The Internet of Things in Transportation. [online]. Available at 2020. Al Nuaimi, E., Al Neyadi, H., Mohamed, N., Al-Jaroodi, J., 2015. Applications of big data to smart cities. *J. Internet Serv. Appl.* 6 (1), 1–15.

[12] Alagarsamy, S., Kandasamy, R., Subbiah, L. and Palanisamy, S., 2019. Applications of Internet of Things in Pharmaceutical Industry. Available at SSRN 3441099.

[13] Alam, S., Chowdhury, M.M., Noll, J., 2011. Interoperability of security-enabled internet of things. *Wireless Pers. Commun.* 61 (3), 567–586.

[14] Alcaraz, C., Najera, P., Lopez, J., Roman, R., 2010. Wireless sensor networks and the internet of things: Do we need a complete integration? *1st International Workshop on the Security of the Internet of Things (SecIoT'10).*

[15] Ali, Z.H., Ali, H.A., Badawy, M.M., 2015. Internet of Things (IoT): definitions, challenges and recent research directions. *Int. J. Comp. Appl.* 128 (1), 37–47.

[16] Alrawais, A., Alhothaily, A., Hu, C., Cheng, X., 2017. Fog computing for the internet of things: security and privacy issues. *IEEE Internet Comput.* 21 (2), 34–42.

[17] Aono, K., Lajnef, N., Faridazar, F. and Chakrabartty, S., 2016, May. Infrastructural health monitoring using self-powered internet-of-things. In *2016 IEEE international symposium on circuits and systems (ISCAS)* (pp. 2058–2061). IEEE.

[18] Armbrust, M., Fox, A., Griffith, R., Joseph, A.D., Katz, R., Konwinski, A., Lee, G., Patterson, D., Rabkin, A., Stoica, I., Zaharia, M., 2010. A view of cloud computing. *Commun. ACM* 53 (4), 50–58.

[19] Armentia, A., Gangoiti, U., Priego, R., Estévez, E., Marcos, M., 2015. Flexibility support for homecare applications based on models and multi-agent technology. *Sensors* 15 (12), 31939–31964.

[20] Arunjyothi, B., Harikrishna, B., 2020. Automated railway gate control using internet of things. In: *Soft Computing: Theories and Applications.* Springer, Singapore, pp. 501–513.

[21] Aslam, S., Michaelides, M.P., Herodotou, H., 2020. Internet of ships: a survey on architectures, emerging applications, and challenges. *IEEE Internet Things J.* 7 (10), 9714–9727.

[22] Atlam, H.F. and Wills, G.B., 2019. Technical aspects of blockchain and IoT. In *Advances in Computers* (Vol. 115, pp. 1-39). Elsevier. Atlam, H.F., Walters, R.J., Wills, G.B., 2018. Fog computing and the internet of things: a review. *Big Data Cognitive Comput.* 2 (2), 10.

[23] Awoyemi, B.S., Alfa, A.S., Maharaj, B.T., 2020. Resource optimization in 5G and internetof-things networking. *Wireless Pers. Commun.* 111 (4), 2671–2702.

[24] Aziz, A.A., Mohamad, K.A., Alias, A., 2020. Obstacle detection system for railways using IoT sensors. Evol. *Elec. Electron. Eng.* 1 (1), 57–63.

[25] Badarinath, R., Prabhu, V.V., 2017, September. Advances in Internet of Things (IoT) in manufacturing. In *IFIP International Conference on Advances in Production Management Systems* (pp. 111–118).

[26] Bansal, N., Lal, T., 2019. A Brief Review on the Future and Challenges of Internet of Things (IoT). *Pannonian Conference on Advances in Information Technology (PCIT 2019).*

[27] Veszprém, Hungary. Bellavista, P., Cardone, G., Corradi, A., Foschini, L., 2013. Convergence of MANET and WSN in IoT urban scenarios. *IEEE Sens. J.* 13 (10), 3558–3567.

[28] Besher, K.M., Nieto-Hipolito, J.I., Buenrostro-Mariscal, R., Ali, M.Z., 2021. Spectrum Based Power Management for Congested IoT Networks. *Sensors* 21 (8), 2681.

[29] Bessis, N., Dobre, C. (Eds.), 2014. *Big Data and Internet of Things: A Roadmap for Smart Environments* (Vol. 546). Springer International Publishing, Basel, Switzerland.

[30] Bogaard, P., 2020. IoT Proving Its Worth to Rail Industry at a Time of Crisis. [online]. Available: https://www.railtech.com/ digitalisation/2020/04/14.

[31] https://www.polarismarketresearch.com/industry-analysis/railway-cybersecurity-market

[32] L., Warren, E. and Chapman, V., 2016. Using the internet of things to monitor low adhesion on railways. In *Proceedings of the Institution of Civil Engineers: Transport* (Vol. 169, No. 5, pp. 321–329).

[33] Thomas Telford Ltd. Chen, C.W., 2020. Internet of video things: Next-generation IoT with visual sensors. *IEEE Internet Things J.* 7 (8), 6676–6685.

[34] Shah, I. A., Jhanjhi, N. Z., Amsaad, F., & Razaque, A. (2022). The Role of Cutting-Edge Technologies in Industry 4.0. In *Cyber Security Applications for Industry 4.0* (pp. 97–109). Chapman and Hall/CRC.

[35] Chen, Y., Han, F., Yang, Y.H., Ma, H., Han, Y., Jiang, C., Lai, H.Q., Claffey, D., Safar, Z., Liu, K.R., 2014b. Time-reversal wireless paradigm for green internet of things: An overview. *IEEE Internet Things J.* 1 (1), 81–98.

[36] Choi, N., Kim, D., Lee, S.J., Yi, Y., 2017. A fog operating system for user-oriented iot services: Challenges and research directions. *IEEE Commun. Mag.* 55 (8), 44–51.

[37] Chu, Y., Pan, L., Leng, K., Fu, H.C., Lam, A., 2020. Research on key technologies of service quality optimization for industrial IoT 5G network for intelligent manufacturing. *Int. J. Adv. Manuf. Technol.* 107 (3), 1071–1080.

[38] Shah, I. A., Jhanjhi, N. Z., Humayun, M., & Ghosh, U. (2022). Impact of COVID-19 on Higher and Post-secondary Education Systems. In *How COVID-19 Is Accelerating the Digital Revolution* (pp. 71–83). Springer, Cham.

[39] Darshan, K.R. and Anandakumar, K.R., 2015. A comprehensive review on usage of Internet of Things (IoT) in healthcare system. In *2015 International Conference on Emerging Research in Electronics, Computer Science and Technology (ICERECT)* (pp. 132–136). IEEE.

[40] Ujjan, R. M. A., Pervez, Z., Dahal, K., Bashir, A. K., Mumtaz, R., & González, J. (2020). Towards sFlow and adaptive polling sampling for deep learning based DDoS detection in SDN. *Future Generation Computer Systems, 111,* 763–779.

[41] Deng, N., 2012, August. RFID technology and network construction in the internet of things. In *2012 International Conference on Computer Science and Service System* (pp. 979–982). IEEE.

[42] D'Errico, L., Franchi, F., Graziosi, F., Rinaldi, C. and Tarquini, F., 2017, July. Design and implementation of a children safety system based on IoT technologies. In *2017 2nd International Multidisciplinary Conference on Computer and Energy Science (SpliTech)* (pp. 1–6). IEEE.

[43] Ujjan, R. M. A., Pervez, Z., & Dahal, K. (2018, June). Suspicious traffic detection in SDN with collaborative techniques of snort and deep neural networks. In *2018 IEEE 20th International Conference on High Performance Computing and Communications; IEEE 16th International Conference on Smart City; IEEE 4th International Conference on Data Science and Systems (HPCC/SmartCity/DSS)* (pp. 915–920). IEEE.

[44] Dillon, T., Wu, C. and Chang, E., 2010, April. Cloud computing: issues and challenges. In *2010 24th IEEE International Conference on Advanced Information Networking and Applications* (pp. 27–33). IEEE.

[45] Dirnfeld, R., Flammini, F., Marrone, S., Nardone, R. and Vittorini, V., 2020. Low-power wide-area networks in intelligent transportation: Review and opportunities for smart-railways. In *2020 IEEE 23rd International Conference on Intelligent Transportation Systems (ITSC)* (pp. 1–7). IEEE.

[46] Li Y, *et al.* Rail component detection, optimization, and assessment for automatic rail track inspection. *IEEE Trans Intell Transp Syst* 2014;15(2):760–70.

[47] Shah, I. A., Jhanjhi, N. Z., Amsaad, F., & Razaque, A. (2022). The Role of Cutting-Edge Technologies in Industry 4.0. In *Cyber Security Applications for Industry 4.0* (pp. 97–109). Chapman and Hall/CRC.

[48] Zarembski AM. Some examples of big data in railroad engineering. In: *Big Data (Big Data), 2014 IEEE International Conference on.* New York, USA: IEEE; 2014.

[49] Aytekin C, *et al.* Railway fastener inspection by real-time machine vision. *IEEE Trans Syst Man Cybern Syst Hum* 2015;45(7):1101–7.

[50] Atzori L, Iera A, Morabito G. The internet of things: a survey. *Comput Netw* 2010;54(15):2787–805.

[51] Seife C. Big data: the revolution is digitized. *Nature* 2015;518(7540):480.

[52] The Internet of Railway Things Security. Whitepaper. Technische Universitat Darmstadt, June 2020. https://www1.deutschebahn.com/resource/blob/5664326/57803c929dde6d12a3a206cf33421675/IoRT_Security-short-data.pdf

[53] Khaitan S, Mccalley J. Design techniques and applications of cyberphysical systems: a survey. *IEEE Syst J* 2015;9(2):350–65.

[54] Shah, I. A., Wassan, S., & Usmani, M. H. (2022). E-Government Security and Privacy Issues: Challenges and Preventive Approaches. In *Cybersecurity Measures for E-Government Frameworks* (pp. 61–76). IGI Global.

[55] Ujjan, R. M. A., Taj, I., & Brohi, S. N. (2022). E-Government Cybersecurity Modeling in the Context of Software-Defined Networks. In *Cybersecurity Measures for E-Government Frameworks* (pp. 1–21). IGI Global.

[56] Ujjan, R. M. A., Pervez, Z., Dahal, K., Bashir, A. K., Mumtaz, R., & González, J. (2020). Towards sFlow and adaptive polling sampling for deep learning based DDoS detection in SDN. *Future Generation Computer Systems, 111,* 763–779.

[57] Dawson, M., & Walker, D. (2022). Argument for Improved Security in Local Governments Within the Economic Community of West African States. *Cybersecurity Measures for E-Government Frameworks,* 96–106.

[58] Gaur, L., Ujjan, R. M. A., & Hussain, M. (2022). The Influence of Deep Learning in Detecting Cyber Attacks on E-Government Applications. In *Cybersecurity Measures for E-Government Frameworks* (pp. 107–122). IGI Global.

[59] Jhanjhi, N. Z., Ahmad, M., Khan, M. A., & Hussain, M. (2022). The Impact of Cyber Attacks on E-Governance during the COVID-19 Pandemic. In

Cybersecurity Measures for E-Government Frameworks (pp. 123–140). IGI Global.

[60] Ujjan, R. M. A., Hussain, K., & Brohi, S. N. (2022). The Impact of Blockchain Technology on Advanced Security Measures for E-Government. In *Cybersecurity Measures for E-Government Frameworks* (pp. 157–174). IGI Global.

[61] Shah, I. A., Jhanjhi, N. Z., Humayun, M., & Ghosh, U. (2022). Impact of COVID-19 on Higher and Post-secondary Education Systems. In *How COVID-19 Is Accelerating the Digital Revolution* (pp. 71–83). Springer, Cham.

[62] Kiran, S. R. A., Rajper, S., Shaikh, R. A., Shah, I. A., & Danwar, S. H. (2021). Categorization of CVE Based on Vulnerability Software by Using Machine Learning Techniques. *International Journal, 10*(3).

[63] Umrani, S., Rajper, S., Talpur, S. H., Shah, I. A., & Shujrah, A. (2020). Games based learning: A case of learning physics using Angry Birds. *Indian Journal of Science and Technology, 13*(36), 3778–3784.

[64] Tuysuz, M. F., & Trestian, R. (2020). From serendipity to sustainable green IoT: Technical, industrial and political perspective. *Computer Networks, 182*, 107469.

[65] Srinivasan, K., Garg, L., Datta, D., Alaboudi, A. A., Jhanjhi, N. Z., Agarwal, R., & Thomas, A. G. (2021). Performance comparison of deep cnn models for detecting driver's distraction. *CMC-Computers, Materials & Continua, 68*(3), 4109–4124.

[66] Khalil, M. I., Jhanjhi, N. Z., Humayun, M., Sivanesan, S., Masud, M., & Hossain, M. S. (2021). Hybrid smart grid with sustainable energy efficient resources for smart cities. *Sustainable Energy Technologies and Assessments, 46*, 101211.

[67] Khalil, M. I., Jhanjhi, N. Z., Humayun, M., Sivanesan, S., Masud, M., & Hossain, M. S. (2021). Hybrid smart grid with sustainable energy efficient resources for smart cities. *Sustainable Energy Technologies and Assessments, 46*, 101211.

[68] Shafiq, M., Ashraf, H., Ullah, A., Masud, M., Azeem, M., Jhanjhi, N., & Humayun, M. (2021). Robust cluster-based routing protocol for IoT-assisted smart devices in WSN. *Computers, Materials & Continua, 67*(3), 3505–3521.

[69] Lim, M., Abdullah, A., & Jhanjhi, N. Z. (2021). Performance optimization of criminal network hidden link prediction model with deep reinforcement learning. *Journal of King Saud University-Computer and Information Sciences, 33*(10), 1202–1210.

[70] Ujjan, R. M. A., Pervez, Z., Dahal, K., Bashir, A. K., Mumtaz, R., & González, J. (2020). Towards sFlow and adaptive polling sampling for deep learning based DDoS detection in SDN. *Future Generation Computer Systems, 111*, 763–779.

8

Emerging Electric Vehicles and Challenges

Areeba Laraib[1]* and Raja Majid Ali Ujjan[2]

[1]Mehran University of Engineering and Technology, Shaheed Zulfiqar Ali Bhutto Campus, Khairpur Mir's, Pakistan
[2]School of Computer, Engineering & Physical Science, University, Paisley, Scotland

Abstract

Researchers and companies predict that 126 million electric vehicles will be on the road by 2030. Improved air quality, less noise pollution and greenhouse gas emissions, and greater long-term energy security are just a few of the many benefits of electric vehicles, representing an exciting development in intelligent mobility. However, security considerations must be prioritised when implementing any new technology affecting our highways' security. Electric vehicles, for example, might have enormous benefits for the economy as a whole if they were to be introduced to underdeveloped countries. The battery and the battery management system make up as much as 80% of an electric car, and their importation is mandated by law, as reported by PwC India. Because of this aspect, there are ample chances for manufacturers to leave hidden entry points where hackers can sneak in and steal information or cause harm. 30 US companies, including IT heavyweights Apple and Amazon, face this issue. The potential dangers extend far beyond any one car or even one manufacturer. Through the Internet of Things, a compromised EV could potentially compromise the charging station, the entire car network, and the power system. While a widespread threat to IT cybersecurity could be disastrous for the public image and cost millions to rectify, an attack on the car industry could have the same effect, with a genuine and terrible impact on human lives. Researchers have demonstrated that it is possible to duplicate these cards and use them to charge a vehicle, with the cost being billed to the original account. Threats to drivers' privacy could also emanate from the USB connections found at charging stations. Logs and data can be copied onto a flash drive, giving an attacker access to the data on the OCPP server and private information about

---

*Corresponding author: Areebalareb.sw8@muetkhp.edu.pk

Imdad Ali Shah and Noor Zaman Jhanjhi (eds.) Cybersecurity in the Transportation Industry, (165–186) © 2024 Scrivener Publishing LLC

setting point users, such as their ID numbers and locations. The primary object of this chapter is to focus on electric vehicle security issues and challenges and provide required recommendations for new researchers and companies.

Keywords: Electric vehicle, security issues and challenges, IoT and emerging technologies

8.1 Introduction

As technology improves and expands human life, so do the dangers that threaten it. In every aspect of our lives, we require safety, whether to protect our family, health, possessions, or anything else of value. With the advancement of information technology, there has been a dramatic increase in online dangers. Cybersecurity measures aid protection against these cyberattacks. When discussing protecting hardware, software, and data connected to the internet, we talk about cybersecurity. Both businesses and individuals use data centres and other digital system security technologies. With the ever-increasing volume of data—much of it sensitive or confidential—and the increasing number of people, devices, and programmes in today's businesses, the importance of cybersecurity has only grown. The high level of sophistication worsens the situation that cyberattackers employ. Cyber vulnerabilities and challenges are shown in Figure 8.1.

Economists predict that demand for electric vehicles will rise in 2021, despite challenges caused by COVID-19 in the automobile industry. Millions of battery-powered cars will hit the streets in the next few years. The auto industry has made great strides toward mass-producing autonomous automobiles, which do not have a human driver behind the wheel. To create such cars, Hyundai, Tesla, and Google are at the forefront. While the EV business is helping to lessen the industry's overall environmental impact, new cybersecurity threats are emerging. Experts say that companies need to address security risks before electric vehicles can be deployed on a large scale. Autonomous systems can be safeguarded from cyberattacks using a variety of machine learning algorithms. Machine learning methods of many types are used to secure autonomous systems [1–4]. These algorithms allow the car to adapt to its owner's driving style gradually. When something goes wrong with the owner's pattern algorithm, an alert is sent to the owner, who then requests the user's credentials. Figure 8.2 presents the Controller Area Network (CAN) bus attack interfaces.

However, some hackers can spoof user credentials and bypass this initial safeguard. Experts can counter this using deep learning and machine

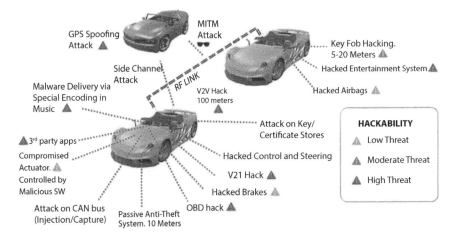

GPS Spoofing
Attack ⚠

MITM
Attack
🔊

Key Fob Hacking.
5-20 Meters ⚠

Side Channel
Attack

RF LINK

Hacked Entertainment System⚠

Malware Delivery via
Special Encoding in
Music ⚠

V2V Hack
100 meters
⚠

Hacked Airbags ⚠

⚠ 3ʳᵈ party apps

Attack on Key/
Certificate Stores

HACKABILITY

⚠ Low Threat

Compromised
Actuator. ⚠
Controlled by
Malicious SW

Hacked Control and Steering

V21 Hack ⚠

⚠ Moderate Threat

⚠ High Threat

Hacked Brakes ⚠

Attack on CAN bus
(Injection/Capture)

Passive Anti-Theft
System. 10 Meters

OBD hack ⚠

Figure 8.1 Cyber vulnerabilities and challenges [5].

learning to detect anomalies in ever-expanding databases. Additionally, data collected via vehicle-to-vehicle communication can be analysed to determine if it represents "normal driving behaviour" or a hostile attack. Cybersecurity experts in the industry of self-driving machines might expect more problems as the number of self-driving cars, drones, and automated industrial machines grow. Significant improvements have been made in various areas in the recent decade that are important to electric car manufacturing, application, and marketing [6–9]. Research activities have also grown, which has led to a rise in electric vehicle–related positions and ideas. This section provides a brief overview of the most important issues surrounding EVs that have been discussed in the existing body of literature. Differentials that stand out in this survey are also noted. Some of the current literature examines broad topics, including the historical development of electric vehicles, provides several classifications based on design and engine characteristics and assesses the effect of these vehicles on the electrical grid. [9–11] examine EV development from the mid-19th century to the present. A second step they take is to categorise the automobiles based on their powerplant configurations. Finally, their project examines how charging electric vehicles affects the power infrastructure. To the same end, Richardson [12, 13] investigates how EVs may alter the power system's necessary output, efficiency, and capacity. Moreover, he analyses the financial and ecological results of using electric cars. Electric vehicle charging technologies and their effects on electrical grids are discussed. The authors additionally examine delayed

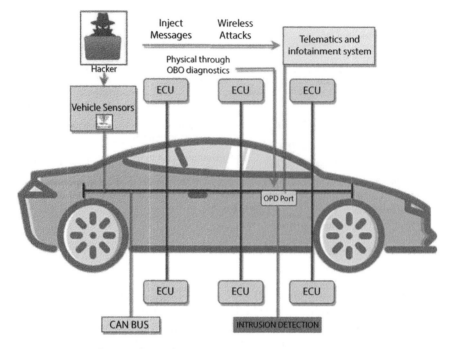

Figure 8.2 CAN bus attack interfaces.

loading, coordinated charging, and intelligent charge planning. Finally, they investigate the financial returns of V2G technology, considering different charging strategies.

The chapter focuses on the following points:

- Peer-reviewed the advanced electric vehicles
- Security issues and challenges in electric vehicles
- Different attacks on electric vehicles
- Electric Vehicle Cyber-Physical Systems
- Security issues and challenges in electric vehicles.

8.2   Literature Review

The industry has mandated the quick construction of the requisite infrastructure to keep up with the surging demand for electric vehicles (EVs). Defending internet-enabled systems and the interconnected vital infrastructure from potential cyber assaults is essential for successfully deploying an EV charging ecosystem that meets customer needs.

To gather a representative sample of EV charging station management systems, we designed a system lookup and collection technique (EVCSMS). Additionally, we conducted the first-ever comprehensive security and vulnerability research on the identified EVCSMS and their respective software and firmware implementations by employing reverse engineering and penetration testing techniques. Figure 8.3 presents the taxonomy of the literature review.

Rapid growth in the number of electric vehicles (EVs) on the road over the past several years has spurred the introduction of valuable new tools and infrastructure. There are already over 6.3 million electric vehicles on the road, with over 800,000 public charging sites and an estimated 6.5 million home chargers, according to a recent report by the International Energy Agency. Additionally, the predicted expansion in EV adoption will lead to linear growth in the number of deployed EVCS needed to meet customer needs and improve service quality. In this vein, the IoT paradigm spurred the development of EVCS management systems (EVCSMS) that provide new features, including remote monitoring, management, scheduling, and user billing [14–16]. An essential worry for consumers and network operators is the security and management problems posed by the IoT paradigm, even though it has been demonstrated to be helpful in various areas of our lives.

8.3 Methodology

There are four platforms used for the collected data for this chapter; the procedure flowchart for gathering data is shown in Figure 8.4. We used the keyword "Emerging Electric Vehicles, Security Issues and Challenges." We selected these databases because they contain many research papers, book chapters and online information on numerous subjects.

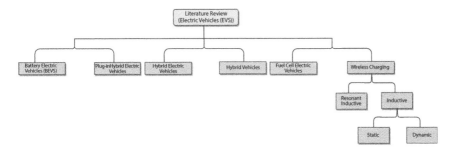

Figure 8.3 The taxonomy of the literature review.

As a relatively new and expansive attack surface, the EV charging eco-system represents an enticing target for exploitation by both powerful corporations and well-funded individuals and groups [17–20]. Given the danger they pose to power grid stability, we evaluate the effects of several different assault scenarios and focus on attacks that cause frequency insta-bility. To be more specific, these assaults happen when there is an imbal-ance in the power grid's demand and supply, leading to a sudden decrease or rise in the system frequency. We undertake our study under the assump-tion that the adversary has control over a sizable number of compromised EVCS that are then coordinated to request charging and discharging simultaneously to destabilise or cripple the power system. Electric supply/ demand balance and system frequency, represented by generator speed, are used as grid stability and reliability measures. The grid can only remain stable if it operates within a narrow frequency band. An unstable and inef-ficient system is the result of a frequency deviation. Given the impossibility of studying the effects of such massive assaults on a simulated world.

8.3.1   Electric Vehicles and Security Issues

Recent climate change has increased the need to find environmentally friendly replacements for polluting technologies. Transportation using

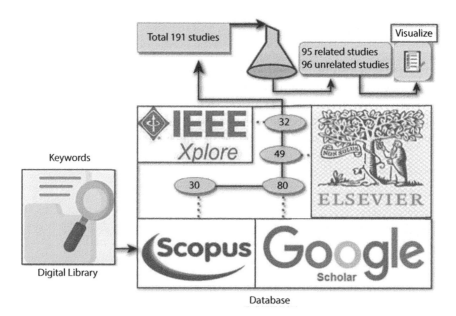

Figure 8.4 Flow chart of data collection.

fossil fuels is a significant contributor to atmospheric carbon dioxide levels. There is a push for battery-powered electric vehicles (EVs) as an eco-friendlier option. The percentage of new EV sales in some countries is rising [21–24]. Further growth in EV uptake is predicted over the coming years. Governments are proposing a ban on the sale of fossil-fuel vehicles, and many electric vehicle supply equipment (EVSE) are already being deployed in public charging infrastructures. In addition, recent technological developments have removed the obstacles that keep consumers from adopting EVs, such as the need for a standard charging infrastructure and limited range. The proliferation of EVs necessitates a careful examination of the safety of transportation and infrastructure. But there are other parts to EVs as well. In fact, [25–27] an EV incorporates elements that regulate hardware and software for efficient electric energy management. Several studies have demonstrated the dangers of cyberattacks on car systems and the viability of remote infotainment system hijacking. The in-vehicle network architecture used by many currently available automobiles—the Controller Area Network (CAN)—has already been shown to be insecure. Figure 8.5 presents an overview of vehicle-to-grid (V2G) threats.

Lastly, confidentiality must be ensured to prevent snooping passengers from learning personal details about the driver, like where she goes and what she does. Security and privacy must be built in from the start to stop these and other threats. Multiple facets of in-car communication were the focus of studies into vehicle security [29–33]. However, electric vehicles (EVs) feature unique hardware that is radically different than traditional vehicles and can be exploited. Which includes a battery pack used to power the vehicle's electronics, such as the infotainment system and accelerator pedal. Therefore, examining the dangers posed by these parts inside the car is crucial. In addition to traditional vehicles, the electricity grid requires specialised equipment for regulation. However, researchers focused on the vulnerabilities of the EV charging infrastructure to attacks while ignoring the dangers posed by the vehicles.

To provide security guarantees and interoperability, the automotive industry must adopt cybersecurity standards. There was a comprehensive analysis of the existing standards, including design and validation, in [34–36]. The unique characteristics of EVs, the key parts of an electric vehicle, are ignored by these norms. Not all the technologies or attacks were related to EVs, but all of them were discussed. In addition, other papers provide technical overviews of the EV ecosystem [37–40]. However, only some of them give thought to safety. The literature contains several publications that analyse various aspects of EVs in isolation. Cybersecurity risks to electric vehicles' onboard charging systems were summarised. While their

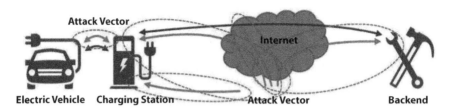

Figure 8.5 Overview of V2G threat, adapted from [28].

research into this component's security is thorough, it ignores the potential impact these attacks have on the EV's other out-of-the-ordinary parts. There is no comprehensive picture of the EV ecosystem here. Also, the dangers to privacy are not mentioned. The first debate over whether EVs qualify as CPS is provided [41–44]. The authors detail a variety of possible attacks, both from within the vehicle and when exchanging data with the charging station. While emphasising the Cyber-Physical System (CPS) exemplified by the power electronics in EVs, neither of these works considers the unique features of EVs, such as the BMS. Neither of these groups addressed the potential effects of these attacks on the rest of the EV, nor did they address the WPT-related concerns. Most research on electric vehicle cybersecurity has concentrated on the charging process and network. The dangers of a hardwired electric vehicle charging network are outlined in the research. The negotiation and activation of a charging session present several security risks, which are discussed, and investigate the communications between the various parties involved. The WPT option was ignored in favour of their other billing options.

8.4   Overview of Electric Vehicle Cyber-Physical System

To allow the effective and intelligent functioning of electric cars, information and communication technologies (ICT) and physical systems are integrated with electric vehicles (EVs) to create an electric vehicle cyber-physical system (EV-CPS). It combines the computer systems that regulate and enhance the performance of an electric vehicle's physical elements, including the battery, motor, and charging infrastructure. By combining electric cars with cutting-edge information and communication technology, EV-CPS enables smart and efficient management of energy [45–47], charging infrastructure, and transportation networks. It attempts to enhance the entire user experience while boosting the performance, dependability, and sustainability of electric cars. An overview of Cyber-physical attacks in the physical system layer are shown in Figure 8.6.

Approved New Work Item 21435 Road Vehicles -- Cybersecurity Engineering" standard. Summary information about the suggestions made by these manuals can be found in [49–51]. Alongside the auto industry's efforts, academics have also been publishing papers on vehicle network security in recent years. [52] demonstrated the typical in-vehicle network architecture of a modern vehicle. The brake system, engine control unit, steering control unit, powertrain control, body and comfort control, in-car infotainment, and telematics systems are all considered in this design [53–55]. Using this framework, several studies have covered the cyberse-curity of automobiles and discussed various strategies for protecting them from malware assaults.

8.5   Discussion

With the increased demand for cleaner and more energy-efficient trans-portation alternatives, electric vehicles (EVs) have emerged as the future

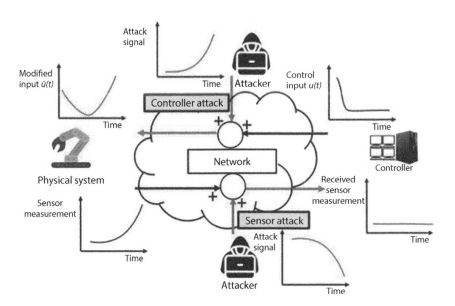

Figure 8.6 Overview of cyber-physical attacks in the physical system layer, adapted from [48].

of transportation worldwide. Cleaner air is possible with the widespread use of EVs because they use no fossil fuels [56–58]. When using a dynamic charging station, the EV must engage with several entities during the charging process.

8.5.1 Vehicle Charging Security Issues

The security mechanisms and procedures put in place to guarantee the integrity and safety of the electric vehicle (EV) charging infrastructure and the charging process are referred to as vehicle charge security. It entails safeguarding the hardware used for charging, the battery of the vehicle, and the information transmitted while charging. Authentication methods are put in place to stop illegal usage of the charging system. Users often need to verify their identity using tools like RFID cards and smartphone applications [59–65]. By implementing these security measures, it may be possible to ensure the integrity and safety of the charging process, giving EV owners peace of mind and promoting the widespread adoption of electric vehicles. An overview of the electric vehicle system is shown in Figure 8.7.

A modern Proterra electric bus can accept a 500 kW charge. As a result, bus fleets will have an overall charging profile that is highly pulsed and unpredictable. Light-duty electric vehicles and electrified bus fleets with weak powertrain systems are both possible threats to electrical infrastructure [66–69]. While these assumptions are based on location data, it is unclear if they can be applied universally to other geographic areas. This is why there have been recent initiatives to discover real-time EV charging characteristics.

8.6 Electric Vehicles (EV) Security Challenges

The components and protocols used in EVs present unique security and privacy issues that are addressed in this section. Some concerns are batteries and battery management systems. We talk about the difficulties with the controller and the charger. Given that the CAN bus does not foresee secure by-design solutions, its security has been the subject of substantial research [70–72]. However, the potential effects of such attacks on EVs have never been investigated. Since CAN and LIN buses carry all in-vehicle communications, we explore how their weaknesses can be leveraged to compromise EV-specific parts. An overview of EV security challenges is shown in Figure 8.8.

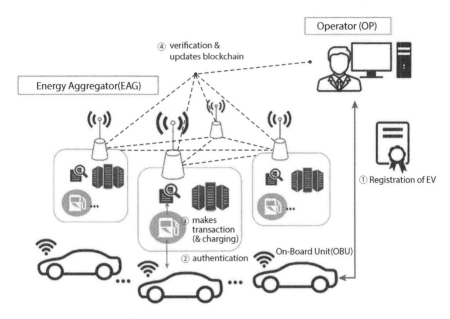

Figure 8.7 Overview of EV charging system, adapted from [63].

8.6.1 Battery and BMS

The electric vehicle's battery pack should be treated with care. In the worst-case scenario, it could start a fire or possibly explode. Passengers can be seriously injured, and the owner and manufacturer can suffer reputational and financial injury because of such incidents. However, even moderate cyberattacks can result in costly consequences, such as shortened battery life that necessitates an early battery replacement [73–75]. The battery management system (BMS) controls the battery pack and talks to the other

Component	Type of attack	Component	Type of attack
Battery and BMS	DoS	**Controller and Charger**	MitM
	Tempering		DoS
	Malicious Code Injection		Malicious Code Injection
	Spoofing, Replaying, and MitM		Eavesdropping, and Side Channels

Figure 8.8 Overview of EV security challenges.

ECUs on the vehicle bus. Once again, multiple cyberattacks have shown that this route is weak.

- Denial of Service: The BMS's job is to monitor the batteries and control the flow of electricity. A similar scenario to that of a Denial of Service (DoS) attack against a website may occur if an attacker forges and sends many requests to the BMS controller [76]. If the BMS is overworked, it may take longer to respond to valid queries, or it may stop responding altogether. Depending on what the BMS is asking for and how the requesting device handles not receiving a response, this could have a number of outcomes. If the battery's power is not correctly cut off in the event of malicious conduct or physical interference, the battery could be damaged. The battery may be damaged beyond repair if a DoS prevents it from reaching a safe operating temperature [77]. This is because the DoS could target sensor readings like temperature and impede cooling device activation. This attack could trigger anxiety about running out of juice, and drivers' safety could be put at risk in the event of an unexpected EV stop. If the BMS is equipped with flow control, it may be spared from processing excessive unnecessary requests. In this scenario, source authentication can be used to determine the reliability of a message's sender. There is evidence that a variant of "time-lock puzzles" could provide a solution for flow control. In addition, rate restriction can lessen the impact of a DoS attack [77], and intrusion detection methods can help spot an oncoming attack before it causes harm. Extreme DoS assaults against the BMS can be mitigated using controller redundancy.
- Tampering: Depending on the tampered component, a short circuit could be triggered, potentially starting a fire that would be disastrous for the car and any passengers inside. Both the battery and BMS should be considered in this light because they control excessive voltages [78]. There may also be secondary effects from tampering, such as the BMS losing contact with the battery or failing to supply the battery with full power when charging. Attacks like these may involve severing cables.
- Malicious Code Injection: Reverse engineering the software is a tactic that attackers can use to look for security flaws and create exploits for them [79]. EV software can be updated

wirelessly or over the charging cord to address security vulner-abilities. This, however, poses a security risk because upgrades to the programme require access to the entire EV network. A hacker could take control of the BMS by inserting malware into software updates. It's possible for an attacker to disrupt the vehicle's usual operation if they get access to some or all of its controls. One way in which malware can cripple an EV is by preventing the battery management system (BMS) from drawing power from the battery. The BMS may be coerced into demanding more power than necessary to hasten the dis-charge procedure as a countermeasure. The software also gives the attacker the ability to monitor the driver's system, which could lead to privacy breaches. Controlled access to the EV's internal network is essential for preventing code insertion and its consequences. Authentication from outside sources is one possible solution. An effective injection necessitates immedi-ate attention to locating the source and lessening its impact. To this end, the in-vehicle components could be validated with the help of remote attestation and collective expansion [80]. In addition, anomaly and intrusion detection methods could be used to spot car network threats. Integrity checks on the new software, perhaps using a blockchain, can reveal the injection of malicious updates.

- Spoofing, Replaying, and Man-in-the-Middle: These attacks alter messages such that the driver is given misleading infor-mation about the battery's SoC, making it unsafe for the driver to operate the vehicle. By pretending to be the BMS or altering data in transit, an attacker can send false data to the charging system. Because of this, the EV's battery or electrical system could be harmed during the charging process. In addition, an adversary can report misleading information to stop the BMS from exchanging the right amount of energy from the battery to the EV, for instance, by decreasing the current demand. In a battery exhaustion assault, the attacker draws power from the battery quicker than expected, draining it; in an overcharging attack, they significantly reduce the battery's lifespan by forcing it to charge above its capacity also problematic [81]. Finally, a Man-in-the-Middle (MitM) attack might result in bat-tery degradation due to over-discharging since an attacker changed the voltage settings of the battery pack. Giving the battery and BMS a unique identifier and requiring source authentication and message integrity protection can help deter these attacks. To prevent MitM attacks and to help spot current threats, an intrusion detection system can be installed [82]. Using redundant controllers can increase the BMS's resistance to hostile attacks while it is being charged. It is recommended to use blockchain technology to authenticate users and manage who has access to sensitive data shared by the BMS with other devices in the EV.

Chapter's Contributions

Several cyber-physical security issues associated with EVs may affect driver safety. We have found that some of the methods of attack and protection described here can be used on other types of EV assets as well. Given the time and space constraints, however, we will only cover the ones we think are most compelling. While several potential dangers are associated with the charging infrastructure, those associated with the in-car network pose the most significant risk to passengers. Electroshocking the driver is possible in EVs because the electric component can be tampered with or hindered. It becomes more challenging to ensure that data from the cyber and physical worlds is consistent as the number of cyber features in EVs grows. Lastly, from a CPS perspective, substantial issues still arise from the growing interest in using the WPT technology for EVs.

Regarding security, EVs have several unique challenges, but one of the most significant is denial-of-service attacks. It's notoriously hard to prevent and can affect almost every part of an EV. DoS attacks can damage a region's electric vehicle charging infrastructure (EVSEs), impacting more than just one vehicle. All entities within the vehicle need to be linked to a specific identity, and the information flow between them (and the resulting traffic) should be conditional on the vehicle's current location to reduce the likelihood of security breaches. In fact, it's possible that under the influence of certain physical stimuli, an ECU needs to increase the rate at which it sends data. All ECUs will receive adequate funding at the same time. Future defences against DoS for vehicular networks must, therefore, consider physical considerations and the potential impact on the entire electrical grid. Potential tampering with EV components could endanger the user's safety and harm other parts of the vehicle's system. Anomaly detection capabilities or the ability to cut off voltage or current flow in the event of tampering should be built into every part of the vehicle. Potentially useful in the future might be the collective verification of several components, which would render the manipulation of any one unit useless.

The cybersecurity of EVs is becoming more difficult to ensure as the capabilities of attackers rise. The functionality of EVs could be severely compromised if an attacker combines various attacks. It is crucial to incorporate into EV frameworks the collection of information from different sources, combining the cyber and physical worlds, to increase the protection mechanisms. Data from various sensors and actuators could be used to validate message integrity, making information manipulation more difficult. Just as network data shared over the bus might be combined with physical signals from sensors better to represent the EV's condition, intrusion detection techniques could do the same thing. This measure will also hinder attacks against mechanical systems that rely on actuators controlled by electronic control units.

8.7   Conclusion

Electric vehicles are an exciting breakthrough in smart mobility because they have numerous positive impacts, including cleaner air, less noise pollution, reduced greenhouse gas emissions, and increased long-term energy security. However, safety must always come first when introducing new technologies that could compromise the safety of our roads. We gave a brief rundown of the parts that make up an EV, emphasising the parts that make them unique. We laid the foundation for knowing how in-car communication networks function and what gadgets require interoperability. We discussed the background information needed to understand both technologies and how they can be used. Both the security and privacy concerns of in-vehicle communications and charging infrastructure were addressed. We looked at the issue of security and privacy from the standpoint of the user and the system as a whole (CPS). Then, we recommended future paths and addressed potential countermeasures for making the EV ecosystem safer and more private for everyone involved. In conclusion, the current state of EV technology provides a sizable attack surface for cybercriminals to exploit. As a result, it is crucial to design technologies that consider the CPS character of EVs to guarantee complete safety. In the future, it will be essential to consider EV-specific parts like the battery and the charger as potential data sources for the vehicle's condition.

8.8   Future Work

Computers can predict battery charge and discharge curves with a certain degree of certainty. These simulations can be put to immediate use by serving as a reference for finding packets that announce an altered SoC. One advantage electric vehicles have over older vehicles is the sophistication of the software that controls them. Unfortunately, this raises the risk that a vehicle will be the target of a cyberattack. Malware insertion into EV parts is one possible form of attack. To ensure the safety of the entire EV, remote attestation can be used to check the state of each part individually. However, remote attestation measures need to consider the time-sensitive nature of the information transferred and the restricted resources of EV components.

References

[1] Z. Shahan, 16 Countries Now Over 10% Plugin Vehicle Share, 6 Over 20%, *Clean Technica*, September 5, 2021, https://cleantechnica.com/2021/09/05/16-countries-now-over-10-plugin-vehicle-share-6-over-20/.

[2] A. Madhani and T. Krisher, Biden Pushes Electric Vehicle Chargers as Energy Costs Spike. *U.S. News*, November 17, 2021, https://www.usnews.com/news/business/articles/2021-11-17/biden-pushes-electric-vehicle-chargers-as-energy-costs-spike.

[3] P. Gordon, Netherlands aims to ban conventionally-fueled vehicles by 2050. *Smart Energy International*, Feb 4, 2019. https://www.smart-energy.com/industry-sectors/electric-vehicles/netherlands-aims-to-ban-conventionally-fueled-vehicles-by-2050/

[4] T. Capuder, D. M. Sprčić, D. Zoričić, and H. Pandžić, Review of challenges and assessment of electric vehicles integration policy goals: Integrated risk analysis approach, *International Journal of Electrical Power & Energy Systems*, vol. 119, p. 105894, 2020.

[5] El-Rewini, Zeinab, et al. Cybersecurity challenges in vehicular communications. *Vehicular Communications* 23 (2020): 100214.

[6] C. Miller and C. Valasek, Remote exploitation of an unaltered passenger vehicle, *Black Hat USA*, vol. 2015, no. S 91, 2015.

[7] C. Schmittner and G. Macher, Automotive cybersecurity standards relation and overview, in *International Conference on Computer Safety, Reliability, and Security*. Springer, 2019, pp. 153-165.

[8] M. Scalas and G. Giacinto, Automotive cybersecurity: Foundations for next-generation vehicles, in *2019 2nd International Conference on new Trends in Computing Sciences (ICTCS)*. IEEE, 2019, pp. 1-6.

[9] R. Gottumukkala, R. Merchant, A. Tauzin, K. Leon, A. Roche, and P. Darby, Cyber-physical system security of vehicle charging stations, in *2019 IEEE Green Technologies Conference (GreenTech)*. IEEE, 2019, pp. 1-5.

[10] A. Bahrami, EV charging definitions, modes, levels, communication protocols and applied standards, *Changes*, vol. 1, pp. 10-01, 2020.

[11] H. S. Das, M. M. Rahman, S. Li, and C. Tan, "Electric vehicles standards, charging infrastructure, and impact on grid integration: A technological review," *Renewable and Sustainable Energy Reviews*, vol. 120, p. 109618, 2020.

[12] A. Khalid, A. Sundararajan, A. Hernandez, and A. I. Sarwat, Facts approach to address cybersecurity issues in electric vehicle battery systems, in *2019 IEEE Technology & Engineering Management Conference (TEMSCON)*. IEEE, 2019, pp. 1-6.

[13] Khatri, N., Shrestha, R., & Nam, S. Y. (2021). Security issues with in-vehicle networks, and enhanced countermeasures based on blockchain. *Electronics*, *10*(8), 893.

[14] A. Chandwani, S. Dey, and A. Mallik, Cybersecurity of onboard charging systems for electric vehicles—review, challenges and countermeasures, *IEEE Access*, vol. 8, pp. 226 982-226 998, 2020.

[15] S. Acharya, Y. Dvorkin, H. Pandžić, and R. Karri, Cybersecurity of smart electric vehicle charging: A power grid perspective, *IEEE Access*, vol. 8, pp. 214 434–214 453, 2020.

[16] J. Ye, L. Guo, B. Yang, F. Li, L. Du, L. Guan, and W. Song, "Cyber–physical security of powertrain systems in modern electric vehicles: Vulnerabilities, challenges, and future visions," *IEEE Journal of Emerging and Selected Topics in Power Electronics*, vol. 9, no. 4, pp. 4639-4657, 2020.

[17] J. Antoun, M. E. Kabir, B. Moussa, R. Atallah, and C. Assi, A detailed security assessment of the ev charging ecosystem, *IEEE Network*, vol. 34, no. 3, pp. 200-207, 2020.

[18] S. Sripad, S. Kulandaivel, V. Pande, V. Sekar, and V. Viswanathan, Vulnerabilities of Electric Vehicle Battery Packs to Cyberattacks on Auxilary Components. November 2017. https://www.researchgate.net/publication/321095614_Vulnerabilities_of_Electric_Vehicle_Battery_Packs_to_Cyberattacks_on_Auxiliary_Components#.

[19] Z. Garofalaki, D. Kosmanos, S. Moschoyiannis, D. Kallergis, and C. Douligeris, Electric vehicle charging: a survey on the security issues and challenges of the open charge point protocol (ocpp), *IEEE Communications Surveys & Tutorials*, 2022.

[20] P. Van Aubel and E. Poll, Security of ev-charging protocols, arXiv preprint arXiv:2202.04631, 2022.

[21] P. R. Babu, B. Palaniswamy, A. G. Reddy, V. Odelu, and H. S. Kim, A survey on security challenges and protocols of electric vehicle dynamic charging system, *Security and Privacy*, vol. 5, no. 3, 2022.

[22] Y. Fraiji, L. B. Azzouz, W. Trojet, and L. A. Saidane, Cyber security issues of internet of electric vehicles, in *2018 IEEE Wireless Communications and Networking Conference (WCNC)*. IEEE, 2018, pp. 1-6.

[23] Many cars have a hundred million lines of code. *MIT Technology Review*. [Online]. Available: https://www.technologyreview.com/2012/12/03/181350/many-cars-have-a-hundred-million-lines-of-code/

[24] K. Cho, J. Kim, D. Y. Choi, Y. H. Yoon, J. H. Oh, and S. E. Lee, An FPGA-based ECU for remote reconfiguration in automotive systems, *Micromachines*, vol. 12, no. 11, p. 1309, 2021.

[25] M. Bozdal, M. Samie, S. Aslam, and I. Jennions, Evaluation of CAN bus security challenges, *Sensors*, vol. 20, no. 8, p. 2364, 2020.

[26] Road vehicles — Local Interconnect Network (LIN) — Part 8: Electrical physical layer (EPL) specification: LIN over DC powerline (DCLIN), International Organization for Standardization (ISO), Standard, Mar. 2019.

[27] C. Corbett, E. Schoch, F. Kargl, and F. Preussner, Automotive ethernet: Security opportunity or challenge? Sicherheit 2016-Sicherheit, Schutz und Zuverlassigkeit, 2016.

[28] telematicswire:https://www.telematicswire.net/wp-content/uploads/2021/02/TWlogo.png

[29] S. Halder, A. Ghosal, and M. Conti, Secure over-the-air software updates in connected vehicles: A survey, *Computer Networks*, vol. 178, p. 107343, 2020.

[30] F. Un-Noor, S. Padmanaban, L. Mihet-Popa, M. N. Mollah, and E. Hossain, A comprehensive study of key electric vehicle (EV) components, technologies, challenges, impacts, and future direction of development, *Energies*, vol. 10, no. 8, p. 1217, 2017.

[31] L. Guo and J. Ye, Cyber-physical security of electric vehicles with four motor drives, *IEEE Transactions on Power Electronics*, vol. 36, no. 4, pp. 4463-4477, 2020.

[32] S. S. Ravi and M. Aziz, Utilization of electric vehicles for vehicleto-grid services: progress and perspectives, *Energies*, vol. 15, no. 2, p. 589, 2022.

[33] Shah, I. A., Jhanjhi, N. Z., Amsaad, F., & Razaque, A. (2022). The Role of Cutting-Edge Technologies in Industry 4.0. In *Cyber Security Applications for Industry 4.0* (pp. 97-109). Chapman and Hall/CRC.

[34] Y. Li, Y. Wang, M. Wu, and H. Li, Replay Attack and Defense of Electric Vehicle Charging on GB/T 27930-2015 Communication Protocol, vol. 07, no. 12, pp. 20-30.

[35] International Standard Organization, "ISO 15118-8:2020: Road vehicles — vehicle to grid communication interface — part 8: Physical layer and data link layer requirements for wireless communication," Standard, Sep. 2022.

[36] ——, "ISO 15118-20:2022: Road vehicles — vehicle to grid communication interface — part 20: 2nd generation network layer and application layer requirements," Standard, Apr. 2022.

[37] What is Autocharge? Fastned FAQ. [Online]. Available: https://support.fastned.nl/hc/en-gb/articles/115012747127-Whatis-Autocharge-

[38] "ISO 15118-1:2019: Road vehicles —Vehicle to grid communication interface — Part 1: General information and use-case definition," International Organization for Standardization (ISO), Standard, Apr. 2019.

[39] L. Buschlinger, M. Springer, and M. Zhdanova, Plug-and-patch: Secure value added services for electric vehicle charging, in *Proceedings of the*

14th International Conference on Availability, Reliability and Security, 2019, pp. 1-10.

[40] "SAE Electric Vehicle and Plug in Hybrid Electric Vehicle Conductive Charge Coupler," Society of Automotive Engineers (SAE), Standard, Apr. 2019.

[41] Z. J. Lee, G. Lee, T. Lee, C. Jin, R. Lee, Z. Low, D. Chang, C. Ortega, and S. H. Low, Adaptive charging networks: A framework for smart electric vehicle charging, IEEE Transactions on Smart Grid, vol. 12, no. 5, pp. 4339-4350, 2021.

[42] "IEEE Standard Technical Specifications of a DC Quick Charger for Use with Electric Vehicles," IEEE Std 2030.1.1-2015, pp. 1-97, 2016. 16.

[43] Z. Zhang, H. Pang, A. Georgiadis, and C. Cecati, Wireless power transfer—an overview, *IEEE Transactions on Industrial Electronics*, vol. 66, no. 2, pp. 1044-1058, 2018.

[44] H. Wang and K. W. E. Cheng, An improved and integrated design of segmented dynamic wireless power transfer for electric vehicles, *Energies*, vol. 14, no. 7, p. 1975, 2021.

[45] P. Machura, V. De Santis, and Q. Li, Driving range of electric vehicles charged by wireless power transfer, *IEEE Transactions on Vehicular Technology*, vol. 69, no. 6, pp. 5968-5982, 2020.

[46] L. F. Roman and P. R. Gondim, Authentication protocol in ctns for a cwdwpt charging system in a cloud environment, *Ad Hoc Networks*, vol. 97, p. 102004, 2020.

[47] F. Corti, A. Reatti, M. C. Piccirilli, F. Grasso, L. Paolucci, and M. K. Kazimierczuk, Simultaneous wireless power and data transfer: Overview and application to electric vehicles, in *2020 IEEE International Symposium on Circuits and Systems (ISCAS)*. IEEE, 2020, pp. 1-5.

[48] Shah, I. A. (2022). Cybersecurity Issues and Challenges for E-Government During COVID-19: A Review. *Cybersecurity Measures for E-Government Frameworks*, 187-222.

[49] Ujjan, R. M. A., Pervez, Z., & Dahal, K. (2018, June). Suspicious traffic detection in SDN with collaborative techniques of snort and deep neural networks. In *2018 IEEE 20th International Conference on High Performance Computing and Communications; IEEE 16th International Conference on Smart City; IEEE 4th International Conference on Data Science and Systems (HPCC/SmartCity/DSS)* (pp. 915-920). IEEE.

[50] Kumar, T., Pandey, B., Mussavi, S. H. A., & Zaman, N. (2015). CTHS based energy efficient thermal aware image ALU design on FPGA. *Wireless Personal Communications*, 85, 671-696.

[51] Shafiq, M., Ashraf, H., Ullah, A., Masud, M., Azeem, M., Jhanjhi, N., & Humayun, M. (2021). Robust cluster-based routing protocol for IoT-assisted smart devices in WSN. *Computers, Materials & Continua*, 67(3), 3505-3521.

[52] Adeyemo, V. E., Abdullah, A., JhanJhi, N. Z., Supramaniam, M., & Balogun, A. O. (2019). Ensemble and deep-learning methods for two-class and

multi-attack anomaly intrusion detection: an empirical study. *International Journal of Advanced Computer Science and Applications, 10*(9).

[53] Kok, S. H., Abdullah, A., & Jhanjhi, N. Z. (2022). Early detection of crypto-ransomware using pre-encryption detection algorithm. *Journal of King Saud University - Computer and Information Sciences, 34*(5), 1984-1999.

[54] R. L. Rivest, A. Shamir, and D. A. Wagner, Time-lock puzzles and timed-release crypto. Technical Report, Massachusetts Institute of Technology, 1996.

[55] M. Kuerban, Y. Tian, Q. Yang, Y. Jia, B. Huebert, and D. Poss, Flowsec: Dos attack mitigation strategy on sdn controller, in *2016 IEEE International Conference on Networking, Architecture and Storage (NAS)*. IEEE, 2016, pp. 1-2.

[56] C. Young, J. Zambreno, H. Olufowobi, and G. Bloom, Survey of automotive controller area network intrusion detection systems, *IEEE Design & Test*, vol. 36, no. 6, pp. 48-55, 2019.

[57] S. Bogosyan and M. Gokasan, Novel strategies for security-hardened bms for extremely fast charging of bevs, in *2020 IEEE 23rd International Conference on Intelligent Transportation Systems (ITSC)*. IEEE, 2020, pp. 1-7.

[58] Z. Sun, Y. Han, Z. Wang, Y. Chen, P. Liu, Z. Qin, Z. Zhang, Z. Wu, and C. Song, Detection of voltage fault in the battery system of electric vehicles using statistical analysis, *Applied Energy*, vol. 307, p. 118172, 2022.

[59] R. Gennaro, A. Lysyanskaya, T. Malkin, S. Micali, and T. Rabin, Algorithmic tamper-proof (atp) security: Theoretical foundations for security against hardware tampering, in *Theory of Cryptography Conference*. Springer, 2004, pp. 258-277.

[60] "J2464: Electric and Hybrid Electric Vehicle Rechargeable Energy Storage System (RESS) Safety and Abuse Testing. Society of Automotive Engineers (SAE), Standard, Aug. 2021.

[61] P. Kiley, Reverse Engineering the Tesla Battery Management System to Increase Power Available, *Blackhat*, p. 28, 2020. [Online]. Available: https://i.blackhat.com/USA-20/Wednesday/us-20- Kiley-Reverse-Engineering-The-Tesla-Battery-Management-SystemTo-Increase-Power-Available.pdf

[62] P. Rughoobur and L. Nagowah, A lightweight replay attack detection framework for battery depended on iot devices designed for healthcare, in *2017 International Conference on Infocom Technologies and Unmanned Systems (Trends and Future Directions) (ICTUS)*. IEEE, 2017, pp. 811-817.

[63] Kim, M., Park, K., Yu, S., Lee, J., Park, Y., Lee, S. W., & Chung, B. (2019). A secure charging system for electric vehicles based on blockchain. *Sensors, 19*(13), 3028.

[64] Shah, I. A., Wassan, S., & Usmani, M. H. (2022). E-Government Security and Privacy Issues: Challenges and Preventive Approaches. In *Cybersecurity Measures for E-Government Frameworks* (pp. 61-76). IGI Global.

[65] Kumar, T., Pandey, B., Mussavi, S. H. A., & Zaman, N. (2015). CTHS based energy efficient thermal aware image ALU design on FPGA. *Wireless Personal Communications, 85,* 671-696.

[66] Shafiq, M., Ashraf, H., Ullah, A., Masud, M., Azeem, M., Jhanjhi, N., & Humayun, M. (2021). Robust cluster-based routing protocol for IoT-assisted smart devices in WSN. *Computers, Materials & Continua, 67*(3), 3505-3521.

[67] Shah, I. A., Habeeb, R. A. A., Rajper, S., & Laraib, A. (2022). The Influence of Cybersecurity Attacks on E-Governance. In *Cybersecurity Measures for E-Government Frameworks* (pp. 77-95). IGI Global.

[68] Lim, M., Abdullah, A., & Jhanjhi, N. Z. (2021). Performance optimization of criminal network hidden link prediction model with deep reinforcement learning. *Journal of King Saud University - Computer and Information Sciences, 33*(10), 1202-1210.

[69] Adeyemo, V. E., Abdullah, A., JhanJhi, N. Z., Supramaniam, M., & Balogun, A. O. (2019). Ensemble and deep-learning methods for two-class and multi-attack anomaly intrusion detection: an empirical study. *International Journal of Advanced Computer Science and Applications, 10*(9).

[70] Shah, I. A., Jhanjhi, N. Z., Humayun, M., & Ghosh, U. (2022). Health Care Digital Revolution During COVID-19. In *How COVID-19 Is Accelerating the Digital Revolution* (pp. 17-30). Springer, Cham.

[71] Ujjan, R. M. A., Taj, I., & Brohi, S. N. (2022). E-Government Cybersecurity Modeling in the Context of Software-Defined Networks. In *Cybersecurity Measures for E-Government Frameworks* (pp. 1-21). IGI Global.

[72] Kok, S. H., Abdullah, A., & Jhanjhi, N. Z. (2022). Early detection of crypto-ransomware using pre-encryption detection algorithm. *Journal of King Saud University - Computer and Information Sciences, 34*(5), 1984-1999.

[73] Umrani, S., Rajper, S., Talpur, S. H., Shah, I. A., & Shujrah, A. (2020). Games based learning: A case of learning physics using Angry Birds. *Indian Journal of Science and Technology, 13*(36), 3778-3784.

[74] Ujjan, R. M. A., Khan, N. A., & Gaur, L. (2022). E-Government Privacy and Security Challenges in the Context of Internet of Things. In *Cybersecurity Measures for E-Government Frameworks* (pp. 22-42). IGI Global.

[75] Muzafar, S., Humayun, M., & Hussain, S. J. (2022). Emerging Cybersecurity Threats in the Eye of E-Governance in the Current Era. In *Cybersecurity Measures for E-Government Frameworks* (pp. 43-60). IGI Global.

[76] Chhajed, G. J., & Garg, B. R. (2022). Applying Decision Tree for Hiding Data in Binary Images for Secure and Secret Information Flow. In *Cybersecurity Measures for E-Government Frameworks* (pp. 175-186). IGI Global.

[77] Dawson, M., & Walker, D. (2022). Argument for Improved Security in Local Governments within the Economic Community of West African States. *Cybersecurity Measures for E-Government Frameworks,* pp. 96-106.

[78] Gaur, L., Ujjan, R. M. A., & Hussain, M. (2022). The Influence of Deep Learning in Detecting Cyber Attacks on E-Government Applications. In

Cybersecurity Measures for E-Government Frameworks (pp. 107-122). IGI Global.

[79] Jhanjhi, N. Z., Ahmad, M., Khan, M. A., & Hussain, M. (2022). The Impact of Cyber Attacks on E-Governance During the COVID-19 Pandemic. In *Cybersecurity Measures for E-Government Frameworks* (pp. 123-140). IGI Global.

[80] Hussain, M., Talpur, M. S. H., & Humayun, M. (2022). The Consequences of Integrity Attacks on E-Governance: Privacy and Security Violation. In *Cybersecurity Measures for E-Government Frameworks* (pp. 141-156). IGI Global.

[81] L. Guo, J. Ye, and B. Yang, Cyberattack detection for electric vehicles using physics-guided machine learning, *IEEE Transactions on Transportation Electrification*, vol. 7, no. 3, pp. 2010-2022, 2020.

[82] Ujjan, R. M. A., Hussain, K., & Brohi, S. N. (2022). The Impact of Blockchain Technology on Advanced Security Measures for E-Government. In *Cybersecurity Measures for E-Government Frameworks* (pp. 157-174). IGI Global.

9

Autonomous Shipping: Security Issues and Challenges

Imdad Ali Shah

School of Computing Science, Taylor's University, Kuala Lumpur, Selangor, Malaysia

Abstract

Autonomous shipping is a developing technology with the potential to radically alter the shipping sector by introducing unmanned vessels. While autonomous shipping has several potential advantages, including higher efficiency, decreased costs, and enhanced safety, it also faces some security concerns and future obstacles. Connectivity, data sharing, and digital systems are crucial for autonomous ships. This reliance increases the likelihood of cyber threats like hacking, data loss, and unwanted interference. Autonomous ships' safe and secure functioning depends on their being shielded from cyber threats. Navigation, propulsion, and cargo management are just a few systems that make up an autonomous ship. Hackers can potentially exploit flaws in any system. It is crucial to identify and remedy these vulnerabilities to protect the ship's operations from threats that could interrupt or compromise them. Sensors like global positioning systems (GPS), radar, and lidar let autonomous ships get a clear picture of their surroundings and make sound navigational choices. However, the signals from these sensors can be intentionally disrupted (in the case of jamming) or spoofed (in the case of spoofing) by malicious actors. If an attack of this kind compromises the ship's navigation system, collisions and other accidents may happen. For autonomous shipping to be widely adopted, it must first earn the people's trust. Worries about cybersecurity, the loss of maritime jobs, and the ships' ability to respond to the unexpected may hinder the public's adoption of autonomous ships. Successful adoption of autonomous shipping requires establishing public trust through open testing, regulatory monitoring, and clear communication. In order to effectively address existing security concerns and future problems, the marine industry, technology providers, regulatory agencies, and cybersecurity experts will need to

Email: shahsyedimdadali@gmail.com

Imdad Ali Shah and Noor Zaman Jhanjhi (eds.) Cybersecurity in the Transportation Industry, (187–210) © 2024 Scrivener Publishing LLC

work together. The full potential of autonomous shipping while maintaining its security and safety will depend on ongoing research, development, and testing of autonomous shipping technology and the adoption of international standards and laws. The primary objective of this chapter is to focus on emerging technologies in Autonomous Shipping and Security issues. We provided solutions and recommendations to new researchers and concerned companies.

Keywords: Autonomous shipping, artificial intelligence, IoT, GPS, security issues and challenges

9.1   Introduction

Self-driving ships, often called unmanned ships or autonomous shipping, are cutting-edge innovations with the potential to radically alter the shipping sector. Automated ship navigation and control rely more on high-tech sensors, AI, and automation than human pilots. While autonomous shipping has the potential to greatly enhance efficiency, cut costs, and safeguard passengers, it also presents a number of security concerns and new problems. Autonomous ships are susceptible to cyberattacks because they rely heavily on networked systems and networks. Malicious actors may try to access onboard systems without authorization or alter sensor data.

When hackers attack the shipping industry, it can have a big effect on how ships work, how safe they are, and on the global supply chain. Here are some ways hackers can impact the shipping industry:

Disruption of shipping operations: Hackers can disrupt shipping operations by targeting the computer systems that control vessel navigation and communication and the strategies that manage cargo loading and unloading. This can cause delays, damage, or even accidents [1–3].

Cybersecurity breaches: Cybersecurity breaches can lead to the theft of sensitive information, such as cargo manifests, customer data, and financial information. This can compromise the security of the supply chain and result in significant financial losses. Ransomware attacks involve the encryption of critical data, which can only be unlocked by paying a ransom to hackers. This can cause considerable disruption to shipping operations and result in financial losses. Figure 9.1 presents the vessel and port infrastructure.

Digitization, operational integration, and automation are becoming increasingly important in the marine industry worldwide. The leaders in the shipbuilding and operating industries are using cutting-edge technology and systems that go beyond traditional ship design to make ships with levels of remote control, communication, and connection that

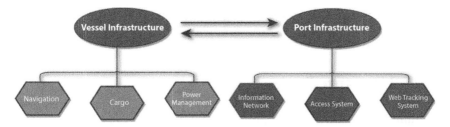

Figure 9.1 Vessel & port infrastructure.

have never been seen before [4–7]. Many ongoing initiatives are putting autonomous vessels' capabilities to the test. The Mayflower's effort to sail the Atlantic Ocean without human intervention using solar power and artificial intelligence technologies was the first of its kind. Even though the ship's initial effort to cross the Atlantic was unsuccessful, it plans to give it another go by February 2022. European Regulation EU 2016-679 states that cyber-enabled ships are among the most vital infrastructures primarily relying on digital services, and that deliberate interruption of their operations may cause financial and environmental harm and jeopardise human safety. Although a growing body of literature exists in this field, maritime cybersecurity must be thoroughly explored. In this article, we first catalogue the security problems and dangers that today's shipping sector is subject to, explicitly emphasizing the shipboard infrastructure. One of the most recent and ground-breaking developments is blockchain technology. Regarding its potential impact on society, many see blockchain as the internet's successor. With blockchain, we can move beyond the internet of information and into the internet of values. These days, data kept on paper, in hard drives, or in the cloud is not as safe as it once was [8–10]. They can easily be manipulated and changed. Due to various factors, the public no longer has faith in such databases. Rather than relying on a central authority to verify transactions, blockchain technology can facilitate the development of a trustworthy environment. The government, businesses, or anybody else can avoid becoming involved because of the way the system is set up. Alternatively, confidence may be established simply by using the system as intended. The distributed ledger technology known as blockchain is designed to prevent fraud, hacking, and other forms of framework manipulation.

The chapter focuses on the following points:

- Autonomous Shipping
- Types of Autonomous Shipping

- Security Issues and Challenges in Autonomous Shipping
- Navigation Control.

9.2   Literature Review

Common cyber threats to shipping automation systems include malware, ransomware, and denial-of-service attacks. These attacks can exploit vulnerabilities in ship systems, steal sensitive information, and disrupt critical ship operations. To mitigate the risks of cyberattacks on ship automation systems, ship owners and operators must implement robust cybersecurity measures. These measures include regular system updates and patching, strong access control policies, training and awareness programs for the crew, and continuous monitoring and threat intelligence gathering [11–13]. Furthermore, ship automation systems should be designed and built with cybersecurity in mind. This means incorporating security features into the system's design, such as firewalls, intrusion detection systems, and encryption technologies. Figure 9.2 presents the modern automation system.

Hackers can target vessels carrying hazardous cargo control systems, such as oil. This can result in spills or other ecological disasters. Hackers can significantly impact the shipping industry and the global supply chain. Shipping companies need to implement robust cybersecurity measures and stay vigilant against potential threats. The marine infrastructure has two main hubs found at ports and aboard ships. We can see a visual

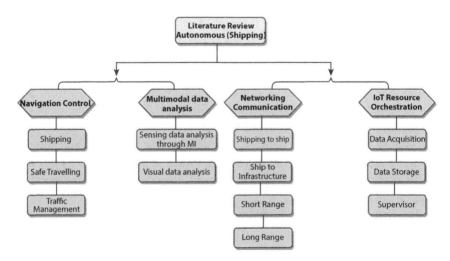

Figure 9.2 The modern automation system.

representation of the different platforms, how they connect, and how their services work together [14]. Simply put, a blockchain is a distributed ledger of all the transactions that have ever taken place within the blockchain's computer networks. Many separate transactions are contained within each chain block. Each participant's ledger is updated whenever a new transaction is on the blockchain. Cryptocurrencies are a prominent example of the widespread use of blockchain technology. When people think about blockchain applications, they usually think of Bitcoin, which is both well-known and divisive. Nonetheless, blockchain technology is not contentious in and of itself, and its potential applications in financial and non-financial areas have been widely acknowledged [15]. The introduction of a fully autonomous ship that is also secure and dependable will mark the culmination of the shipping industry's digitalization trend. Two interconnected artificial intelligence systems that act as the ship's navigator and engineer and have situational awareness, planning, and control abilities could achieve complete autonomy. Although there have been several efforts to create onboard systems, the shore facilities are not yet equipped to handle this new technology. The purpose of the study is to outline the novel approaches and technology required to create a cutting-edge vessel traffic management system. To deal with dangers and system failures without human intervention onboard, the proposed systems will aim for perfect data collection and processing, offer input to decision-making systems, and advise evasive actions [16–18]. The system is made up of three interconnected levels. The first is an artificially intelligent instrument that uses situational awareness and obstacle avoidance techniques to find and steer autonomous ships. The second is a platform for orchestration and management that was created to coordinate the outputs of AI algorithms and the sensing-actuation infrastructure that were made available by many ships, mustering edge and distributed computing approaches to meet the demanding specifications of the hostile maritime environment.

Rotating crews on ships, at ports, and at third parties can have varying degrees of knowledge about cybersecurity. They may not be conversant with best practices for ensuring the security of linked systems. Any adversary hoping to compromise a ship's systems, steal sensitive data, or sabotage its operations might benefit from a lack of a cybersecurity culture. Hence, raising marine industry awareness and knowledge of genuine cyber dangers is crucial [19–21]. Cybersecurity awareness training, education, and certification for the applicable portions of the vessel's operation are among the most effective means of achieving this goal. Turn-by-turn directions are the standard feature of navigation systems, which normally employ a map to show the user where they currently are and where they need to go. Real-time traffic data might also be used to help people get around slow spots and locate the quickest routes. It is possible to search for restaurants, gas stations, and other points of interest, as well as save favourite destinations, on some navigation systems [22–24]. Drivers, hikers, and bikers alike can now be found with a navigation system installed in their vehicles. They've also grown in significance for use by organizations like the armed forces, delivery services, and logistics firms, all of which rely heavily on precise location data.

Technical systems that use electronic displays to present digital information to end users are known as electronic displays and information systems. Advertising, transportation, education, healthcare, and many more fields make use of such systems. A device that converts electrical signals into visible visuals is called an electronic display. They come in a variety of forms, such as plasma displays, organic light-emitting diode displays, liquid crystal displays, and inorganic light-emitting diode displays. In contrast, information systems are digital infrastructures that are designed to gather, process, store, and disseminate data. They're able to perform these tasks thanks to software and technology that can be customized to match individual requirements. Electronic displays and information systems working together can create potent tools that provide consumers with up-to-the-moment data [25–27]. The arrival and departure times of trains and buses can be shown digitally at a transportation hub. When plans shift, an information system can immediately reflect the new status of the data. The advent of electronic displays and information systems has revolutionized the way we interact with digital content, making it more accessible, engaging, and user-friendly than ever before.

Location and time may be determined from a GPS receiver anywhere on or near Earth thanks to this satellite-based navigation system. Satellites in orbit, ground-based control centers, and GPS receivers all work together to pinpoint precise locations and measure exact distances. Numerous applications have been found for global positioning system (GPS) technology, including marine and air navigation, land and sea mapping, animal monitoring, and personal navigation during outdoor pursuits like hiking and camping. Smartphones, automotive navigation systems, and fitness trackers, to name a few, all rely heavily on global positioning systems [28, 29]. Although the United States' government operates and maintains the GPS satellite network, anyone with a GPS receiver can access and use the satellites' signals.

There are advantages and disadvantages to addressing cargo security at sea. Protecting the integrity of the global supply chain requires measures to increase the safety of cargo transported by water. As a result, foreign trade and the economy as a whole can benefit from this increase in consumer and business optimism. Recent technological advancements have enabled the improvement of cargo security. Container tracking systems, X-ray scanning equipment, and electronic seals are just a few examples of the technical advancements that have made it feasible to better monitor and identify potential security issues [30, 31]. Protecting cargo on the open ocean requires cooperative international action. There is a window of opportunity for nations to work together, share intelligence, and set common standards and best practices to successfully lessen security problems. Public-private collaborations can strengthen maritime cargo security. Governments, shipping companies, port operators, and logistics providers may all work together to improve security, share data, and develop contingency strategies. To address these challenges, it is necessary to invest in technological advancement, capacity training, international cooperation, and the ongoing review and modification of security standards. By taking measures to prevent these dangers to marine cargo, international trade can be made more secure and efficient. Hacking and other shipping security issues can have far-reaching consequences for the economy. Hackers are more likely to launch attacks as the number of internet-connected ships increases [32]. It is possible for hackers to get access to ship systems and disable them, steal sensitive data, or even take command of the vessel. Cybercriminals can target ships with advanced equipment and seize command of them. They utilize malware to take over a ship's systems or GPS spoofing to misdirect ships. In order to steal money or sensitive information, hackers may attack shipping businesses. They could also employ hacking methods to get where they need to go on the ship without being detected. It is possible for hackers to interrupt the shipping process by attacking shipping coordination systems. Attacks against ships transporting oil or other potentially harmful cargo pose a threat to the environment. Recently, hackers have emerged as a major threat to the maritime industry, with several high-profile attacks generating headlines around the world. These assaults can take numerous forms, including theft of sensitive information or intellectual property, and disruption of supply lines. Together, hackers infiltrate a company's network and hold sensitive data hostage using ransomware. If hackers get access to a company's network, they might potentially steal sensitive information, rearrange shipping timetables, and even seize control of the ship's navigation systems. To counteract these assaults, shipping businesses need to beef up their security systems. System updates, security patches, and stringent password rules are all part of this, as is frequent training for staff members on how to recognize and respond to any threats [33]. To further strengthen the safety of their operations, they should look into implementing cutting-edge technology like blockchain or machine learning. While hacking assaults on shipping are becoming increasingly worrying, there are measures that businesses may take to protect themselves. Shipping firms face a number of threats to their ships and cargo that can only be mitigated by investing in cybersecurity technologies and techniques. The primary goal of this chapter is to analyze new technologies and make precise suggestions to the relevant organizations.

9.3   Evaluation of Autonomous Shipping

The term "autonomous shipping" describes the practice of using unmanned vessels and systems to transfer cargo from one location to another. Safety, efficiency, cost-effectiveness, regulatory compliance, and environmental impact are only some of the factors that must be taken into account when determining the viability and efficacy of autonomous shipping [34]. In autonomous shipping, safety comes first. Analyze the dependability of autonomous systems as well as their propensity to recognize dangers and take appropriate action in response. Think about things like emergency response procedures, redundancy in case of system breakdowns, and collision avoidance [35]. Optimal route planning, decreased fuel usage and reduced human error are just a few of the ways in which autonomous shipping could boost productivity. Find out how well autonomous systems can meet deadlines while maintaining high levels of speed and accuracy. Think about how it will affect the effectiveness of the supply chain as a whole and its resilience in the face of interruptions [36]. All autonomous vessels will need to adhere to local and international maritime legislation and determine whether or not autonomous systems can achieve compliance with these regulations and any other legal and liability concerns connected to autonomous operations. Figure 9.3 presents an overview of NA for an autonomous ship.

Determine how much damage autonomous shipping causes to the environment than conventional shipping does [37]. Think about things like how much gas you use, how much pollution you produce, and how much more efficient your vehicle could be. Check for environmental compliance and assess the overall sustainability benefits [38]. Find out how well-developed and trustworthy the technologies are that enable autonomous shipping. Think about things like sensor precision, network speed, data processing power, and safety precautions. Evaluate the scalability and widespread use of these technologies [39]. Examine the obstacles that must be overcome in order to make the transition to autonomous shipping. Think about the

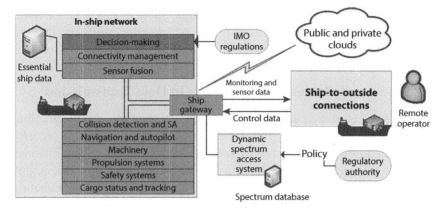

Figure 9.3 Overview of NA for an autonomous ship.

individuals who will be working in the sector, the resources that will be required to sustain the industry, and the significance of working together. Find out if it is realistic to employ fully autonomous ships [40]. Think about autonomous shipping's possibilities in the long run and how it might affect the shipping sector. Examine new developments, R&D initiatives, and technological improvements that might improve the capabilities of autonomous shipping.

9.3.1   Overview of Data Transmission

When two or more devices or systems exchange data back and forth, this is known as data transmission. Data transmission is the process of moving digital information from one location to another through a network. Wires (like Ethernet cables and fibre optics) and waves (like Wi-Fi, cellular networks, and satellite communication) can both be used to transmit data. Data transmission often involves encoding information as a series of binary digits (0s and 1s) before sending it as electrical impulses, light signals, or radio waves. Important players in the process include the source of the data, the channel through which it travels, and the final destination. Different modes of data transmission exist, including simplex, half-duplex, and full-duplex. No response or feedback is given or received during data transmission in simplex mode. Data can be sent in both directions in half-duplex mode, but only one direction at a time. Full-duplex mode allows for bidirectional data transmission [41, 42]. Error detection and repair procedures, data compression, encryption for security, and flow control to manage the rate of data transfer are only some of the techniques and protocols used to assure accurate and efficient data transmission. These safeguards improve transfer rates and reliability while minimising the likelihood of data loss during transmission.

9.3.2   Security Issues and Challenges in Data Transmission

To protect the privacy, authenticity, and accessibility of sent information, numerous security risks and obstacles must be overcome. These security issues can only be solved by taking a comprehensive approach that includes not only technical solutions but also user education and awareness, frequent security audits, and adherence to best practices in data transmission security. Secure data transfer relies heavily on user authentication and authorization. The term "challenges in data transmission" is used to describe the problems and issues that arise during the transfer of data [43]. Data transfer security, efficiency, and dependability are all threatened by these potential problems. Figure 9.4 presents the average cost of a data breach worldwide from 2014 to 2022.

In 2022, the average total cost of a data breach throughout the world reached a new high of $4.35 million, an increase of $0.11 million from 2017. There was a 2.6% rise in spending from $4.24 million in 2021 to $4.35 million in 2022.

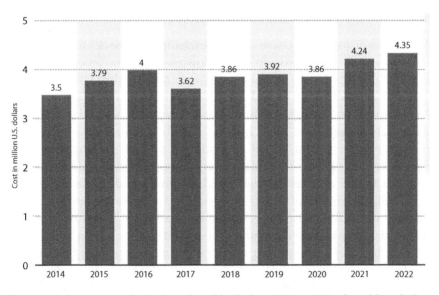

Figure 9.4 Average cost of a data breach worldwide from 2014 to 2022, adapted from [26].

9.4   Evaluation of the IoT in Autonomous Shipping

Assessing the efficacy, and overall impact of IoT technologies in the context of autonomous ships constitute the evaluation of IoT in autonomous shipping. The study's goal is to find out if and how the Internet of Things (IoT) solutions improve autonomous shipping in terms of security, dependability, and efficiency [44]. Examine the security, latency, and reach of the networks utilized by IoT devices on board self-driving ships. Evaluate how well you can connect to and keep in touch with land-based infrastructure, other vessels, and remote monitoring centres [45]. Analyze how well various sensors on autonomous ships work together and how effective they are. Navigational, environmental, collision avoidance, cargo monitoring, and other sensors fall under this category. Test the precision, dependability, and speed with which these sensors can gather data in real time [46]. Analyze how well Internet of Things platforms deal with the mountains of data produced by the sensors on an autonomous ship. Evaluate the safety and efficacy of data processing, storage, and transmission [47]. Determine how well IoT systems can facilitate autonomous decision-making on board ships. Assess how well algorithms and machine learning models process sensor data, spot anomalies, identify dangers, and trigger relevant actions like route corrections and system maintenance. Figure 9.5 shows

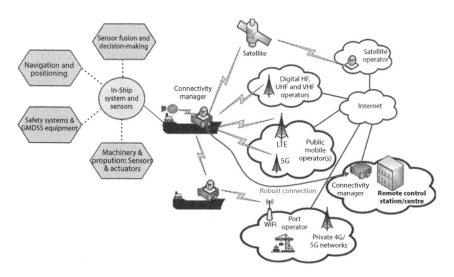

Figure 9.5 Connectivity manager for the integrated satellite-terrestrial system in a future maritime scenario.

the connectivity manager for the integrated satellite-terrestrial system in a future maritime scenario.

These features, along with the shipping gateway itself, are the subject of ongoing study and improvement. The proposed integrated satellite-terrestrial architecture can make use of numerous conventional 5G features, such as quality-of-service control, prioritization, and network slicing, to guarantee end-to-end service and a reliable connection, for instance, between the ship and the remote operator. However, due to the complexity involved in integrating so many networks, new logic and features must be developed to meet the needs of the shipping industry. Prioritizing safety/critical data during a crisis ensures that it will be supplied without delay, while less urgent data can be delayed. [48] Analyze the safety precautions taken to safeguard the Internet of Things infrastructure onboard autonomous ships. Analyze how susceptible the Internet of Things gadgets, networks, and databases are to cyberattacks. Analyze how well security measures like passwords, encryption, and access control are working [49]. Analyze the degree to which autonomous maritime IoT systems can communicate with one another. In order to guarantee the interoperability and seamless integration of numerous devices and systems onboard ships, it is important to evaluate the observance of industry standards and protocols [50]. Analyze how Internet of Things innovations affect the efficacy and effectiveness of autonomous shipping processes. Analyze the IoT systems to see if they lead to savings on gasoline, money spent on repairs, better route optimization, and more efficient operations.

9.5   Overview of Cybersecurity in Automation Ship

Cybersecurity plays a key role in autonomous shipping, where self-navigating vessels are used for transportation and logistics. Safe, secure, and secret operations for autonomous ships depend on various cyber factors that must be taken into account, as they do for any autonomous system. Various cyber dangers, such as illegal access, data breaches, malware, ransomware, and system manipulations, are a concern for autonomous shipping systems. These dangers can result in risks like operations disruption, cargo theft, vessel hijacking, and navigational interference. In order to function properly, autonomous ships require elaborate networks and means of communication. It is crucial to protect against cyber assaults and illegal access by securing these networks. Firewalls, intrusion detection systems, and encryption techniques that can withstand malicious attacks are essential for protecting the ship's data transmissions [51]. The navigation data, sensor readings, and operational information generated and exchanged by autonomous ships are enormous. To avoid tampering or theft, this information must be safely kept, transported, and processed. To keep private data safe, you need encryption, permissions, and safe data transport methods [52]. Security should be a primary consideration while developing the software and systems that power autonomous ships. Potential security holes must be patched and updated regularly through software updates and vulnerability assessments [53]. Only authorized users should be able to access sensitive data and systems in autonomous shipping systems, hence, strong authentication procedures are a must. This includes things like using strong passwords, multiple authentication factors, and role-based access controls.

In the marine industry, GPS and navigational systems are widely used, making them prime targets for cyberattacks that attempt to exploit design weaknesses and disrupt businesses that rely on them (55). The potential for bodily harm, in addition to breaches in data and service protocols, makes the danger posed by these assaults moderate to high. Several assaults [54] have been documented as trying to take advantage of this technology cluster, such as using fake GPS signals to redirect a ship without raising red flags with the system administrator. In a similar occurrence in South Korea, more than a thousand planes and seven hundred ships had their GPS signals disrupted for almost a week. Because of flaws in GPS and navigation system architecture and standards, these hacks might be considered moderately to highly complex. Several critical security holes and vulnerabilities exist in satellite communication systems (SATCOMs), such as those used to connect ships and the mainland over the internet.

9.6   Cybersecurity Challenges in Automation Ship

Several cybersecurity issues threaten the reliability and security of autonomous shipping and must be resolved. Connectivity is key for autonomous ships, which use satellites, wireless networks, and the IoT. These lines of communication may be weak spots that hackers can exploit. Autonomous shipping systems are vulnerable to malware and other forms of malicious software. Malware infection in the control systems or network infrastructure of an autonomous ship can cause malfunctions, a loss of command, or even the manipulation of ship functions. Ransomware attacks can potentially encrypt crucial ship systems and hold them for ransom. [56] There is always a chance that hackers or pirates will gain access to an autonomous ship. If an intruder gains physical access to a ship, they may try to alter the ship's systems, sensors, or navigational controls, putting everyone on board in peril. Physical tampering can cause serious problems, so it's important to include safeguards like access controls, surveillance systems, and tamper-evident technologies [57]. To prevent manipulation, autonomous ships must secure data such as navigation coordinates, sensor readings, and operational details. Data integrity and privacy must be protected to avoid tampering that could compromise important information or disrupt ship operations [58]. Cybersecurity threats to the supply chain can arise from autonomous shipping systems due to the number of suppliers and vendors involved. Attackers may be able to get access to your system through any number of holes in the security procedures of your third-party vendors. There is a risk of introducing vulnerabilities into the autonomous shipping system due to a tainted component or a software update from a supplier. [59] Since autonomous shipping is still a developing sector, there aren't yet widely accepted cybersecurity requirements. Implementing uniform security measures across various autonomous shipping platforms might be difficult in the absence of well-defined standards and best practices. Due to the absence of uniformity, systems may be more vulnerable to attacks. [60] Strong network security, encrypted communication protocols, regular vulnerability assessments, incident response plans, and cross-industry cooperation to standardize best practices are all necessary to combat today's sophisticated cyber threats. To keep ahead of the ever-changing dangers in the cybersecurity arena, continuous monitoring, threat information, and proactive security measures are essential.

9.7   Discussion

Severe cybersecurity events in the maritime sector have occurred in recent years. Increasing automation and artificial intelligence open new routes for cyberattacks. Spoofing technology for vessels is cheap, and obtaining and downloading online is getting simpler. It has also been reported that navigational errors have led to several ship crashes and maritime mishaps. A container ship carrying 8,250 TEU was attacked in its entirety in February 2017 while sailing from Cyprus to Djibouti. The commander could not restore navigational systems for nearly 10 hours while the assailant had control. Hackers blocked the global positioning system (GPS) signal, causing some signs to die and others to get erroneous data [61–63]. South Korea stated that more than 280 warships had suffered navigational system failures. If GPS technology fails, the ship's crew, passengers, and surrounding environment are all in danger. Only recently, malware has infiltrated the network that controls a U.S. Navy ship's systems. Electronic chart updates, cargo data management, and on-shore-to-ship communications are typical uses of this network. The maritime sector has been an appealing target for ransomware attacks in recent years. In 2020, the Hermes 2.1 ransomware affected two ships. Many administrative workstations were infected after opening a Word file with macros that had been sent via email [64–66]. Several Greek shipping firms fell victim to a ransomware assault in 2021 that propagated through the networks of an IT consulting firm. As a result of this intrusion, shipowners, ship management, and the shipping industry were exposed to the realities of IT supply chain risk. Two or three days later, one ship was kidnapped in the Gulf of Oman, and up to six others reported losing control. Cyberpiracy was the term used to describe these occurrences. Another cyber incident involved the infection of an ECDIS on a brand-new dry bulk ship, which prevented it from leaving port for many days. In this case, the cause and mode of infection are uncertain.

Several studies have suggested that blockchain technology might be used to enhance the control and security of autonomous boats. It is argued that blockchain technology's fundamental features—traceability, transparency, immutability, and decentralization—make it possible for ships and shore control centres to communicate and store data safely and reliably. Data loss, tampering with data by hostile actors, and data hijacking are all potential problems that may be avoided with this technology [67–70]. The receiver may identify such attempts to prevent the unauthorised generation or alteration of navigation data. Since a hacker wouldn't have access to the key needed to construct a fake authentication message, that would be impossible. The International Maritime Organisation (IMO) warned of the risks posed by a loss of ECDIS functionality and emphasised the need for backup systems. These backups should be used in addition to standard paper charts because they cannot replace ECDIS's features. To lessen the impact of an ECDIS failure, many respectable shipping firms opt to install a second ECDIS on board. Since ships generate so much data, it's usually best to use authentication and access control systems that are both fast and reliable.

Chapter's Contribution

Through the use of unmanned vessels, autonomous shipping has the potential to drastically change the maritime industry. Although autonomous shipping has a number of potential benefits, such as increased efficiency, lower costs, and more safety, it also has certain security issues and upcoming challenges. For autonomous ships, connectivity, data sharing, and digital systems are essential. Due to this reliance, cyber threats like hacking, data loss, and uninvited interference are more likely to occur. Protecting autonomous ships from cyberattacks is essential to ensuring their safe and secure operation. An autonomous ship is made up of many different systems, including navigation, propulsion, and cargo management. Any system can have vulnerabilities that hackers could use. To safeguard the ship's operations from dangers that could disrupt or jeopardize them, it is imperative to recognize and address these vulnerabilities. Self-navigating ships can receive a good image of their surroundings and make wise navigational decisions thanks to sensors like GPS, radar, and lidar. However, hostile actors have the ability to spoof (in the case of spoofing). Such an attack might jeopardize the ship's navigation system, which could lead to accidents and other mishaps. Autonomous shipping must first gain the public's trust in order to be broadly accepted. Concerns about cybersecurity, the loss of marine jobs, and the ships' capacity to handle the unexpected may hinder the public's adoption of autonomous ships. In order for autonomous shipping to be widely adopted, it is necessary to build public trust through transparent testing, regulatory oversight, and open communication. The marine industry, technology suppliers, regulatory bodies, and cybersecurity specialists will need to collaborate in order to successfully address current security risks as well as upcoming issues. Continuous research, development, and testing of autonomous shipping technology as well as the implementation of global norms and rules will be required to realize autonomous shipping's full potential while ensuring its security and safety. The evaluation of IoT (Internet of Things) technologies in the context of autonomous ships consists of determining their effectiveness and overall impact. The purpose of the project is to determine whether and how IoT solutions might increase the efficiency, dependability, and security of autonomous shipping. Review the networks' reach [71–74], security, and latency as IoT devices on autonomous ships use them. Analyze your ability to maintain contact with other vessels, distant monitoring stations, and land-based infrastructure. Analyze the efficiency and coordination of the numerous sensors on autonomous ships. This category includes sensors for navigation, the environment, collision avoidance, cargo monitoring, and other purposes. Check the accuracy, dependability, and speed of these sensors' abilities to collect data in realtime. Find out how successfully IoT systems can help ships make autonomous decisions. Analyze how well algorithms and machine learning models handle sensor data, detect abnormalities, recognize threats, and initiate appropriate actions like route adjustments and system upkeep.

Cybersecurity is crucial in autonomous shipping, as self-navigating ships are employed for logistics and transportation. As with any autonomous system, autonomous ship operations depend on various cyber aspects that must be considered. Autonomous shipping systems need to be aware of a number of cyber threats, including unauthorized access, data breaches, malware, ransomware, and system manipulation. These hazards can lead to threats including cargo theft, vessel hijacking, operations disruption, and navigational interference. Autonomous ships require complex networks and communication systems to operate effectively. It is essential to secure these networks in order to defend against cyberattacks and unauthorized access. Data transfers aboard the ship must be protected using firewalls, intrusion detection systems, and encryption methods that can survive malicious attacks. A huge amount of navigational data, sensor data, and operational data are produced and exchanged by autonomous ships. This information must be handled, stored, and moved properly to prevent theft or tampering [75, 76]. We require encryption, permissions, and secure data transit techniques to keep private data secure. When creating the software and systems that drive autonomous ships, security should come first. Regular software updates and vulnerability analyses are required to patch and update any potential security gaps. Strong authentication processes are necessary because only authorized individuals should be able to access sensitive data and systems in autonomous shipping systems. Role-based access controls, leveraging multiple authentication mechanisms, and using strong passwords, are all necessary.

9.8   Conclusion

Autonomous shipping is a developing technology with the potential to radically alter the shipping sector by introducing unmanned vessels. While autonomous shipping has several potential advantages, including higher efficiency, decreased costs, and enhanced safety, it also faces some security concerns and future obstacles. Connectivity, data sharing, and digital systems are crucial for autonomous ships. This reliance increases the likelihood of cyber threats like hacking, data loss, and unwanted interference. Autonomous ships' safe and secure functioning depends on their being shielded from cyber threats. Navigation, propulsion, and cargo management are just a few systems that make up an autonomous ship. Hackers can potentially exploit flaws in any system.

9.9   Future Work

Identifying and remedying these vulnerabilities is crucial to protect the ship's operations from threats that could interrupt or compromise them. Sensors like global positioning systems (GPS), radar, and lidar let autonomous ships get a clear picture of their surroundings and make sound navigational choices. However, the signals from these sensors can be intentionally disrupted. Autonomous ships produce and exchange a lot of navigational data, sensor data, and operational data. This information must be handled, stored, and moved properly to prevent theft or tampering. We require encryption, permissions, and secure data transit techniques to keep private data secure. When creating the software and systems that drive autonomous ships, security should come first. Regular software updates and vulnerability analyses are required to patch and update any potential security gaps. Strong authentication processes are necessary because only authorized individuals should be able to access sensitive data and systems in autonomous shipping systems. Also essential are role-based access controls, leveraging multiple authentication mechanisms, and using strong passwords.

References

[1] DiRenzo, J.; Goward, D.A.; Roberts, F.S. The little-known challenge of maritime cybersecurity. In *Proceedings of the 2015 6th International Conference on Information, Intelligence, Systems and Applications (IISA), Corfu, Greece, 6–8 July 2015*; pp. 1–5.

[2] Jensen, L. Challenges in maritime cyber-resilience. *Technol. Innov. Manag. Rev.* 2015, 5, 35. [CrossRef]

[3] Alcaide, J.I.; Llave, R.G. Critical infrastructures cybersecurity and the maritime sector. *Transp. Res. Procedia* 2020, 45, 547–554. [CrossRef]

[4] Fell, J. Mayflower tribute set to sail unmanned [automated marine transport]. *Eng. Technol.* 2015, 10, 42–44. [CrossRef]

[5] Demonstration Test of World's First Unmanned Operation of Small Tourism Boat Successfully Completed at Sarushima, Yokosuka. Nippon Foundation, January 11, 2022. Available online: https://www.nippon-foundation.or.jp/en/news/articles/2022/20220111-67000.html (accessed on 14 January 2022).

[6] Gu, Y.; Goez, J.C.; Guajardo, M.; Wallace, S.W. Autonomous vessels: State of the art and potential opportunities in logistics. *Int. Trans. Oper. Res.* 2021, 28, 1706–1739. [CrossRef]

[7] Gu, Y.; Wallace, S.W. Operational benefits of autonomous vessels in logistics—A case of autonomous water-taxis in Bergen. *Transp. Res. Part E Logist. Transp. Rev.* 2021, 154, 102456. [CrossRef]

[8] Werle, D.; Boudreau, P.R.; Brooks, M.R.; Butler, M.J.; Charles, A.; Coffen-Smout, S.; Griffiths, D.; McAllister, I.; McConnell, M.L.; Porter, I.; *et al.* The Future of Ocean Governance and Capacity Development. In *The Future of Ocean Governance and Capacity Development*; Brill Nijhoff: Leiden, The Netherlands, 2019; pp. 1–4.

[9] Shah, I. A., Sial, Q., Jhanjhi, N. Z., & Gaur, L. (2023). Use Cases for Digital Twin. In *Digital Twins and Healthcare: Trends, Techniques, and Challenges* (pp. 102–118). IGI Global.

[10] Tam, K.; Jones, K. Cyber-risk assessment for autonomous ships. In *Proceedings of the 2018 International Conference on Cybersecurity and Protection of Digital Services (Cybersecurity), Scotland, UK, 11–12 June 2018*; pp. 1–8.

[11] Höyhtyä, M., Huusko, J., Kiviranta, M., Solberg, K., & Rokka, J. (2017, October). Connectivity for autonomous ships: Architecture, use cases, and research challenges. In *2017 International Conference on Information and Communication Technology Convergence (ICTC)* (pp. 345–350). IEEE.

[12] Shah, I. A., Habeeb, R. A. A., Rajper, S., & Laraib, A. (2022). The Influence of Cybersecurity Attacks on E-Governance. In *Cybersecurity Measures for E-Government Frameworks* (pp. 77–95). IGI Global.

[13] Adeyemo, V. E., Abdullah, A., JhanJhi, N. Z., Supramaniam, M., & Balogun, A. O. (2019). Ensemble and deep-learning methods for two-class and multi-attack anomaly intrusion detection: an empirical study. *International Journal of Advanced Computer Science and Applications, 10*(9).

[14] Kok, S. H., Abdullah, A., & Jhanjhi, N. Z. (2022). Early detection of crypto-ransomware using pre-encryption detection algorithm. *Journal of King Saud University - Computer and Information Sciences, 34*(5), 1984–1999.

[15] Verma, S., Kaur, S., Rawat, D. B., Xi, C., Alex, L. T., & Jhanjhi, N. Z. (2021). Intelligent framework using IoT-based WSNs for wildfire detection. *IEEE Access, 9*, 48185–48196.

[16] Bhutani, A.; Gottel, B.; Van, N.T.P.; Mukhopadhyay, S.; Demir, V. *Advances in Radar Technology*; Scientific Research Publishing: Wuhan, China, 2021; p. 245.

[17] Kuzmichev, A.P.; Smirnov, V.G.; Zakhvatkina, N.Y.; Bychkova, I.A. Use of Satellite Communication Systems for Collecting and Transmitting Data on the State of the Arctic Sea Ice Cover. In *Proceedings of the 2021 IEEE International Geoscience and Remote Sensing Symposium IGARSS, Brussels, Belgium, 11–16 July 2021*; pp. 5732–5734.

[18] Shah, I. A., Jhanjhi, N. Z., Humayun, M., & Ghosh, U. (2022). Health Care Digital Revolution During COVID-19. In *How COVID-19 Is Accelerating the Digital Revolution* (pp. 17–30). Springer, Cham.

[19] Stouffer, K.; Falco, J.; Scarfone, K. *Guide to Industrial Control Systems (ICS) Security*. NIST Spec. Publ. 2011, 800, 16.

[20] Shah, I. A. (2022). Cybersecurity Issues and Challenges for E-Government During COVID-19: A Review. *Cybersecurity Measures for E-Government Frameworks*, 187–222.

[21] Kazak, N.; Frolova, S. Ship Automation and Control Systems. In *Proceedings of the IX All-Russian Science-Practical Conference of Students, Postgraduates and Young Scientists, Kerch, Crimea, 6 May 2020*; p. 46.

[22] Ujjan, R. M. A., Pervez, Z., Dahal, K., Bashir, A. K., Mumtaz, R., & González, J. (2020). Towards sFlow and adaptive polling sampling for deep learning based DDoS detection in SDN. *Future Generation Computer Systems, 111,* 763–779.

[23] Menhat, M.N.; Zaideen, I.M.M.; Yusuf, Y.; Salleh, N.H.M.; Zamri, M.A.; Jeevan, J. The impact of Covid-19 pandemic: A review on maritime sectors in Malaysia. *Ocean. Coast. Manag.* 2021, 105638. [CrossRef] [PubMed]

[24] Chang, C.; Wenming, S.; Wei, Z.; Changki, P.; Kontovas, C. Evaluating cybersecurity risks in the maritime industry: A literature review. In *Proceedings of the International Association of Maritime Universities (IAMU) Conference, Tokyo, Japan, 30 October–1 November 2019.*

[25] Shah, I. A., Wassan, S., & Usmani, M. H. (2022). E-Government Security and Privacy Issues: Challenges and Preventive Approaches. In *Cybersecurity Measures for E-Government Frameworks* (pp. 61–76). IGI Global.

[26] Ujjan, R. M. A., Taj, I., & Brohi, S. N. (2022). E-Government Cybersecurity Modeling in the Context of Software-Defined Networks. In *Cybersecurity Measures for E-Government Frameworks* (pp. 1–21). IGI Global.

[27] Kumar, T., Pandey, B., Mussavi, S. H. A., & Zaman, N. (2015). CTHS based energy efficient thermal aware image ALU design on FPGA. *Wireless Personal Communications, 85,* 671–696.

[28] Shafiq, M., Ashraf, H., Ullah, A., Masud, M., Azeem, M., Jhanjhi, N., & Humayun, M. (2021). Robust cluster-based routing protocol for IoT-assisted smart devices in WSN. *Computers, Materials & Continua, 67*(3), 3505–3521.

[29] Performance optimization of criminal network hidden link prediction model with deep reinforcement learning.

[30] Ujjan, R. M. A., Pervez, Z., & Dahal, K. (2018, June). Suspicious traffic detection in SDN with collaborative techniques of snort and deep neural networks. In *2018 IEEE 20th International Conference on High Performance Computing and Communications; IEEE 16th International Conference on Smart City; IEEE 4th International Conference on Data Science and Systems (HPCC/SmartCity/DSS)* (pp. 915–920). IEEE.

[31] Shah, I. A., Jhanjhi, N. Z., Humayun, M., & Ghosh, U. (2022). Health Care Digital Revolution During COVID-19. In *How COVID-19 Is Accelerating the Digital Revolution* (pp. 17–30). Springer, Cham.

[32] Almusaylim, Z. A., Zaman, N., & Jung, L. T. (2018, August). Proposing a data privacy aware protocol for roadside accident video reporting service using 5G in Vehicular Cloud Networks Environment. In *2018 4th International*

Conference on Computer and Information Sciences (ICCOINS) (pp. 1–5). IEEE.

[33] Singhal, V., Jain, S. S., Anand, D., Singh, A., Verma, S., Rodrigues, J. J., ... & Iwendi, C. (2020). Artificial intelligence enabled road vehicle-train collision risk assessment framework for unmanned railway level crossings. *IEEE Access, 8,* 113790–113806.

[34] Zaman, N. (Ed.). (2012). *Wireless Sensor Networks and Energy Efficiency: Protocols, Routing and Management: Protocols, Routing and Management.* IGI Global.

[35] Ujjan, R. M. A., Pervez, Z., Dahal, K., Bashir, A. K., Mumtaz, R., & González, J. (2020). Towards sFlow and adaptive polling sampling for deep learning based DDoS detection in SDN. *Future Generation Computer Systems, 111,* 763–779.

[36] Shah, I. A., Sial, Q., Jhanjhi, N. Z., & Gaur, L. (2023). The Role of the IoT and Digital Twin in the Healthcare Digitalization Process: IoT and Digital Twin in the Healthcare Digitalization Process. In *Digital Twins and Healthcare: Trends, Techniques, and Challenges* (pp. 20–34). IGI Global.

[37] Ujjan, R. M. A., Taj, I., & Brohi, S. N. (2022). E-Government Cybersecurity Modeling in the Context of Software-Defined Networks. In *Cybersecurity Measures for E-Government Frameworks* (pp. 1–21). IGI Global.

[38] Muzafar, S., Humayun, M., & Hussain, S. J. (2022). Emerging Cybersecurity Threats in the Eye of E-Governance in the Current Era. In *Cybersecurity Measures for E-Government Frameworks* (pp. 43–60). IGI Global.

[39] Dawson, M., & Walker, D. (2022). Argument for Improved Security in Local Governments within the Economic Community of West African States. *Cybersecurity Measures for E-Government Frameworks,* 96–106.

[40] Gaur, L., Ujjan, R. M. A., & Hussain, M. (2022). The Influence of Deep Learning in Detecting Cyber Attacks on E-Government Applications. In *Cybersecurity Measures for E-Government Frameworks* (pp. 107–122). IGI Global.

[41] Jhanjhi, N. Z., Ahmad, M., Khan, M. A., & Hussain, M. (2022). The Impact of Cyber Attacks on E-Governance During the COVID-19 Pandemic. In *Cybersecurity Measures for E-Government Frameworks* (pp. 123–140). IGI Global.

[42] Hussain, M., Talpur, M. S. H., & Humayun, M. (2022). The Consequences of Integrity Attacks on E-Governance: Privacy and Security Violation. In *Cybersecurity Measures for E-Government Frameworks* (pp. 141–156). IGI Global.

[43] Ujjan, R. M. A., Hussain, K., & Brohi, S. N. (2022). The Impact of Blockchain Technology on Advanced Security Measures for E-Government. In *Cybersecurity Measures for E-Government Frameworks* (pp. 157–174). IGI Global.

[44] John, R. GPS Flaw Could Let Terrorists Hijack Ships, Planes. *Fox News Tech,* July 26, 2013 Available online: http://www.foxnews.com/tech/2013/07/26/

exclusive-gps-flaw-could-let-terrorists-hijack-ships-planes.html (accessed on 31 January 2022).

[45] Meland, P.; Bernsmed, K.; Wille, E.; Rødseth, Ø.; Nesheim, D. A retrospective analysis of maritime cybersecurity incidents. *Int. J. Mar. Navig. Saf. Sea Transp.* 2021, 15, 4. [CrossRef]

[46] Analytica, O. Global maritime security risks rise with GNSS use. In *Emerald Expert Briefings; Oxford Analytica*: Oxford, UK, 2019; Volume 1.

[47] Coffed, J. The Threat of GPS Jamming: The Risk to an Information Utility; Report of EXELIS: Herndon, VA, USA, 2014; pp. 6–10.

[48] Schmidt, D.; Radke, K.; Camtepe, S.; Foo, E.; Ren, M. A survey and analysis of the GNSS spoofing threat and countermeasures. *ACM Comput. Surv.* 2016, 48, 1–31. [CrossRef]

[49] Chhajed, G. J., & Garg, B. R. (2022). Applying Decision Tree for Hiding Data in Binary Images for Secure and Secret Information Flow. In *Cybersecurity Measures for E-Government Frameworks* (pp. 175–186). IGI Global.

[50] Svilicic, B.; Kamahara, J.; Celic, J.; Bolmsten, J. Assessing ship cyber risks: A framework and case study of ECDIS security. *WMU J. Marit. Aff.* 2019, 18, 509–520. [CrossRef]

[51] Wu, Z.; Pan, Q.; Yue, M.; Ma, S. An Approach of Security Protection for VSAT Network. In *Proceedings of the 2018 17th IEEE International Conference on Trust, Security and Privacy in Computing and Communications/12th IEEE International Conference on Big Data Science and Engineering (TrustCom/ BigDataSE), New York, NY, USA, 1–3 August 2018*; pp. 1511–1516.

[52] Santamarta, R. Maritime Security: Hacking into a Voyage Data Recorder (VDR). *IOActive*, December 9, 2015. Available online: https://ioactive.com/ maritime-security-hacking-into-a-voyage-data-recorder-vdr/ (accessed on 10 January 2022).

[53] Pavur, J.; Moser, D.; Strohmeier, M.; Lenders, V.; Martinovic, I. A tale of sea and sky on the security of maritime VSAT communications. In *Proceedings of the 2020 IEEE Symposium on Security and Privacy (SP), San Francisco, CA, USA, 18–21 May 2020*.

[54] Tam, K.; Jones, K. MaCRA: A model-based framework for maritime cyber-risk assessment. *WMU J. Marit. Aff.* 2019, 18, 129–163. [CrossRef]

[55] Heffner, C. Exploiting Surveillance Cameras Like a Hollywood Hacker. *PrivacyPC*. Available online: https://privacy-pc.com/articles/exploiting-network-surveillance-cameras-like-a-hollywood-hacker.html (accessed on 10 January 2021).

[56] Bugeja, J.; Jonsson, D.; Jacobsson, A. An investigation of vulnerabilities in smart connected cameras. In *Proceedings of the 2018 IEEE International Conference on Pervasive Computing and Communications Workshops (PerCom Workshops), Athens, Greece, 19–23 March 2018*; pp. 537–542.

[57] Shoultz, D. Securely Connected Vessels: Vessel Communications and Maritime Cybersecurity. Technical Report. 2017. Available online: https:// www.maritimeprofessional.com/blogs/post/securely-connected-vessels-vessel-communicationsand-maritime15176 (accessed on 9 July 2021).

[58] Caprolu, M.; Di Pietro, R.; Raponi, S.; Sciancalepore, S.; Tedeschi, P. Vessels cybersecurity: Issues, challenges, and the road ahead. *IEEE Commun. Mag.* 2020, 58, 90–96. [CrossRef]

[59] Al-Mhiqani, M.N.; Ahmad, R.; Yassin, W.; Hassan, A.; Abidin, Z.Z.; Ali, N.S.; Abdulkareem, K.H. Cyber-security incidents: A review cases in cyber-physical systems. *Int. J. Adv. Comput. Sci. Appl.* 2018, 1, 499–508.

[60] Jones, M. Spoofing in the Black Sea: What Really Happened? *GPS World,* October 11, 2017. Available online: https://www.gpsworld.com/spoofing-in-the-black-sea-what-really-happened/ (accessed on 31 January 2022).

[61] Borger, J. Pentagon Orders Temporary Halt to US Navy Operations after Second Collision. *Guardian,* August 21, 2017. Available online: https://www.theguardian.com/us-news/2017/aug/21/us-destroyer-uss-john-s-mccain-damaged-after-collision-with-oil-tanker (accessed on 31 January 2022).

[62] Cohen, Z. US Navy Ship Collides with South Korean Fishing Boat. CNN, May 10, 2017. Available online: https://edition.cnn.com/2017/05/09/politics/fishing-vessel-hits-us-navy-ship-south-korea/index.html (accessed on 31 January 2022).

[63] Roberts, F.S.; Egan, D.; Nelson, C.; Whytlaw, R. Combined cyber and physical attacks on the maritime transportation system. *NMIOTC Marit. Interdiction Oper. J.* 2019, 18, 22.

[64] Oruc, A.; MIMarEST, M.S.M. Claims of State-Sponsored Cyberattack in the Maritime Industry. In *Proceedings of the 15th International Naval Engineering Conference & Exhibition, Delft, The Netherlands, 6–8 October 2020.*

[65] Winder, D. U.S. Coast Guard Issues Alert after Ship Heading into Port of New York Hit by Cyberattack. *Forbes,* July 9, 2019. Available online: https://www.forbes.com/sites/daveywinder/2019/07/09/u-s-coast-guard-issues-alert-after-ship-heading-into-port-of-new-york-hit-by-cyberattack/?-sh=61b920e741aa (accessed on 31 January 2022).

[66] Cooper, H. Chinese Hackers Steal Unclassified Data from Navy Contractor. *New York Times,* June 8, 2018. Available online: https://www.nytimes.com/2018/06/08/us/politics/china-hack-navy-contractor-.html (accessed on 31 January 2022).

[67] Cyberattack Hits Multiple Greek Shipping Firms. *Maritime Executive,* November 3, 2021. Available online: https://www.maritime-executive.com/article/cyberattack-hits-multiple-greek-shipping-firms (accessed on 3 February 2022).

[68] Bebbington, T. Cyberattack or Coincidence? *SeatradeMaritime,* August 6, 2021. Available online: https://www.seatrade-maritime.com/opinions-analysis/cyberattack-or-coincidence (accessed on 3 February 2022).

[69] The Guidelines on Cybersecurity Onboard Ships. International Chamber of Shipping, 2021. Available online: https://www.ics-shipping.org/wp-content/uploads/2021/02/2021-Cyber-Security-Guidelines.pdf (accessed on 3 February 2022).

[70] Nicaise, V. Cybermarétique: A Short History of Cyberattacks against Ports. *StormShield*, October 15, 2021. Available online: https://www.stormshield.com/news/cybermaretique-a-short-history-of-cyberattacks-against-ports/ (accessed on 3 February 2022).

[71] Team, E. Maersk Line: Surviving from a Cyber Attack. Available online: https://safety4sea.com/cm-maersk-line-survivingfrom-a-cyberattack/ (accessed on 3 February 2022).

[72] Rosehana Amin, R.D.; Jones, D. Part 1: A Very Modern Form of Piracy: Cybercrime against the Shipping Industry—Rapidly Developing Risks. Available online: https://www.lexology.com/library/detail.aspx?g=b4d-c3b52-40b5-4700-afee-a95d09b7b6d3 (accessed on 3 February 2022).

[73] Elliott, L. Port of Houston Target of Suspected Nation-State Hack. *NBC News*, September 24, 2021. Available online: https://www.nbcnews.com/tech/security/port-houston-target-suspected-nation-state-hack-rcna2249 (accessed on 3 February 2022).

[74] Silverajan, B.; Ocak, M.; Nagel, B. Cybersecurity attacks and defences for unmanned smart ships. In *Proceedings of the 2018 IEEE International Conference on Internet of Things (iThings) and IEEE Green Computing and Communications (GreenCom) and IEEE Cyber, Physical and Social Computing (CPSCom) and IEEE Smart Data (SmartData), Halifax, NS, Canada, 30 July–3 August 2018*; pp. 15–20.

[75] Bothur, D.; Zheng, G.; Valli, C. A critical analysis of security vulnerabilities and countermeasures in a smart ship system. In *Proceedings of the 15th Australian Information Security Management Conference, Perth, Australia, 5–6 December 2017*.

[76] Zhou, X.; Liu, Z.; Wu, Z.; Wang, F. Quantitative processing of situation awareness for autonomous ships navigation. *Int. J. Mar. Navig. Saf. Sea Transp.* 2019, 13, 25–31. [CrossRef]

10

IoT-Based Smart Transportation Industry: Security Challenges

Imdad Ali Shah

School of Computing Science, Taylor's University, Kuala Lumpur,
Selangor, Malaysia

Abstract

The IoT-based smart transport sector has completely altered our understanding of transportation networks. The Internet of Things (IoT) allows us to connect users, infrastructure, and vehicles to manage traffic more effectively while also enhancing safety and minimising environmental impact. For the smart transportation ecosystem to maintain its integrity, confidentiality, and availability, a number of security issues must be resolved along with these advantages. Intelligent transportation systems depend on IoT devices, including sensors, actuators, and communication modules. These devices are susceptible to a range of assaults, including physical theft, tampering, and unauthorised access. To avoid disturbances in the system, it is essential to ensure the security of these devices. Smart transportation systems generate a lot of data from various sources, such as user devices, infrastructure, and vehicles. Sensitive data, including location information, unique identifiers for individuals, and payment information, is frequently included in this data. This data must be shielded against unauthorised access, interception, and manipulation to ensure user privacy and stop misuse. IoT devices in smart transportation systems communicate information and commands using wireless communication protocols. In order to avoid eavesdropping, man-in-the-middle attacks, and unauthorised access to the system, it is essential to secure these communication routes. These dangers can be reduced by putting strong encryption, authentication, and access control measures in place. Integration of numerous components, including cars, traffic control systems, infrastructure sensors, and backend servers, is required for smart transportation systems. Due to the ecosystem's complexity, it is difficult to guarantee the security of these linked systems. Strong security measures must be put in place throughout the infrastructure because flaws in one part

Email: shahsyedimdadali@gmail.com

Imdad Ali Shah and Noor Zaman Jhanjhi (eds.) Cybersecurity in the Transportation Industry,
(211–240) © 2024 Scrivener Publishing LLC

could potentially affect the entire system. The purchase and integration of multiple hardware and software components from various vendors is a requirement for smart transportation systems. To avoid the inclusion of harmful or hacked components that could jeopardise the entire system, it is essential to ensure the supply chain's security. This problem can be solved by doing extensive security assessments and putting supply chain risk management procedures in place. The primary object of this chapter is to peer-review on smart transportation industry, security issues and challenges. Our recommendation helps new researchers and transportation industries.

Keywords: IoT-based smart transportation, supply chain, security issues and challenges and logistics industry

10.1   Introduction

The Internet of Things (IoT) has changed a number of industries, including smart transport. IoT-based smart transportation systems make use of infrastructure, sensors, and connected devices to boost efficiency, promote sustainable mobility, and improve traffic management. To maintain the integrity and safety of these systems, there are important security concerns that must be resolved, just like with any technology that depends on connectivity and data sharing. The security issues that the IoT-based smart transport sector must deal with are examined in this chapter. It explores potential threats and weaknesses related to supply chain security, privacy issues, software and firmware security, device security, data security, communication security, system integration, remote access, and system security [1]. To establish successful strategies and countermeasures, stakeholders—including transportation authorities, system integrators, and cybersecurity experts—need to have a thorough understanding of these issues. The IoT-based smart transportation sector can put in place the necessary safeguards and create a robust ecosystem by having a thorough understanding of security issues. This will inspire user trust, improve operational efficiency, and pave the way for a future of connected and intelligent transportation. Figure 10.1 shows an overview of V2x Communication Multi-Technology Dissemination Robustness Enhancement.

For boosting national and corporate competitiveness, logistics is essential in fostering economic development. High prices and inefficiency continue to be problems in the logistics business today. With the advent of intelligent logistics, there will be new ways to address these issues [2, 3]. The Internet of Things has the potential to generate massive amounts of data, allowing researchers to delve into the intricate webs of connections

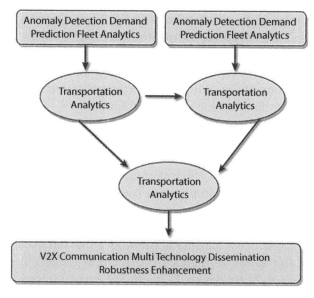

Figure 10.1 Overview of V2x communication multi-technology dissemination robustness enhancement.

between the transactions reflected in these numbers using a variety of statistical and computational methods. These characteristics aid in pushing forward the growth of intelligent supply chain management. We give a systematic research review using IoT technology for smart logistics. Figure 10.2 shows an overview of IoT in transportation.

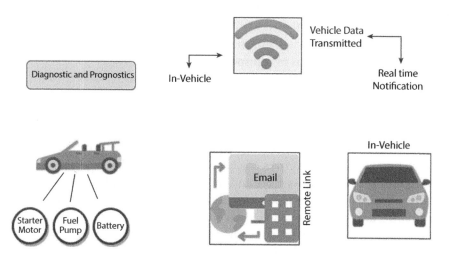

Figure 10.2 Overview of IoT in transportation.

Logistics is a significant contributor to GDP growth and a critical factor in national and corporate competitiveness. Logistics costs have come down in recent years, but they remain expensive because of the difficulty in managing supply chains and the price of labour [4, 5]. The United States, for instance, is one of the most logistics-efficient countries in the world, spending $1.64 trillion on logistics in 2018, up 12.4% from the previous year and equivalent to roughly 9% of the United States' $20.5 trillion GDP, as reported in the Council of Supply Chain Management Professionals' 30th annual State of Logistics Report. Logistics expenses can be as high as 26% of GDP in the least efficient countries. When logistics costs are high, it can have a negative impact on a country's ability to compete globally in the manufacturing sector. Consequently, in academia and industry, there is a pressing need to increase logistics efficiency while decreasing logistics costs. Intelligent logistics is a new idea that has been introduced recently. The foundation of smart logistics is cutting-edge information and communication technologies (ICT) [6–9]. The current integrated logistics system can become a reality by collecting and analysing data from all logistics in real time. Time and money can be saved using intelligent logistics, which can increase visibility from beginning to finish, enhance logistical processes like shipping and receiving, sorting and storing, and provide information services, among other things. It may help lessen the impact of logistics on the environment. Still, there are a lot of obstacles to overcome before smart logistics can become a reality.

The chapter focuses on the following points:

- Peer-reviewed on the IoT-based transportation industry
- IoT transportation systems
- IoT security issues and challenges
- IoT applications in transportation systems.

10.2   Literature Review

The Internet of Things (IoT) is experiencing explosive growth in transportation because it improves efficiency, cuts costs, enhances security and increases accessibility. As more and more cities and municipalities worldwide adopt wireless technology for use in traffic management, emergency response, and pedestrian and bicycle safety, it is expected that the Internet of Things will have far-reaching consequences. The automobile industry, including EV charging stations and connected car technologies, will also see significant improvements thanks to the IoT and public transportation systems [10–13]. The IoT is being used increasingly in transportation systems, helping to make cities more efficient and easier to run in terms of fixed and mobile infrastructure. Cellular networks' stability now approaches traditional wired networks, creating new possibilities possible in stationary applications like traffic lights, cameras, and intersection management. Some studies have been conducted on the role of the IoT in intelligent logistics in the recent past [14–16]. Most of them concentrate on IoT infrastructure and various IoT-based innovative logistics applications. Only a few of these studies focus on wireless communication technology, intelligent logistics development, and related difficulties. Current surveys have yet to report the state and problems of IoT technology in intelligent logistics, looking at the significant IoT technologies supporting automated logistics processes. They launch RFID- and WSN-enabled smart products [17–19]. Then, they zero in on how the Internet of Things might help with design and runtime modifications that account for the inevitable and unpredictable shifts in business operations. Figure 10.3 shows a taxonomy of literature review.

We analyse many key IoT technologies and their evolution and deployment in smart logistics using a patent roadmap visualisation technique.

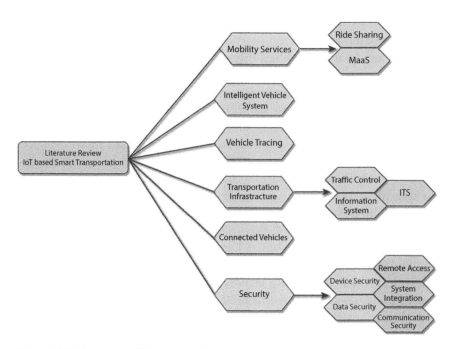

Figure 10.3 Taxonomy of literature review.

The authors provide only superficial answers to the question of where the subject should go from here, and they fail to address any of the critical challenges that have plagued it thus far [20–23]. Another study introduces the use of IoT in the relevant industries and analyses the effect of IoT on logistics information in the LSSC [24–26] to create the IoT-based architecture of the LSSC and forecast the potential of its use. This survey examines the effects of the IoT on logistics data, including logistics and service flow, information flow, and financial flow. Still, it does not focus on the usage of IoT in other domains of smart logistics or the challenges that come with it. It evaluated cloud computing and the IoT's salient properties and proposed cloud- and IoT-based solutions for implementing real-world logistics data exchange. Because of their exclusive focus on IoT analysis and implementation, the authors have ignored the potential of other technologies like RFID, WSN, and AI to enhance smart logistics (artificial intelligence). They showed the necessity for five IoT technologies to be implemented before IoT-based products and services can be successfully rolled out to the market [27–30]. We also take a look at the technological and administrative challenges. While a more comprehensive introduction to IoT-related technologies and a discussion of IoT's problems are provided, wireless communication technologies and IoT's logistics applications are only briefly discussed. One study discusses the first application of IoT-based smart logistics and its benefits and limitations [31–35]. When designing Internet-of-Things-based solutions for smart logistics, we consider them all. Instead of just being a standard survey, this study aims to serve as a road map for applications, issues, and the future of IoT technologies in smart logistics.

In comparison to similar surveys, ours is more intuitive and straightforward [36–38]. Having experience with smart logistics is a rapidly developing area of study that will significantly impact the logistics industry in the coming years. Here, we briefly introduce the ideas behind smart logistics, covering their definition, history, key applications, and prospective solutions [39–41]. The term "smart logistics" has been coined, but there is still no agreement on what it means in the academic community. The original concept behind "smart products" and "smart services" was that consumers might delegate some control responsibilities to the products and services. According to Uckelmann, "smart logistics" is the distribution of "smart" goods and services using information technology. Based on these characteristics, which Uckelmann elaborates upon, the term "smart logistics" is used to designate Uckelmann's preferred logistics management method. The phrase "smart logistics" describes a logistics system that helps firms adjust more quickly to market changes and meet their customers' needs and preferences. Logistics is defined as the management of an organization's

supply chain or an external supply chain's movement of materials and information from origin to destination. To represent the growing significance
of technological innovation to logistical performance, the idea of "smart
logistics" develops throughout time [42–44]. Smart logistics is a term used
in the logistics field to refer to activities that are better planned, controlled,
or regulated than conventional approaches. Though academics can't agree
on a common definition of "smart logistics," they agree on a few central
tenets: the concept integrates and optimises the logistics system through
thorough analysis, timely processing, and self-adjustment, and it makes
use of cutting-edge information and communication technologies. Figure
10.4 shows the IoT security challenges.

Industrial safety management is one of the most visible and essential
positions in the business world. It stands to gain even more prominence
and importance from the technological improvements and benefits that the
IoT provides. Therefore, the IoT paradigm's promise of a unified information gathering and management system that is both intelligent and timely is
appealing for critical industrial areas like safety management. For instance,
the worker death rate is consistently high due to the inherent dangers of

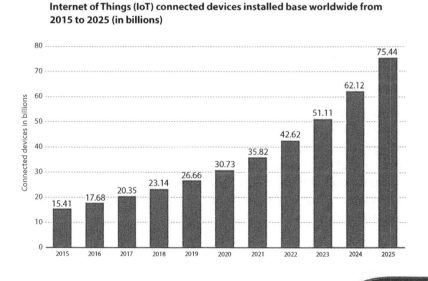

Figure 10.4 The IoT security challenges [24].

working in deep mines and high-voltage switchgear installations [45, 46]. Even a minor deviation from established Standard Operating Procedures (SOPs) might have catastrophic results in life-or-death fields. As we've already established, the Industrial Internet of Things (IIoT) facilitates coordination between IT and OT while increasing the degree to which industrial operations are automated. Furthermore, such systems improve event traceability by storing sensed data from machines and other intelligent devices on centralised servers, which record employees' access to machines and their operational status over time [47]. Information useful for condition monitoring and predictive maintenance can be gleaned from such logs and data collected from industrial machinery over time. Accidents caused by broken or badly maintained machinery and equipment can be avoided if businesses have timely access to accurate information on the condition of their machines. In addition, robots have played an increasingly important role in factory automation in recent years. However, because of the development of Internet of Things–based technologies and Industry 4.0, robots have recently seen a considerable uptick. In various sectors, these alterations may improve worker safety by taking people out of potentially dangerous situations.

10.3   Evaluation of IoT in the Transportation System

With the convergence of movement, robotics, and data analytics as the driving forces of change in technology and business, the IoT has the potential to alter the data and information gathered by transportation systems radically. The term IoT is used to describe the interconnection of electronic devices that allow for the monitoring and control of mechanical ones, as well as the incorporation of embedded sensors, actuators, and other devices that can report on network activity in real time. Incorporating IoT technology into the transportation industry has the potential to improve efficiency and effectiveness. The IoT is at the centre of forces revolutionising transportation to make it safer, more efficient, easier to maintain, and better at managing traffic. An overview of IoT in the transportation system is shown in Figure 10.5.

- More efficient
  Reduced-price public transportation expands capacity using sensors, cameras, and communication networks and improves traveller security and convenience while decreasing expenses and dangers.

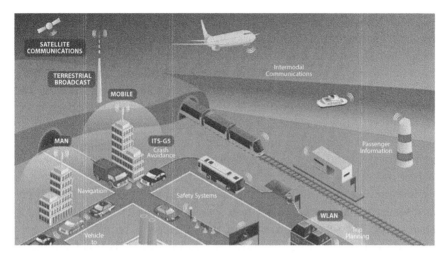

Figure 10.5 Overview of IoT in the transportation system [48].

- Dynamic roadside message signs
  These signs are used for high-tech transit networks that automatically update information like road conditions, tolls, traffic jams, and trip times based on data collected by sensors and cameras.
- Autonomous vehicles
  AVs have advanced sensing and prediction capabilities, the capacity to exchange information with other cars and their surroundings, and the speed and agility to respond in real time to various situations that may arise on the road.
- Video surveillance solutions
  They use high-definition CCTV cameras to keep airports and train stations safe, like keeping an eye on passport control and crowd movement around the clock. The early identification of suspicious behaviour and lost luggage can be automated by using intelligent video analysis software.

10.4   IoT Security Issues and Challenges

Users reaped many benefits from the IoT, but it also presented specific difficulties. Cybersecurity and privacy threats are of particular concern to researchers and security experts. Combining the two creates a severe problem for many private and public entities. IoT technology is vulnerable, as has been shown by recent high-profile cyberattacks. This is a problem since the interconnectedness of networks in the Internet of Things also means accessibility from the anonymous and untrusted internet, which necessitates new forms of security [49–53]. Known difficulties, such as protecting users' personal information, significantly impact developing solutions for the Internet of Things. Unfortunately, however, users frequently need more recognition of the security repercussions after a breach has happened, at which point it is sometimes too late to prevent severe consequences, such as the loss of vital data. As users' privacy continues to be breached by recurring security breaches, customers' tolerance for shaky protection is dwindling. Recent research on consumer-grade Internet of Things privacy and security found it wanting. There were many weak spots in today's car electronics. The security problem in the IT sector is familiar, but adopting the Internet of Things has posed new difficulties. As this technology continues to become more passive and integrated into our everyday lives, consumers must believe that Internet of Things devices and their services are secure from flaws. Data streams left unprotected by poorly secured Internet of Things devices and services present a significant entry point for cybercriminals and put customers' personal information at risk. Figure 10.6 presents an overview of security challenges.

Because of how interconnected IoT devices are, a single improperly secured or linked item might compromise the safety and stability of the internet on a global scale. The problem of using so many similar devices in the IoT is the direct cause of this behavior. The capacity of some devices to mechanically bond with others means that users and developers of IoT have a responsibility to ensure that neither they nor the internet is vulnerable to attack. To overcome these obstacles, the IoT has adopted a collaborative strategy [54–57]. For instance, the IoT is susceptible to a wide range of authentication-related threats, which continue to be a major problem when providing security for many applications. In the case of authentication, its protection against threats like denial-of-service (DoS) or replay assaults is spotty at best. Owing to the popularity of unsafe applications due to their natural diversity of data gathering in the IoT environment, information security has emerged as one of the most significant vulnerable areas in the authentication of IoT. Consider the case of contactless credit cards as an illustration. Without the authentication of IoT, these cards can read card numbers and names, allowing hackers to use the cardholder's bank account information and identity to make purchases. Man-in-the-middle attacks are commonplace in the IoT, in which a third party takes over a communication channel to pretend to be one of the devices in a network transaction to steal sensitive information. Since the attacker in a

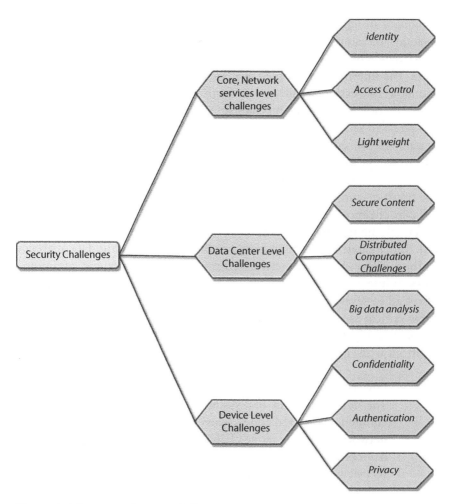

Figure 10.6 Overview of security challenges.

man-in-the-middle attack doesn't need to know the victim's true identity, he or she can successfully fool the bank server into thinking the transaction is legitimate [58–60]. The degree to which the Internet of Things can honour people's need for privacy will determine how optimistically we view its potential benefits. The IoT could be held back from reaching its full potential by worries about privacy and the possible dangers that come along with it. Knowing that the user's privacy rights would be respected is crucial to the user's trust in the Internet of Things, the connected device, and the linked services. A lot of effort is being put into ensuring that privacy concerns, such as the proliferation of surveillance and tracking, are rethought in light of the Internet of Things. Reasons for privacy worries include data sampling and distribution in the IoT can be carried out practically anywhere thanks to the pervasiveness of intelligence-integrated artefacts. The internet's widespread availability is also crucial to comprehend the issue. Accessing sensitive data from anywhere globally will become notably easier if no unique mechanism is implemented to prevent this.

Increased security threats and difficulties in managing massive amounts of data are two side effects of the Internet of Things. Transportation agencies must update their network architectures to include more intelligence, automation, and security measures to solve these problems. Companies in the transportation industry want a network infrastructure that is scalable, reliable, cheap, and can handle a lot of data traffic safely. To reach its full potential, the Internet of Things draws on various tools and services [61–64]. This includes everything from hardware in the field to data analytics to the wired and wireless networks through which equipment communicates. While these parts make the Internet of Things so effective, they can also lead to severe problems if none fails to function correctly. One of the most critical aspects of managing a successful IoT project is ensuring all parts are compatible and functioning properly. Challenges that businesses confront while introducing IoT systems include the following:

- Power Management
  The devices that an IoT system uses are one of its major components. Wired and wireless IoT devices can be used in networks in a wide range of configurations. Although wired devices are simple, they can only connect to the network and receive power through a hardline. Devices that run on batteries and are wireless offer much greater flexibility. Sadly, they also have their own difficulties, such as power needs and network access.
- Connectivity Solutions
  The networked gadgets that can transmit and receive information comprise the backbone of an IoT system. With this link, the system is sound. Any deployment will need help to maintain a strong connection with IoT devices.
- Identifying a location to develop and integrate software
  Notwithstanding their versatility, there is no one-size-fits-all answer regarding the Internet of Things management solutions. That's why most businesses need the help of developers and integrators to craft a system that's tailor-made for their specific requirements. Searching in an industry saturated

with so-called "experts" can be challenging to zero in on a reputable and competent provider.
- Obtaining IoT devices
The availability and accessibility of IoT devices present another challenge for businesses. As critical components of the whole, the gadgets must be of the highest quality and ideally suited to the task. It can be challenging to determine which systems are compatible and can communicate with one another when there are so many options and firms to select from.
- Success Factors for Deploying an IoT Infrastructure
While designing and implementing an IoT system can be highly challenging, companies worldwide have recognised it as a powerful resource that, if executed properly, can yield excellent returns on investment. Installing an efficient IoT system can be challenging without a dependable partner to offer guidance and assistance throughout the project.

With the proliferation of sensors and linked devices, the attack surface of a network grows exponentially as IoT gains traction in the transportation sector. Many IoT devices are produced without security in mind or designed by organisations that need to comprehend current security needs, making the IoT particularly vulnerable. As a result, Internet of Things technologies is rapidly becoming the transportation sector's most vulnerable point.

10.5   Evaluation of IoT Application in Transportation

In recent years, there has been a rise in the transportation sector's use of the Internet of Things. Allied Market Research reported that an estimated $328 billion will be spent on the IoT in transportation by 2023. Ticketing, security, surveillance, and telematics systems are examples of how IoT devices are used in the transportation sector to provide safe and effective public transit in urban areas. IoT in the transportation industry is a vast system of interconnected sensors, actuators, smart objects, and other computing infrastructure. Data from the real world is gathered and sent across the network to be processed by specialised software. With the help of Internet of Things–enabled technology and intelligent solutions, the transportation sector's operations have been revolutionised [65–68]. Also, as the number of cars on the road continues to rise, metropolitan transportation

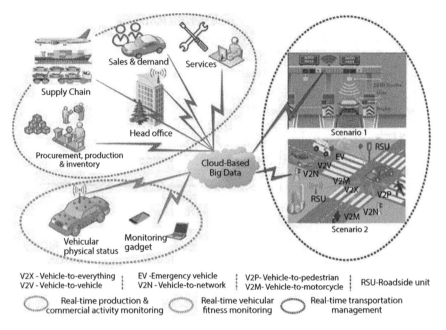

Figure 10.7 Shows the evaluation of IoT applications in transportation [69].

systems are getting increasingly intricate. Cities need to adopt IoT-based transportation systems if their residents are to reap the full range of safety and efficiency gains available through these systems. Figure 10.7 shows the evaluation of IoT applications in transportation.

- Efficient Traffic Management
  Most Internet of Things deployments have been spotted in traffic management, the most significant subset of the transportation industry. Traffic and vehicle-related data in the millions and billions of gigabytes per day are being created by CCTV cameras. This information is sent to traffic management centres so that drivers can be monitored more closely and those who break the law can be fined. Several IoT applications have been developed to better manage traffic and reduce the likelihood of accidents, including smart parking, an automatic traffic signal system, and intelligent accident aid.
- Automated Toll and Ticketing
  The conventional methods of collecting tolls and issuing tickets are becoming antiquated and failing to ease

traffic congestion. Toll booths on major thoroughfares have become overrun due to the surge in traffic, forcing drivers to wait in line for extended periods. Due to a lack of personnel and equipment, the toll booths cannot instantly handle many drivers. With the Internet of Things applied to transportation, automated tolls can be enacted in place of the more labour-intensive and time-consuming manual systems.

The most advanced cars on the market today all come complete with IoT connectivity. Every car, even one kilometre from the toll station, can be clearly seen thanks to IoT devices. As a result, the barriers might be lowered to let cars through. Older vehicles lack Internet of Things connectivity, but owners can still accept automatic payments through the vehicle's digital wallet by using their cell phones. This demonstrates how easily older vehicles may be connected to the Internet of Things to enable automated toll and ticketing.

- Transportation Monitoring

  Important transportation company assets can be tracked in real time. In addition to following a vehicle's whereabouts, IoT gadgets may keep tabs on its driver's habits and provide feedback on things like speed and idle time. The Internet of Things has reduced fleet management system running, fuel, and maintenance costs. When it comes to keeping tabs on the transportation system, it's safe to say that real-time tracking has made it much simpler to put good judgement into practice by letting drivers know immediately if there are any problems with their vehicle and giving them time to take preventative measures.

- Enhanced Security of Public Transport

  Public transportation safety is one of the most promising applications of the Internet of Things in this sector. Cities may monitor traffic offences and enforce laws by using IoT devices to maintain tabs on all modes of transportation. As a bonus to public transit management, IoT can enhance safety measures. Some examples are automated fare collection and integrated tickets, passenger information systems, and vehicle fare collection for vehicles. These tools improve the efficiency of managing public transportation and traffic congestion. Thanks to the Internet of Things, public transportation may now be managed in real time. Since then, transportation companies have been able to better connect with their customers and meet their information needs by implementing passenger information displays and mobile apps. Undoubtedly, the Internet of Things has improved the safety and effectiveness of public transportation.

10.6   Discussion

The manufacturing, transportation, and utilities sectors, which rely heavily on physical assets, have the highest Internet of Things adoption rates. Whether fixed or mobile, these assets are increasingly becoming integrated into a networked environment where they may exchange and learn from critical data. Moving assets like trucks and ships are making an indelible mark on the logistics and transportation sectors by becoming integral nodes in the Internet of Things network [70–74]. Before the term "Internet of Things" was invented, the manufacturing and transportation sectors were among the first to embed connected technologies. These industries were quick to adopt new technologies, and their success has paved the way for other sectors to improve their supply chain management and other end-to-end operations.

Improved telemetry capabilities and monitoring solutions made possible by the Internet of Things have revolutionised the logistics sector. Its connected market around the world is expanding rapidly, too. At a value of $10.04 billion in 2016, the market is projected to grow to $41.30 billion by the end of 2021. More than 32% every year is an impressive pace of expansion. The Internet of Things is a boon for the logistics industry. A logistics firm could adjust its approach and produce better results by adopting it. First, we'll examine the four cornerstones of a typical logistics firm before we go into the Internet of Things applications in this sector.

- Communications Systems
  This method allowed logistics managers and truck drivers to be in regular contact. Using mobile phones helped improve communication between the two parties and facilitate the exchange of data that could impact the timely shipment of the goods.
- Vehicle Tracking
  Vehicle tracking solutions often keep tabs on where the trucks are until they reach their final destination. With GPS

monitoring devices, logistics companies can monitor their trucks and calculate an accurate delivery window.

- Supply Chain Monitoring System
  Supply chain monitoring systems aid the logistics sector. Equally true is the inverse of this statement. Logistics firms oversee the whole supply chain, from procuring inputs to disseminating final goods.
- IT Security
  IBM reports that cyberattacks on the transportation industry are on the rise. As a result, logistics companies also need strong IT security measures to safeguard their private data and prevent hacker attacks.
- IoT Use Cases in the Logistics Industry
  In addition to helping with fleet management, the Internet of Things is helpful in logistics because it makes it easier to store goods and monitor stock levels. It makes inventory management more efficient by giving businesses a full view of their supply chain processes. The Internet of Things has the potential to significantly improve the logistics business by strengthening its foundational elements. Here are some ways traditional logistics companies can benefit from the Internet of Things. All logistical operations rely heavily on trucks. In the United States, trucks carry over 70% of all freight. Trucks once had nearly all manufactured goods. Therefore, fleet and logistics firms need tools to keep track of their trucks. As a result, the logistics sector has adopted IoT's location and route management solution. Logistics managers may now track their trucks' whereabouts in real time with the help of this service. It is possible to keep tabs on the trucks' whereabouts from afar using geofencing and GPS monitoring technology [75–78]. This helps logistics companies track where their drivers are and their schedules so that packages get delivered on time. Most vehicle tracking solutions also have a real-time warning system that sends push notifications to managers whenever something unexpected happens, like a storm or an accident on the highway, that could change the delivery schedule.

The incorporation of these functions aids logistics firms in the management and organisation of delivery schedules. Business operations are optimized, and customer satisfaction is 100% since time-consuming roadblocks are immediately identified and removed [79–85]. RFID tags and sensors make it simple for businesses to monitor the whereabouts and condition of their stock. In other words, the Internet of Things makes it possible to create an intelligent warehouse system that helps businesses cut down on waste, keep their inventory secure, and quickly track down items when they are needed. In addition, it assists firms in modernising their warehouse operations, saving labour money and boosting productivity because fewer mistakes are made during manual handling.

Monitoring and managing assets are only two examples of how the Internet of Things may be put to use in the logistics industry. However, its most useful function is identifying potential weak points in these resources [86–90]. Rather than relying just on routine inspections, businesses may now implement predictive and condition-based maintenance thanks to the IoT rather than just relying on routine inspections. The following is an illustration: Organizations can foresee patterns connected to typical truck breakdowns by measuring and evaluating characteristics that characterise the functioning of the trucks. In a similar vein, condition-based maintenance can be used in conjunction with real-time alert systems to prevent unexpected breakdowns. With the help of IoT's predictive applications, businesses can spot flaws long before they cause major damage. The inspection and repair plans of logistics organisations can be optimised, and better decisions can be made. Businesses may minimise losses and maintenance time thanks to the preventative information they gain about their assets. This, in turn, facilitates the smooth running of processes like process execution and product delivery.

When IoT solutions are used in the logistics industry in conjunction with blockchain technology, a digital bill of lading (BOL) is created, introducing a new level of transparency into supply chains. With this BOL, the shipping firm and its clients may track their goods as they make their way to their final destination. Combining these two technologies has led to the development of innovative contract systems (of which BOL is just one component) that track the journey of commodities from their point of origin to the customer's hands [91–95]. Monitoring devices like GPS and sensors are also crucial to this answer. Using a blockchain to store information drastically lowers the risk of loss due to hacking or theft. Because of this, if the conditions specified in the transaction are met, the funds are immediately made available to the consumer. The customer has the right to cancel the agreement if there is a breach of contract, such as spoiled cargo or a delivery delay. This ensures that the contract specifications are subject to mutual oversight, strengthening the supply chain's security, transparency, and traceability.

Chapter's Contribution

Modern technologies, such as the IoT, have made transportation and facility management far more efficient. IoT is a popular network that interconnects various computing gadgets, each with its own identity and the ability to reliably and automatically transmit data across the web. Unfortunately, security issues have been brought about by the rapid development of the IoT. The organisation risks becoming a victim of cybercrime if adequate security measures are not implemented. The framework provides a standardised technique for managing cybersecurity risks across sectors, lowering the risks associated with the Internet of Things.

The transportation industry's IoT use has increased in recent years. According to Allied Market Research, the transportation industry's Internet of Things devices market will reach $328 billion by 2023. IoT and operational technology (OT) are undergoing rapid adoption in the transportation sector. But there is a new set of cyber threats associated with this adaptability. There has been a long list of cybersecurity flaws in IoT and OT systems. In light of this, the transportation sector's increasing reliance on this technology poses serious safety concerns. Further, we discuss the most critical cyber threats facing the transportation sector today.

- Security Issues with IoT and OT Products from Untrusted Sources
  When it comes to the Internet of Things and operational technology (OT) devices, many transportation businesses turn to third parties for help. This dependence on outside sources introduces a potential weak spot. Cybercriminals may use this to their advantage. During development, IoT and OT gadgets are often made without security in mind. Because of this, hackers find them easy prey. Also, these older machines rarely get updates that make them safer. They are vulnerable to threats that have already been found. The shipping industry is facing a big problem. Many companies don't have enough money to protect their IoT and OT infrastructure as well as they should. One example is the WannaCry attack of 2017. It used a hole in Windows XP that Microsoft had stopped fixing a long time ago. Over 200,000 computers in 150 countries were attacked with ransomware. Companies in the transportation industry need to make sure that their Internet of Things and operating technology equipment are safe so that they do not break down in a way that could cause a lot of damage. It is important to work with

OT security companies to make sure that security is a top
priority when new devices are being made.

- Challenges Observing the Target Area
  Connected and operational technology (IoT and OT)
  devices are commonly dispersed over a transportation company's network from end to end, sometimes on a national
  or even international scale. Because of this, it can be challenging for IT and security teams to get a holistic view of the
  company's potential vulnerabilities. Transportation companies cannot protect their networks without knowing what
  can be attacked. As a result, it's hard to see what's going on
  and stop attacks in time. For instance, Maersk, the largest
  container ship operator in the world, was severely impacted
  by the NotPetya attacks in 2017. In total, the attack cost
  Maersk more than $300 million. After the incident, Maersk
  was unable to resume operations for weeks.
  The only way for transportation businesses to stop these
  kinds of attacks is to obtain insight into their attack surface.
  One way to accomplish this is to team up with a group of
  trustworthy OT security providers. Such suppliers can protect networks from intrusion using IoT and OT security
  infrastructure. The networks can see all the devices on the
  network and respond more quickly to any attacks.

- Using Unsafe Methods of Communication
  Unfortunately, insecure protocols are commonly used for
  IoT and OT devices interoperability. Frequently, these protocols have reached the end of their useful lives. The latest
  safeguards for the web and networks are not supported.
  Because of this, hackers can easily eavesdrop on your communications simply by sniffing your network traffic. In 2016,
  for instance, the Mirai botnet assault leveraged vulnerable
  IoT devices to execute a massive, distributed denial of service (DDoS) attack. As a result of the attack, many popular
  websites, like Twitter and Netflix, were down. The problem
  can be easily fixed by requiring secure communications protocols for all IoT and OT devices. Among these methods is
  encrypting communications with a protocol like TLS or SSL.

- ICS Cybersecurity Issues
  Devices connected to the IoT and the operational technology
  domain are frequently used to manage manufacturing facilities, electricity distribution networks, and other industrial

infrastructure. Since these systems are generally insufficiently protected, they are vulnerable to assault. The Stuxnet worm targeted unprotected industrial control systems. The attack on Iran's nuclear enrichment facilities destroyed centrifuges. Inflicting millions of dollars in losses, the worm infiltrated all systems and caused widespread destruction. The transportation sector is vulnerable to similar attacks. Therefore, transportation businesses must implement the highest levels of security for their industrial control systems. Security measures like firewalls and intrusion detection and prevention systems are used as part of this.

- The Existing Security Measures Are Inadequate
  Generally, the security measures for IoT and OT devices are feeble. For the most part, this is because security was not a primary concern throughout the development of these gadgets. This leaves many IoT and OT devices vulnerable to cyberattacks. The Jeep Cherokee (2014) is a well-known target of this kind of vandalism. This breach occurred due to inadequate security measures in the car's media system. Hackers could take control of the vehicle's accelerator, brakes, and throttle because of this vulnerability.
  Businesses in the transportation industry need to have enough security policies to protect their IoT and OT equipment from attacks. IoT and OT devices are becoming increasingly important in transportation. Yet there are several security concerns with these gadgets. These devices could cause more harm than good if adequate safety measures are not taken. Therefore, transportation firms need to be alert to these dangers and employ effective industrial cybersecurity solutions.

10.7   Conclusion

IoT and other recent innovations have greatly improved the effectiveness of transportation and building management. IoT is an increasingly common network that links together various computing devices. Each can maintain its unique identity and consistently and automatically transfer data across the web. Sadly, the rapid expansion of the IoT has resulted in security concerns. Without proper protections, the company could quickly become a victim of cybercrime. It reduces IoT risk since the framework provides a standardized method for managing cybersecurity threats across industries. Internet of Things (IoT) adoption in transportation has recently grown.

10.8   Future Work

Allied Market Research predicts that by 2023 the transportation industry's Internet of Things devices market will be worth $328 billion. When it comes to security, IoT and OT devices are notoriously unreliable. This is mainly attributable to the fact that safety was not a top priority throughout the creation of these devices. Because of this, many IoT and OT gadgets are open to cyberattacks. Sadly, the Jeep Cherokee (2014) is a common target for this damage. This breach occurred because the car's media system lacked proper protection. Intruders exploited this flaw to seize control of the vehicle's throttle, brakes, and accelerator. Transportation companies need robust security measures regarding IoT and operational technology (OT) devices. It's becoming clear that IoT and OT gadgets play a crucial role in the transportation industry. But there are several security issues associated with these devices. These tools could do more harm than good if proper precautions are not taken. Considering these risks, transportation companies must implement robust industrial cybersecurity strategies.

References

[1] Totonchi, A. (2018). Smart buildings based on Internet of Things: A systematic review. *Dep. Inf. Commun. Technol.*

[2] H.N. Rafsanjani, S. Moayedi, C.R. Ahn, M. Alahmad, A load disaggregation framework to sense personalized energy-use information in commercial buildings, *Energy Build.* (2019) 109633.

[3] M. Wang, S. Qiu, H. Dong, Y. Wang, Design an IoT-based building management cloud platform for green buildings, in: *2017 Chin. Autom. Congr. CAC,* 2017: pp. 5663–5667. 10.1109/CAC.2017.8243793.

[4] A. Verma, S. Prakash, V. Srivastava, A. Kumar, S.C. Mukhopadhyay, Sensing, controlling, and iot infrastructure in smart building: a review, *IEEE Sens. J.* 19 (2019) 9036–9046, doi:10.1109/JSEN.2019.2922409.

[5] E. Kim, Y. Cho, G. Kim, Real Time Building Data collecting Using IoT and BIM, 2018.

[6] H.N. Rafsanjani, C.R. Ahn, J. Chen, Linking building energy consumption with occupants' energy-consuming behaviors in commercial buildings: nonintrusive occupant load monitoring (NIOLM), *Energy Build* 172 (2018) 317–327, doi:10.1016/j.enbuild.2018.05.007.

[7] A. Ghahramani, P. Galicia, D. Lehrer, Z. Varghese, Z. Wang, Y. Pandit, Artificial intelligence for efficient thermal comfort systems: requirements, current applications and future directions, *Front. Built Environ* 6 (2020), doi:10.3389/fbuil.2020.00049.

[8] Role and Applications of IoT in Transportation. TechVidvan. https://techvidvan.com/tutorials/role-and-applications-of-iot-in-transportation/.

[9] H.N. Rafsanjani, C. Ahn, K. Eskridge, Understanding the recurring patterns of occupants' energy-use behaviors at entry and departure events in office buildings, *Build. Environ.* 136 (2018) 77–87.

[10] N.H. Motlagh, S.H. Khajavi, A. Jaribion, J. Holmstrom, An IoT-based automation system for older homes: a use case for lighting system, in: *2018 IEEE 11th Conf. Serv.-Oriented Comput. Appl. SOCA*, 2018, pp. 1–6, doi:10.1109/SOCA.2018.8645771.

[11] R. Kanan, O. Elhassan, R. Bensalem, An IoT-based autonomous system for workers' safety in construction sites with real-time alarming, monitoring, and positioning strategies, *Autom. Constr.* 88 (2018) 73–86, doi:10.1016/j.autcon.2017.12.033.

[12] P. Mishra, M. Pradhan, M. Panda, Internet of Things for Remote Healthcare, 2016.

[13] J. Saha, A.K. Saha, A. Chatterjee, S. Agrawal, A. Saha, A. Kar, H.N. Saha, Advanced IOT based combined remote health monitoring, home automation and alarm system, in: *2018 IEEE 8th Annu. Comput. Commun. Workshop Conf. CCWC*, 2018, pp. 602–606, doi:10.1109/CCWC.2018.8301659.

[14] C.K. Metallidou, K.E. Psannis, E.A. Egyptiadou, Energy Efficiency in Smart Buildings: IoT Approaches, *IEEE Access* 8 (2020) 63679–63699, doi:10.1109/ACCESS.2020.2984461.

[15] K. Akkaya, I. Guvenc, R. Aygun, N. Pala, A. Kadri, IoT-based occupancy monitoring techniques for energy-efficient smart buildings, in: *2015 IEEE Wirel. Commun. Netw. Conf. Workshop WCNCW*, 2015, pp. 58–63, doi:10.1109/WCNCW.2015.7122529.

[16] Hussain, M., Talpur, M. S. H., & Humayun, M. (2022). The Consequences of Integrity Attacks on E-Governance: Privacy and Security Violation. In *Cybersecurity Measures for E-Government Frameworks* (pp. 141–156). IGI Global.

[17] A. Daissaoui, A. Boulmakoul, L. Karim, A. Lbath, IoT and big data analytics for smart buildings: a survey, *Procedia Comput. Sci.* 170 (2020) 161–168, doi:10.1016/j.procs.2020.03.021.

[18] Z. Shouran, A. Ashari, T. Priyambodo, Internet of things (IoT) of smart home: privacy and security, *Int. J. Comput. Appl.* 182 (2019) 3–8, doi:10.5120/ijca2019918450.

[19] Jhanjhi, N. Z., Ahmad, M., Khan, M. A., & Hussain, M. (2022). The Impact of Cyber Attacks on E-Governance During the COVID-19 Pandemic. In *Cybersecurity Measures for E-Government Frameworks* (pp. 123–140). IGI Global.

[20] P. Sethi, S.R. Sarangi, Internet of things: architectures, protocols, and applications, *J. Electr. Comput. Eng.* 2017 (2017) e9324035, doi:10.1155/2017/9324035.

[21] F. Van den Abeele, J. Hoebeke, I. Moerman, P. Demeester, Integration of heterogeneous devices and communication models via the cloud in the constrained internet of things, *Int. J. Distrib. Sens. Netw.* 11 (2015) 683425, doi:10.1155/2015/ 683425.

[22] A.R. Al-Ali, I.A. Zualkernan, M. Rashid, R. Gupta, M. Alikarar, A smart home energy management system using IoT and big data analytics approach, *IEEE Trans. Consum. Electron.* 63 (2017) 426–434, doi:10.1109/TCE.2017.015014.

[23] Ujjan, R. M. A., Hussain, K., & Brohi, S. N. (2022). The Impact of Blockchain Technology on Advanced Security Measures for E-Government. In *Cybersecurity Measures for E-Government Frameworks* (pp. 157–174). IGI Global.

[24] Chhajed, G. J., & Garg, B. R. (2022). Applying Decision Tree for Hiding Data in Binary Images for Secure and Secret Information Flow. In *Cybersecurity Measures for E-Government Frameworks* (pp. 175–186). IGI Global.

[25] Kumar, T., Pandey, B., Mussavi, S. H. A., & Zaman, N. (2015). CTHS based energy efficient thermal aware image ALU design on FPGA. *Wireless Personal Communications, 85*, 671–696.

[26] Shafiq, M., Ashraf, H., Ullah, A., Masud, M., Azeem, M., Jhanjhi, N., & Humayun, M. (2021). Robust cluster-based routing protocol for IoT-assisted smart devices in WSN. *Computers, Materials & Continua, 67*(3), 3505–3521.

[27] J. Pan, R. Jain, S. Paul, T. Vu, A. Saifullah, M. Sha, An internet of things framework for smart energy in buildings: designs, prototype, and experiments, *IEEE Internet Things J* 2 (2015) 527–537, doi:10.1109/JIOT.2015.2413397.

[28] W. Tushar, N. Wijerathne, W.-T. Li, C. Yuen, H.V. Poor, T.K. Saha, K.L. Wood, Internet of things for green building management: disruptive innovations through low-cost sensor technology and artificial intelligence, *IEEE Signal Process. Mag.* 35 (2018) 100–110, doi:10.1109/MSP.2018.2842096.

[29] E. Fotopoulou, A. Zafeiropoulos, F. Terroso-Sáenz, U. Şimşek, A. González-Vidal, G. Tsiolis, P. Gouvas, P. Liapis, A. Fensel, A. Skarmeta, Providing personalized energy management and awareness services for energy efficiency in smart buildings, *Sensors* (2017) 17, doi:10.3390/s17092054.

[30] V. Marinakis, H. Doukas, An advanced IoT-based system for intelligent energy management in buildings, *Sensors* 18 (2018), doi:10.3390/s18020610.

[31] D. Minoli, K. Sohraby, B. Occhiogrosso, IoT considerations, requirements, and architectures for smart buildings—energy optimization and next-generation building management systems, *IEEE Internet Things J.* 4 (2017) 269–283, doi:10.1109/JIOT.2017.2647881.

[32] Adeyemo, Victor Elijah, Azween Abdullah, N. Z. JhanJhi, Mahadevan Supramaniam, and Abdullateef O. Balogun. Ensemble and deep-learning methods for two-class and multi-attack anomaly intrusion detection: an

empirical study. *International Journal of Advanced Computer Science and Applications* 10, no. 9 (2019).

[33] H.N. Rafsanjani, A. Ghahramani, Towards utilizing internet of things (IoT) devices for understanding individual occupants' energy usage of personal and shared appliances in office buildings, *J. Build. Eng.* 27 (2020) 100948, doi:10.1016/j.jobe.2019.100948.

[34] Gaur, L., Ujjan, R. M. A., & Hussain, M. (2022). The Influence of Deep Learning in Detecting Cyber Attacks on E-Government Applications. In *Cybersecurity Measures for E-Government Frameworks* (pp. 107–122). IGI Global.

[35] J. Gubbi, R. Buyya, S. Marusic, M. Palaniswami, Internet of Things (IoT): a vision, architectural elements, and future directions, *Future Gener. Comput. Syst.* 29 (2013) 1645–1660, doi:10.1016/j.future.2013.01.010.

[36] D. Miorandi, S. Sicari, F. De Pellegrini, I. Chlamtac, Internet of things: Vision, applications and research challenges, *Ad. Hoc. Netw.* 10 (2012) 1497–1516, doi:10.1016/j.adhoc.2012.02.016.

[37] H.N. Rafsanjani, A. Ghahramani, A.H. Nabizadeh, iSEA: IoT-based smartphone energy assistant for prompting energy-aware behaviors in commercial buildings, *Appl. Energy.* 266 (2020) 114892, doi:10.1016/j. apenergy.2020.114892.

[38] Kok, S. H., Abdullah, A., & Jhanjhi, N. Z. (2022). Early detection of crypto-ransomware using pre-encryption detection algorithm. *Journal of King Saud University - Computer and Information Sciences*, 34(5), 1984–1999.

[39] M. Wei, S.H. Hong, M. Alam, An IoT-based energy-management platform for industrial facilities, *Appl. Energy.* 164 (2016) 607–619, doi:10.1016/j.apenergy. 2015.11.107. [40] A. Khanna, S. Kaur, Evolution of Internet of Things (IoT) and its significant impact in the field of precision agriculture, *Comput. Electron. Agric.* (2019) https://agris.fao.org/agris-search/search.do?recordID=US201900160588. accessed June 22, 2020.

[40] Lim, M., Abdullah, A., Jhanjhi, N. Z., & Supramaniam, M. (2019). Hidden link prediction in criminal networks using the deep reinforcement learning technique. *Computers*, 8(1), 8.

[41] L. Atzori, A. Iera, G. Morabito, The internet of things: a survey, *Comput. Netw.* 54 (2010) 2787–2805, doi:10.1016/j.comnet.2010.05.010.

[42] J. Gubbi, R. Buyya, S. Marusic, M. Palaniswami, Internet of Things (IoT): a vision, architectural elements, and future directions, *Future Gener. Comput. Syst.* 29 (2013) 1645–1660, doi:10.1016/j.future.2013.01.010.

[43] H. Sundmaeker, P. Guillemin, P. Friess, S. Woelfflé, Vision and challenges for realizing the internet of things, Clust. Eur. Res. Proj. Internet Things Eur. Commision. (2010), doi:10.2759/26127.

[44] J. Louis, P.S. Dunston, Integrating IoT into operational workflows for real-time and automated decision-making in repetitive construction operations, *Autom. Constr.* 94 (2018) 317–327, doi:10.1016/j.autcon.2018.07.005.

[45] D. Miorandi, S. Sicari, F. De Pellegrini, I. Chlamtac, Internet of things: vision, applications and research challenges, *Ad. Hoc. Netw.* 10 (2012) 1497–1516, doi:10.1016/j.adhoc.2012.02.016.

[46] Shah, I. A., Jhanjhi, N. Z., Humayun, M., & Ghosh, U. (2022). Health Care Digital Revolution During COVID-19. In *How COVID-19 Is Accelerating the Digital Revolution* (pp. 17-30). Springer, Cham.

[47] Smart IoT desk for personalizing indoor environmental conditions, in: *Proceedings of the 8th International Conference on the Internet of Things*, 2019 n.d.

[48] D. Mocrii, Y. Chen, P. Musilek, IoT-based smart homes: a review of system architecture, software, communications, privacy and security, *Internet Things* 1–2 (2018) 81–98, doi:10.1016/j.iot.2018.08.009.

[49] H. Guo, J. Ren, D. Zhang, Y. Zhang, J. Hu, A scalable and manageable IoT architecture based on transparent computing, *J. Parallel Distrib. Comput.* 118 (2018) 5–13, doi:10.1016/j.jpdc.2017.07.003.

[50] D. Wang, J. Ren, C. Xu, J. Liu, Z. Wang, Y. Zhang, X. Shen, PrivStream: enabling privacy-preserving inferences on IoT data stream at the edge, in: *2019 IEEE 21st Int. Conf. High Perform. Comput. Commun. IEEE 17th Int. Conf. Smart City IEEE 5th Int. Conf. Data Sci. Syst. HPCCSmartCityDSS, 2019*, pp. 1290–1297, doi:10.1109/HPCC/SmartCity/DSS.2019.00180.

[51] W. Tang, J. Ren, K. Deng, Y. Zhang, Secure data aggregation of lightweight Ehealthcare IoT devices with fair incentives, *IEEE Internet Things J* 6 (2019) 8714–8726, doi:10.1109/JIOT.2019.2923261.

[52] Shah, I. A., Jhanjhi, N. Z., & Laraib, A. (2023). Cybersecurity and Blockchain Usage in Contemporary Business. In *Handbook of Research on Cybersecurity Issues and Challenges for Business and FinTech Applications* (pp. 49–64). IGI Global.

[53] M. Tavana, V. Hajipour, S. Oveisi, IoT-based enterprise resource planning: challenges, open issues, applications, architecture, and future research directions, *Internet Things* 11 (2020) 100262, doi:10.1016/j.iot.2020.100262.

[54] J. Ren, H. Guo, C. Xu, Y. Zhang, Serving at the edge: a scalable IoT architecture based on transparent computing, *IEEE Netw.* 31 (2017) 96–105, doi:10.1109/MNET.2017.1700030.

[55] G. Chen, T. Jiang, M. Wang, X. Tang, W. Ji, Modeling and reasoning of IoT architecture in semantic ontology dimension, *Comput. Commun.* 153 (2020) 580–594, doi:10.1016/j.comcom.2020.02.006.

[56] Shah, I. A., Jhanjhi, N. Z., Humayun, M., & Ghosh, U. (2022). Impact of COVID-19 on Higher and Post-secondary Education Systems. In *How COVID-19 Is Accelerating the Digital Revolution* (pp. 71–83). Springer, Cham.

[57] Md.W. Rahman, S.S. Tashfia, R. Islam, Md.M. Hasan, S.I. Sultan, S. Mia, M.M. Rahman, The architectural design of smart blind assistant using IoT with deep learning paradigm, *Internet Things* 13 (2021) 100344, doi:10.1016/j. iot.2020. 100344.

[58] J. Mocnej, A. Pekar, W.K.G. Seah, P. Papcun, E. Kajati, D. Cupkova, J. Koziorek, I. Zolotova, Quality-enabled decentralized IoT architecture with efficient resources utilization, *Robot. Comput.-Integr. Manuf.* 67 (2021) 102001, doi:10.1016/j.rcim.2020.102001.

[59] J. Ariza, K. Garcés, N. Cardozo, J.P.R. Sánchez, F.J. Vargas, IoT architecture for adaptation to transient devices, *J. Parallel Distrib. Comput.* 148 (2021) 14–30, doi:10.1016/j.jpdc.2020.09.012.

[60] H. Elazhary, Internet of Things (IoT), mobile cloud, cloudlet, mobile IoT, IoT cloud, fog, mobile edge, and edge emerging computing paradigms: disambiguation and research directions, *J. Netw. Comput. Appl.* 128 (2019) 105–140, doi:10.1016/j.jnca.2018.10.021.

[61] Muzafar, S., Humayun, M., & Hussain, S. J. (2022). Emerging Cybersecurity Threats in the Eye of E-Governance in the Current Era. In *Cybersecurity Measures for E-Government Frameworks* (pp. 43–60). IGI Global.

[62] Dawson, M., & Walker, D. (2022). Argument for Improved Security in Local Governments Within the Economic Community of West African States. *Cybersecurity Measures for E-Government Frameworks*, 96–106.

[63] P.P. Ray, A survey on internet of things architectures, *J. King Saud Univ. - Comput. Inf. Sci.* 30 (2018) 291–319, doi:10.1016/j.jksuci.2016.10.003.

[64] Introduction to Zigbee Technology, 2011 By element14 https://www. element14.com/community/docs/DOC-37177/l/introduction-to-zigbee-technologyby-element14 accessed June 4, 2020.

[65] LoRaWAN for Smart Buildings. LoRa Alliance®, (n.d.). https://lora-alliance. org/lorawan-verticales markets/buildings (accessed June 3, 2020).

[66] LoRaWAN® Specification v1.0.3. LoRa Alliance®, (n.d.). https://lora-alliance. org/resource-hub/lorawanr-specification-v103 (accessed June 3, 2020).

[67] M. Burhan, R.A. Rehman, B. Khan, B.-S. Kim, IoT elements, layered architectures and security issues: a comprehensive survey, *Sensors* 18 (2018) 2796, doi:10.3390/s18092796.

[68] Shah, I. A., Wassan, S., & Usmani, M. H. (2022). E-Government Security and Privacy Issues: Challenges and Preventive Approaches. In *Cybersecurity Measures for E-Government Frameworks* (pp. 61–76). IGI Global.

[69] Singh, G., Gaur, L., Sharma, S., Disposition of youth in predicting sustainable development goals using the neuro-fuzzy and random forest algorithms. *Human-centric Computing and Information Sciences* 12, June 2021. DOI:10.22967/HCIS.2021.11.024

[70] Y.H. Ho, H.C.B. Chan, Decentralized adaptive indoor positioning protocol using Bluetooth Low Energy, *Comput. Commun.* 159 (2020) 231–244, doi:10.1016/j.comcom.2020.04.041.

[71] Ujjan, R. M. A., Khan, N. A., & Gaur, L. (2022). E-Government Privacy and Security Challenges in the Context of Internet of Things. In *Cybersecurity Measures for E-Government Frameworks* (pp. 22–42). IGI Global.

[72] Shah, I. A., Sial, Q., Jhanjhi, N. Z., & Gaur, L. (2023). Use Cases for Digital Twin. In *Digital Twins and Healthcare: Trends, Techniques, and Challenges* (pp. 102–118). IGI Global.

[73] M. Thiyagarajan, C. Raveendra, Integration in the physical world in IoT using android mobile application, in: *2015 Int. Conf. Green Comput. Internet Things ICGCIoT*, 2015, pp. 790–795, doi:10.1109/ICGCIoT.2015.7380570.

[74] B. Afzal, M. Umair, G. Asadullah Shah, E. Ahmed, Enabling IoT platforms for social IoT applications: vision, feature mapping, and challenges, *Future Gener. Comput. Syst.* 92 (2019) 718–731, doi:10.1016/j.future.2017.12.002.

[75] D. Glaroudis, A. Iossifides, P. Chatzimisios, Survey, comparison and research challenges of IoT application protocols for smart farming, *Comput. Netw.* 168 (2020) 107037, doi:10.1016/j.comnet.2019.107037.

[76] D. Koo, K. Piratla, C.J. Matthews, Towards sustainable water supply: schematic development of big data collection using internet of things (IoT), *Procedia Eng.* 118 (2015) 489–497, doi:10.1016/j.proeng.2015.08.465.

[77] J. Tournier, F. Lesueur, F.L. Mouël, L. Guyon, H. Ben-Hassine, A survey of IoT protocols and their security issues through the lens of a generic IoT stack, *Int. Things* (2020) 100264, doi:10.1016/j.iot.2020.100264.

[78] Y. Jeon, C. Cho, J. Seo, K. Kwon, H. Park, S. Oh, I.-J. Chung, IoT-based occupancy detection system in indoor residential environments, *Build. Environ.* 132 (2018) 181–204, doi:10.1016/j.buildenv.2018.01.043.

[79] C. Perera, A. Zaslavsky, P. Christen, D. Georgakopoulos, Context aware computing for the internet of things: a survey, *IEEE Commun. Surv. Tutor.* 16 (2014) 414–454, doi:10.1109/SURV.2013.042313.00197.

[80] Based on the Internet of things the supermarket chain management information system development and safety stock research - IEEE Conference Publication (n.d.). https://ieeexplore.ieee.org/abstract/document/5529363 (accessed June 10, 2020).

[81] Gaur, L., Afaq, A., Solanki, A., Singh, G., Sharma, S., Jhanjhi, N. Z., ... & Le, D. N. (2021). Capitalizing on big data and revolutionary 5G technology: Extracting and visualizing ratings and reviews of global chain hotels. *Computers and Electrical Engineering*, 95, 107374.

[82] Ujjan, R. M. A., Pervez, Z., & Dahal, K. (2018, June). Suspicious traffic detection in SDN with collaborative techniques of snort and deep neural networks. In *2018 IEEE 20th International Conference on High Performance Computing and Communications; IEEE 16th International Conference on Smart City; IEEE 4th International Conference on Data Science and Systems (HPCC/SmartCity/DSS)* (pp. 915–920). IEEE.

[83] Shah, I. A. (2022). Cybersecurity Issues and Challenges for E-Government During COVID-19: A Review. *Cybersecurity Measures for E-Government Frameworks*, 187–222.

[84] Ujjan, R. M. A., Pervez, Z., Dahal, K., Bashir, A. K., Mumtaz, R., & González, J. (2020). Towards sFlow and adaptive polling sampling for deep learning

based DDoS detection in SDN. *Future Generation Computer Systems, 111,* 763–779.

[85] Ujjan, R. M. A., Taj, I., & Brohi, S. N. (2022). E-Government Cybersecurity Modeling in the Context of Software-Defined Networks. In *Cybersecurity Measures for E-Government Frameworks* (pp. 1–21). IGI Global.

[86] Shah, I. A., Jhanjhi, N. Z., Amsaad, F., & Razaque, A. (2022). The Role of Cutting-Edge Technologies in Industry 4.0. In *Cyber Security Applications for Industry 4.0* (pp. 97–109). Chapman and Hall/CRC.

[87] Sennan, S., Somula, R., Luhach, A. K., Deverajan, G. G., Alnumay, W., Jhanjhi, N. Z., ... & Sharma, P. (2021). Energy efficient optimal parent selection based routing protocol for Internet of Things using firefly optimization algorithm. *Transactions on Emerging Telecommunications Technologies, 32*(8), e4171.

[88] Diwaker, C., Tomar, P., Solanki, A., Nayyar, A., Jhanjhi, N. Z., Abdullah, A., & Supramaniam, M. (2019). A new model for predicting component-based software reliability using soft computing. *IEEE Access, 7,* 147191–147203.

[89] Kiran, S. R. A., Rajper, S., Shaikh, R. A., Shah, I. A., & Danwar, S. H. (2021). Categorization of CVE Based on Vulnerability Software by Using Machine Learning Techniques. *International Journal, 10*(3).

[90] Umrani, S., Rajper, S., Talpur, S. H., Shah, I. A., & Shujrah, A. (2020). Games based learning: A case of learning physics using Angry Birds. *Indian Journal of Science and Technology, 13*(36), 3778–3784.

[91] Humayun, M., Jhanjhi, N. Z., Alruwaili, M., Amalathas, S. S., Balasubramanian, V., & Selvaraj, B. (2020). Privacy protection and energy optimization for 5G-aided industrial Internet of Things. *IEEE Access, 8,* 183665–183677.

[92] Shah, I. A., Sial, Q., Jhanjhi, N. Z., & Gaur, L. (2023). The Role of the IoT and Digital Twin in the Healthcare Digitalization Process: IoT and Digital Twin in the Healthcare Digitalization Process. In *Digital Twins and Healthcare: Trends, Techniques, and Challenges* (pp. 20–34). IGI Global.

[93] Hussain, S. J., Ahmed, U., Liaquat, H., Mir, S., Jhanjhi, N. Z., & Humayun, M. (2019, April). IMIAD: intelligent malware identification for android platform. In *2019 International Conference on Computer and Information Sciences (ICCIS)* (pp. 1–6). IEEE.

[94] Jhanjhi, N. Z., Brohi, S. N., Malik, N. A., & Humayun, M. (2020, October). Proposing a hybrid rpl protocol for rank and wormhole attack mitigation using machine learning. In *2020 2nd International Conference on Computer and Information Sciences (ICCIS)* (pp. 1–6). IEEE.

[95] S Umrani, S Rajper, SH Talpur, IA Shah, A Shujrah. *Indian Journal of Science and Technology,* 2020.

Index

Also of Interest

Check out these other related titles from Scrivener Publishing

AI FOR AUTONOMOUS VEHICLES: The Future of Driverless Technology, Edited by Sathiyaraj Rajendran, Munish Sabharwal, Yu-Chen Hu, Rajesh Kumar Dhanaraj, and Balamurugan Balusamy, ISBN: 9781119847465. This title presents the research prospects and security challenges present in the exciting new field of autonomous vehicles by comprehensively introducing advanced concepts of artificial intelligence (AI) in driverless technology.

Books in the series, "Advances in Cyber Security"

CYBER SECURITY AND DIGITAL FORENSICS: Challenges and Future Trends, Edited by Mangesh M. Ghonge, Sabyasachi Pramanik, Ramchandra Mangrulkar, and Dac-Nhuong Le, ISBN: 9781119795636. Written and edited by a team of world renowned experts in the field, this groundbreaking new volume covers key technical topics and gives readers a comprehensive understanding of the latest research findings in cyber security and digital forensics.

CYBER SECURITY AND NETWORK SECURITY, Edited by Sabyasachi Pramanik, Debabrata Samanta, M. Vinay, and Abhijit Guha, ISBN: 9781119812494. Written and edited by a team of experts in the field, this is the most comprehensive and up to date study of the practical applications of cybersecurity and network security for engineers, scientists, students, and other professionals.

DEEP LEARNING APPROACHES TO CLOUD SECURITY, edited by Pramod Singh Rathore, Vishal Dutt, Rashmi Agrawal, Satya Murthy Sasubilli, and Srinivasa Rao Swarna, ISBN 9781119760528. Covering one of the most important subjects to our society today, this editorial team delves into solutions taken from evolving deep learning approaches, solutions allow computers to learn from experience and understand the world in terms of a hierarchy of concepts.

Other related titles

SECURITY ISSUES AND PRIVACY CONCERNS IN INDUSTRY 4.0 APPLICATIONS, Edited by Shibin David, R. S. Anand, V. Jeyakrishnan, and M. Niranjanamurthy, ISBN: 9781119775621. Written and edited by a team of international experts, this is the most comprehensive and up-to-date coverage of the security and privacy issues surrounding Industry 4.0 applications, a must-have for any library.

MACHINE LEARNING TECHNIQUES AND ANALYTICS FOR CLOUD SECURITY, Edited by Rajdeep Chakraborty, Anupam Ghosh and Jyotsna Kumar Mandal, ISBN: 9781119762256. This book covers new methods, surveys, case studies, and policy with almost all machine learning techniques and analytics for cloud security solutions.

ARTIFICIAL INTELLIGENCE AND DATA MINING IN SECURITY FRAMEWORKS, Edited by Neeraj Bhargava, Ritu Bhargava, Pramod Singh Rathore, and Rashmi Agrawal, ISBN 9781119760405. Written and edited by a team of experts in the field, this outstanding new volume offers solutions to the problems of security, outlining the concepts behind allowing computers to learn from experience and understand the world in terms of a hierarchy of concepts.

SECURITY DESIGNS FOR THE CLOUD, IOT AND SOCIAL NETWORKING, Edited by Dac-Nhuong Le, Chintin Bhatt and Mani Madhukar, ISBN: 9781119592266. The book provides cutting-edge research that delivers insights into the tools, opportunities, novel strategies, techniques, and challenges for handling security issues in cloud computing, Internet of Things and social networking.

DESIGN AND ANALYSIS OF SECURITY PROTOCOLS FOR COMMUNICATION, Edited by Dinesh Goyal, S. Balamurugan, Sheng-Lung Peng and O.P. Verma, ISBN: 9781119555643. The book combines analysis and comparison of various security protocols such as HTTP, SMTP, RTP, RTCP, FTP, UDP for mobile or multimedia streaming security protocol.

Printed and bound by CPI Group (UK) Ltd, Croydon, CR0 4YY

27/10/2024

14580173-0001